Samsung Galaxy Note™
FOR
DUMMIES®

Samsung Galaxy Note™
FOR
DUMMIES®

by Dan Gookin

WILEY

John Wiley & Sons, Inc.

Samsung Galaxy Note™ For Dummies®

Published by
John Wiley & Sons, Inc.
111 River Street
Hoboken, NJ 07030-5774

www.wiley.com

About the Author

Dan Gookin has been writing about technology for over 20 years. He combines his love of writing with his gizmo fascination to create books that are informative, entertaining, and not boring. Having written over 125 titles with 12 million copies in print translated into over 30 languages, Dan can attest that his method of crafting computer tomes seems to work.

Perhaps his most famous title is the original *DOS For Dummies,* published in 1991. It became the world's fastest-selling computer book, at one time moving more copies per week than the *New York Times* number-one bestseller (though, as a reference, it could not be listed on the *Times'* Best Sellers list). That book spawned the entire line of *For Dummies* books, which remains a publishing phenomenon to this day.

Dan's most popular titles include *PCs For Dummies, Word For Dummies, Laptops For Dummies*, and *Troubleshooting & Maintaining Your PC All-in-One For Dummies*. He also maintains the vast and helpful website www.wambooli.com.

Dan holds a degree in Communications/Visual Arts from the University of California, San Diego. He lives in the Pacific Northwest, where he enjoys spending time with his sons playing video games indoors while they watch the gentle woods of Idaho.

Publisher's Acknowledgments

We're proud of this book; please send us your comments at http://dummies.custhelp.com. For other comments, please contact our Customer Care Department within the U.S. at 877-762-2974, outside the U.S. at 317-572-3993, or fax 317-572-4002.

Some of the people who helped bring this book to market include the following:

Acquisitions and Editorial

Sr. Project Editor: Mark Enochs

Acquisitions Editor: Katie Mohr

Copy Editor: Rebecca Whitney

Editorial Manager: Leah Michael

Editorial Assistant: Leslie Saxman

Sr. Editorial Assistant: Cherie Case

Cover Photo: Background image © zhanna ocheret/iStockphoto.com

Cartoons: Rich Tennant (www.the5thwave.com)

Composition Services

Project Coordinator: Sheree Montgomery

Layout and Graphics: Tim Detrick, Christin Swinford

Proofreader: Lauren Mandelbaum

Indexer: Estalita Slivoskey

Publishing and Editorial for Technology Dummies

Richard Swadley, Vice President and Executive Group Publisher

Andy Cummings, Vice President and Publisher

Mary Bednarek, Executive Acquisitions Director

Mary C. Corder, Editorial Director

Publishing for Consumer Dummies

Kathy Nebenhaus, Vice President and Executive Publisher

Composition Services

Debbie Stailey, Director of Composition Services

Contents at a Glance

Table of Contents

Introduction

1 was thrilled when I first learned about the release of the Galaxy Note. I figured that I could write a book about the new device and, because it's much larger than a typical cell phone, write a bigger book — one that's about one-and-a-half times larger than the typical *For Dummies* book.

Alas, I was informed that the book, the one you hold in your hands, would be a normal-size *For Dummies* title. Still, I've managed to cram enough information in here to make using the Galaxy Note an enjoyable and tolerable experience. New devices can be intimidating. I know! So I've written this book to help you get the most from the first-ever hybrid phone/tablet computer.

About This Book

The most important thing to know about this book is that you're not required to read it from cover to cover. I beg you. That's because this book is a reference. It's designed to be used as you need it. Look up a topic in the table of contents or the index. Find something about your phone that vexes you, or something you're curious about. Look up the answer and get on with your life.

Each chapter in this book is written as its own, self-contained unit, covering a specific topic about using your phone. The chapters are further divided into sections representing a task you perform with the phone or explaining how to get something done. Sample sections in this book include

- Checking out the keyboard variations
- Using various S Pen tricks
- Phoning someone you call often
- Adding your phone to Google Voice
- Forwarding a text message
- Talking and video chat
- Uploading a video to YouTube
- Browsing your music library
- Printing to a Bluetooth printer
- Using power saving tools

Every section explains a topic as though it's the first one you've read in this book. Nothing is assumed, and everything is cross-referenced. Technical terms and topics, when they come up, are neatly shoved to the side, where they're easily avoided. The idea here isn't to learn anything. This book's philosophy is to help you look it up, figure it out, and get back to your life.

How to Use This Book

This book follows a few conventions for using your phone, so pay attention!

The main way to interact with your phone is by using its *touchscreen,* which is the glassy part of the phone as it's facing you. Buttons also adorn the phone, all of which are explained in Part I of this book.

You can touch the screen in various ways, which are described in Chapter 3.

Chapter 4 discusses text input — typing — which involves using something called the *onscreen keyboard.* Also covered is using the Galaxy Note S Pen for drawing and text input plus a few special tricks. And, when you tire of typing or drawing, you can always input text on your phone by dictating it.

This book directs you to do things on your phone by following numbered steps. Every step involves a specific activity, such as touching something on the screen; for example:

3. Choose Downloads.

This step directs you to touch the text or item labeled Downloads on the screen. You might also be told to do this:

3. Touch Downloads.

 Various phone options can be turned off or on, as indicated by a gray box with a green check mark in it, as shown in the margin. By touching the box on the screen, you add or remove the green check mark. When the green check mark appears, the option is on; otherwise, it's off.

 The bar codes in the margins are there to help you install recommended apps. To install an app, scan the bar code using the AT&T Code Scanner app that comes preinstalled on your phone. Chapter 18 discusses how to use the app to read bar codes.

Foolish Assumptions

Even though this book was written to provide the gentle handholding required by anyone who is just starting out, or who is easily intimidated, I have made a few assumptions.

Number one: I'm assuming that you're still reading the introduction. That's great. It's much better than getting a foot massage right now or checking the latest Lotto numbers.

My biggest assumptions: You have a Galaxy Note phone. Your cellular service is AT&T. I'm sure that the Galaxy Note will eventually be available to other cellular providers, but for now this book is geared toward the AT&T way of doing things.

More assumptions:

I also assume that you have a computer, either a desktop or laptop. The computer can be a PC (or Windows computer) or a Macintosh. Oh, I suppose it could be a Linux computer instead. In any event, I refer to your computer as *your computer* throughout this book. When directions are specific to a PC or Mac, the book says so.

Programs that run on your Android phone are called *apps*, which is short for *applications.* A single program is an *app.*

Finally, this book assumes that you have a Google account. If you don't, Chapter 2 explains how to configure one. Do so. Having a Google account opens up a slew of useful features, information, and programs that make using your phone more productive.

How This Book Is Organized

This book has been sliced into six parts, each of which describes a certain aspect of the typical Android phone or how it's used.

Part 1: What Is This Thing?

This part of the book serves as an introduction to your phone. Chapters cover setup and orientation and familiarize you with how the phone works. Part I is a good place to start — plus, you discover things in this part that aren't obvious from guessing how the phone works.

Part II: Phone Duties

Nothing is more basic for a phone to do than make calls, which is the topic of the chapters in this part of the book. As you may have suspected, your Galaxy Note can make calls, receive calls, and serve as an answering service for calls you miss. It also manages the names of all the people you know and even those you don't want to know but have to know anyway.

Part III: Keep in Touch

The modern cell phone is about more than simply telephone communications. Part III of this book explores other ways you can use your phone to stay in touch with people, browse the Internet, check your e-mail, do your social networking, exchange text messages, chat by video, and more.

Part IV: Incredible Tasks and Amazing Feats

This part of the book explores the nonphone things your phone can do. For example, your phone can find locations on a map, give you verbal driving directions, take pictures, shoot videos, play music, play games, and do all sorts of other wonderful things that no one would ever think a phone can do. The chapters in this part of the book get you up to speed on those activities.

Part V: Nuts and Bolts

The chapters in this part of the book discuss a spate of interesting topics, from connecting the phone to a computer, using Wi-Fi and Bluetooth networking, and taking the phone overseas and making international calls to customizing and personalizing your phone and the necessary chores of maintenance and troubleshooting.

Part VI: The Part of Tens

Finally, this book ends with the traditional *For Dummies* The Part of Tens, where every chapter lists ten items or topics. For your Galaxy Note, the chapters include tips, tricks, shortcuts, and things to remember, plus a list of some of my favorite Android phone apps.

Icons Used in This Book

This icon flags useful, helpful tips or shortcuts.

This icon marks a friendly reminder to do something.

This icon marks a friendly reminder *not* to do something.

This icon alerts you to overly nerdy information and technical discussions of the topic at hand. Reading the information is optional, though it may win you a pie slice in *Trivial Pursuit.*

Where to Go from Here

Thank you for reading the introduction. Few people do, and it would save a lot of time and bother if they did. Consider yourself fortunate, though you probably already knew that.

Your task now: Start reading the rest of this book — but not the whole thing, and especially not in order. Observe the table of contents, and find something that interests you. Or look up your puzzle in the index. When these suggestions don't cut it, just start reading Chapter 1.

My e-mail address is dgookin@wambooli.com. Yes, that's my real address. I reply to all e-mail I receive, and you get a quick reply if you keep your question short and specific to this book. Although I enjoy saying Hi, I cannot answer technical support questions, resolve billing issues, or help you troubleshoot your phone. Thanks for understanding.

You can also visit my web page for more information or as a diversion: www.wambooli.com.

Occasionally, there are updates to technology books. If this book does have technical updates, they will be posted at:

www.dummies.com/go/samsunggalaxynotefdupdates

Enjoy this book and your Galaxy Note!

Part I
What Is This Thing?

In this part . . .

The Galaxy Note is the Reese's Peanut Butter Cup of mobile gizmos: From the chocolate side comes the modern tablet, a large, slate-like device that does many of the same things you once did on a computer, and on the peanut butter side is the cell phone, the primary 21st century communications device, which suffers from a diminutive screen. Put the two together and you can have something curiously delicious, like the Galaxy Note.

Then again, you don't need a book to tell you how to eat a peanut butter cup. Considering all the amazing things the Galaxy Note can do (and that it's a hybrid device with a writing stylus), reading a book is a good idea. This part contains information, hints, and tips to help get you started.

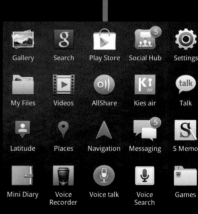

1

A Note for You

*W*hen the geniuses at Samsung named their new hybrid tablet-phone, they chose the word *Galaxy*. That's a given. Many Samsung mobile devices have the name Galaxy in them, which sounds all futuristic and impressive. The word *note*, however, implies different things: A musical tone. Paper money. A mental reminder. The definition that I believe Samsung is after is the verb "to jot down a quick thought or message."

No matter how you define it, the Samsung Galaxy Note is unique. This chapter introduces you to the device, helps you set things up, identifies the pieces and parts, and provides an overall introduction — one that's far more detailed than the tepid *Quick Start* pamphlet and won't frighten the bejeebers out of you.

Out of the Box

The first step toward getting the most from your Galaxy Note is to remove it from its box. I believe that you'll find the phone more responsive after you liberate it from its packaging and set the thing up.

Alas, you probably aren't the first to free the phone from its box. Initial setup was most likely done by the friendly folks at the Phone Store. They've probably configured the Galaxy Note to work with their cellular network, installed something called a SIM card, and walked you through the initial account setup and configuration. If so, great — that's less for you to do.

Whether the phone has been set up or not, I encourage you to rifle through the box to locate and identify these items:

- The phone itself, which may have already been assembled by the Phone Store employee. If not, you'll find the rear cover and battery inside the box, ready to be installed.

- The all-too-brief *Quick Start* pamphlet, the *Health & Safety and Warranty Guide*, and perhaps other miscellaneous and potentially useful pieces of paper

- The charger/data cable, or *USB cable*

- The charger head, which is the wall adapter for the charger/data cable

The phone itself ships with a clingy, static, plastic cover on its screen, back, and sides. The plastic thingy on the front tells you not to text and drive. The rear thingy explains how to remove the back cover. And the plastic thingies on the sides are there just to annoy you because you probably can't tell that they're there. Look extra hard for them and peel them off now.

The most important doodad is the phone itself, which might require some assembly before you can use it; refer to the next section for directions.

- You may have additional items included with your phone purchase, such as a fancy case, flip cover, or car charger or other common accessories that you may have succumbed to purchasing. See the later section "Adding other accessories" for my recommendations.

- The S Pen is found inserted into the phone, so don't panic when you can't locate it loose inside the box. See the later section "Accessing the S Pen" for information.

- One accessory I recommend getting right away is a MicroSD card. See the later section "Adding a MicroSD card" for details.

- Keep the instructions and other information for as long as you own the phone. The phone's box makes an excellent storage place for that stuff — as well as for anything else you don't plan to use right away.

- If anything is missing or appears to be damaged, immediately contact the folks who sold you the phone.

Assembly

The Galaxy Note comes disassembled inside the box. Primarily, the phone is missing its battery and back cover. The Phone Store employee puts everything together for you because the phone must be assembled in order for it to be configured to work with the cellular network.

It rarely happens, but you may be required to perform the initial assembly yourself. If so, this section contains helpful information. Beyond that, you may need to add or upgrade features later, such as a MicroSD card. You'll find that basic information in this section as well, along with the necessary directions for putting everything back together.

Removing the rear cover

To remove the Galaxy Note's rear cover and access all the electronic wonder inside, heed these directions:

1. **Ensure that the phone is turned off.**

   See Chapter 2 for directions. The phone doesn't absolutely have to be turned off, but it reduces the risk of data loss if your goal is removing the MicroSD card.

2. **Flip the phone over and locate the thumbnail notch in the upper-right side of the back cover.**

   Figure 1-1 illustrates where to find the thumbnail hole, though it's specifically called out in Figure 1-2.

3. **Insert your thumbnail into the notch, and carefully pry the back cover from the phone.**

   The cover peels off like a banana skin. The popping noise is normal.

4. **Set aside the cover.**

The Galaxy Note has three items you can access after the back cover is removed, as illustrated in Figure 1-1: the battery, SIM card, and MicroSD card. The following sections offer specific information on each of these items.

See the later section "Reattaching the phone's rear cover" for information on replacing the back cover.

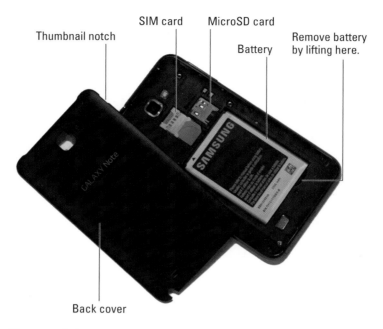

Thumbnail notch SIM card MicroSD card Battery Remove battery by lifting here.

Back cover

Figure 1-1: Galaxy Note guts.

Installing the battery

The first thing to be installed into the Galaxy Note is its battery. If the Phone Store people haven't installed your phone's battery, follow the steps in this section. Or you can heed the directions in the following Tip to replace the phone's battery, should that need ever arise.

Before installing the battery, ensure that you don't need to install other items in your phone. The SIM card and MicroSD card must be installed *before* installing the battery, so install them first, and then come back to this section.

Obey these steps to stick the battery into your phone:

1. **If necessary, remove the battery from its plastic bag.**

2. **Remove the phone's back cover, as discussed in the preceding section.**

3. **Orient the battery.**

   The battery goes in only one way, as illustrated in Figure 1-1. A tiny triangle points up toward the contacts inside the phone. Use the triangle to properly orient the battery.

4. **Insert the battery top side first, and then insert it the rest of the way, as though you're closing the lid on a tiny box.**

   When the battery is properly installed, it's flush with the back of the phone.

After the battery is installed, your next step is to charge it. See the later section "Charge the Battery."

To remove the battery, take off the Galaxy Note's back cover as described in the preceding section. Lift the battery by inserting your thumbnail in the notch in the lower-right corner of the battery compartment, as illustrated in Figure 1-1.

  ✔ If you're replacing the battery, store the original inside a nonmetallic box in a dark, dry location. If you need to dispose of the battery, do so properly; batteries are classified as hazardous waste and should not merely be placed in the trash.

  ✔ Replacement batteries are commonly available, some of which may allow you to use your phone for longer periods between charges. Always ensure that you replace the phone's battery with one that's compatible with the Galaxy Note. Using any old battery as a replacement is a hazard and can damage your phone, you, or innocent bystanders.

Installing the SIM card

Your cellular provider uses the SIM card inside your Galaxy Note to identify it the with the digital cellular network. If the cheerful human at the Phone Store hasn't installed the SIM card into your Galaxy Note, you can do so now by following these steps:

1. **If necessary, remove the phone's back cover. Furthermore, if required, remove the phone's battery.**

2. **Pop the SIM card free from its holder.**

   Press the SIM card until it pops out of the credit-card-size frame.

3. **Insert the SIM card into the SIM card slot inside the Galaxy Note.**

   The SIM card fits in only one way. A silhouette on the SIM card holder inside the phone shows you the proper orientation.

   Insert the SIM card all the way, as illustrated in Figure 1-1.

4. **Replace the battery and the phone's back cover.**

   You're done.

You can skip Step 4 if you need to install a MicroSD card; keep reading in the next section.

- ✔ You rarely, if ever, need to remove the SIM card.

- ✔ A typical way to use a SIM is to replace a broken phone with a new one: You plug the SIM from the old phone into the new phone, and instantly the phone is recognized as your own. Of course, the two phones need to use similar cellular networks for the transplant operation to be successful.

- ✔ SIM stands for Subscriber Identity Module. SIM cards are required for GSM cellular networks and 4G LTE networks.

Adding a MicroSD card

The Galaxy Note doesn't come with a MicroSD card, which is disappointing. The MicroSD card bolsters the internal storage on the Galaxy Note, adding what's called *removable* storage. As with any portable electronic gizmo, the more storage, the better.

Obtain a MicroSD card for your Galaxy Note. The card comes in capacities of 8GB, 16GB, and 32GB. The higher the capacity, the more expensive the card, so buy the largest capacity you can afford.

To install the MicroSD card inside your Galaxy Note, obey these steps:

1. **Remove the phone's back cover and battery.**

   Specific directions are offered earlier in this chapter.

2. **Locate the slot into which you stick the MicroSD card.**

   Use Figure 1-1 as your guide.

3. **Insert the MicroSD card into its slot.**

   The card goes in only one way. The arrow on the card indicates which edge goes in first; the printed side of the card is facing you as you insert the card.

   You may hear a faint clicking sound when the card is fully inserted.

4. **Reinstall the battery (if necessary), and reassemble the Galaxy Note.**

To remove the card, open the phone and remove the battery. Nudge the MicroSD card a tad, until a spring releases the card a few fractions of an inch. Use your fingernail to help grab the card and pull it out the rest of the way.

- ✔ The MicroSD card is a standard form of removable media for portable devices. It's used in mobile phones, cameras, and music players.

- MicroSD cards are teensy! Keep them in a safe place where you won't lose them.
- You can buy a MicroSD card adapter, which allows its data to be read by computers, via either the standard Secure Digital (SD) memory slot or the USB port.
- If you're upgrading to the Galaxy Note from another Android phone, simply remove the MicroSD card from the old phone and install it on the Galaxy Note. By doing so, you instantly transfer your pictures, music, and videos.

Reattaching the phone's rear cover

When you're done rooting around inside your phone, or when it tells you that it's shivering and needs to warm up, you should replace its back cover. The operation works like this:

1. **Line up the bottom of the back cover with the bottom of the Galaxy Note.**

   Start with the back cover up a ways and then slide it down the back of the phone, until you feel it click into place as it lines up.

2. **Working around the back of the phone, gently press the cover into place.**

   The cover snaps as it settles into position.

When the back cover is on properly, it should have no gaps or raised edges. Keep pressing the back cover until you no longer hear any snaps.

Charge the Battery

One of your first duties after assembling your Galaxy Note is to charge its battery. It's cinchy:

1. **If necessary, assemble the charging cord.**

   Connect the charger head (the plug-thing) to the USB cable that comes with the phone. They connect in only one way.

2. **Plug the charger head and cable into a wall socket.**

3. **Plug the phone into the USB cable.**

   The charger cord plugs into the micro-USB connector, found at the phone's bottom side. The connector plugs in only one way.

As the phone charges, the touchscreen displays a large, animated battery icon. It's your clue that the gizmo is connected to a power source and charging. The touchscreen turns off after a few seconds.

- ✒ The Galaxy Note may come with a partially charged battery, often containing enough juice to run setup and get you started. Still, I recommend fully charging the phone before you use it.

- ✒ You can use the phone while it's charging.

- ✒ You can charge the phone in your car, using what was once called a cigarette lighter. Simply ensure that the cell phone charger in your car features the proper connector for your phone or that it's specifically designed for use with your cell phone brand.

- ✒ The phone also charges itself when it's plugged into a computer by way of a USB cable. The computer must be on for charging to work.

- ✒ The Galaxy Note charges more quickly when it's plugged into the wall as opposed to a computer's USB port or a car adapter.

Explore the Galaxy Note

So what is this gizmo you have, this Galaxy Note? Sure it's a phone, but it's probably unlike any other phone you've ever used. To help you get better acquainted, peruse this section and get to know the names of the specific doodads and pieces.

Identifying important things

I'll admit that I use the word *doodad* too often. It's a handy, generic term for just about anything that would otherwise have a technical name. When you use *doodad,* you avoid learning proper terminology, and you run the risk of frustrating other people who may actually know what things are called. Before this happens with your Galaxy Note, examine Figure 1-2 and discover the names of the various doodads on your phone.

The terms referenced in Figure 1-2 are the same terms used elsewhere in this book and in whatever pitiful Galaxy Note documentation exists.

- ✒ The phone's Power Lock button, which turns the phone off or on, is found on the phone's right side as it's facing you, as shown in Figure 1-2.

- ✒ The main area of the phone is its *touchscreen* display. You use the touchscreen with one or more of your fingers to control the phone, which is where it gets the name *touch*screen.

- ✒ Below the touchscreen you'll find four *soft buttons.* See Chapter 3 for more information on how useful they can be.

✔ The *Power / USB connection* is the spot on the phone where you attach the USB cable. You use this cable to charge the phone or to communicate with a computer. See Chapter 20 for information on using the cable to connect to a computer and share files.

✔ The main microphone is found on the bottom of the phone. Even so, it picks up your voice loud and clear. There's no need to hold the phone at an angle for the microphone to work.

✔ The phone's volume is adjusted by using the Volume button on the phone's left side as it's facing you (refer to Figure 1-2). Pressing the top part of the button increases the volume; pressing the bottom part lowers the volume.

✔ The Volume button can also be used as the zoom function when using the phone's camera. See Chapter 14 for more information.

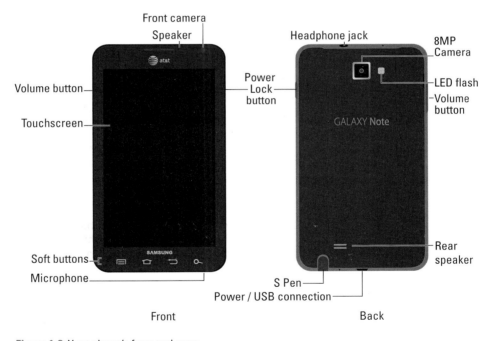

Figure 1-2: Your phone's face and rump.

Accessing the S Pen

Among the things that make the Galaxy Note unique is its *stylus,* or writing implement. Officially, it's the *S Pen,* where the S probably stands for Samsung, but in my world it's "Something else to lose."

The S Pen is found inserted into the bottom of the Galaxy Note, as illustrated earlier, in Figure 1-2. Pull out the pen to reveal the device's full glory, as illustrated in Figure 1-3.

S Pen button

Tip —

Figure 1-3: The S Pen.

You use the S Pen to manipulate items on the screen, to draw more precisely than you can with your finger, but primarily to get the most from the S Memo app, which is discussed in Chapter 17.

Chapter 4 lists a few tricks you can pull by using the S Pen.

When you're done using the S Pen, slide it back into the bottom of the phone for storage.

Using earphones

You don't need to use earphones to get the most from your Galaxy Note, but it helps! If the nice folks who sold you the phone tossed in a pair of earphones, that's wonderful! If they didn't, well then, they weren't so nice, were they?

The most common style of cell phone earphone is the earbud: The buds are set into your ears. The sharp, pointy end of the earphones, which you don't want to stick into your ear, plugs into the top of the phone.

Between the earbuds and the sharp, pointy thing is often found a doodle on which a button sits. The button can be used to mute the Galaxy Note when you're on a call or to start or stop the playback of music when the phone is in its music-playing mode.

You can also use the Doodle button to answer the phone when it rings.

A teensy hole that's usually on the back side of the doodle serves as the phone's microphone. It lets you wear the earphones and talk on the phone while keeping your hands free. If you gesture while you speak, you'll find this feature invaluable.

- You can purchase any standard cell phone headset for use with your phone. Ensure that the headset features a microphone; you need to talk and listen on a phone.

- Some headsets feature extra Doodle buttons. These headsets work fine with your phone, though the extra buttons may not do anything specifically.

- The earbuds are labeled R for right and L for left.

- See Chapter 16 for more information on using your Galaxy Note as a portable music player.

- Fully insert the earphone connector into the phone. The person you're talking with can't hear you well when the earphones are plugged in only partway.

- You can also use a Bluetooth headset with your phone, to listen to a call or some music. See Chapter 19 for more information on Bluetooth.

- Fold the earphones when you don't need them, rather than wrap them in a loop: Hold the earbuds and connector in one hand, and then pull the wire straight out with the other hand. Fold the wire in half, and then in half again. You can then put the earphones in your pocket or on a tabletop. By folding the wires, you avoid creating one of those Christmas-tree-light wire balls that would otherwise happen.

Adding other accessories

Beyond earphones, you can find an entire galaxy of accessories available for your phone. I'm certain that the folks in the Phone Store would be happy to show you a fancy cover or case, but beyond that are some official Samsung accessories. The two in the following sections are worthy of your consideration.

Multimedia Dock

The multimedia dock works like a base station for the Galaxy Note, by propping it up at the perfect angle for viewing videos or using it as a desktop alarm clock. Though the dock may seem kind of ridiculous, it's exactly how I store my Galaxy Note overnight, on my nearby nightstand. As a bonus, the phone charges while it's nestled in the multimedia dock.

Car Mount

Its official name is the Galaxy Note i717 Vehicle Navigation Mount & Car Charger, but it's simply a gizmo that lets you suction-cup the phone to your car's windshield (or any other flat surface). After you secure your phone to the mount, you can use your phone while driving — hands-free. See Chapter 13 for more information on using the Galaxy Note's amazing navigation abilities.

A Home for Your Phone

Thanks to its mobile nature, your Galaxy Note phone can go anywhere. You can find your phone across town or overseas or even in the couch cushions or under a stack of books on the nightstand. Because the phone will no doubt be a necessary part of your life in the near future, finding a better location than the couch cushions is probably a good idea.

Toting your Galaxy Note

It's true that many a wild-eyed stare greets the Galaxy Note because of its dominating size and hybrid tablet-phone nature. Still, the thing fits perfectly in your front pocket, clips easily on a belt, or sits snugly in even the teensiest of party purses. To help it survive in these harsh conditions, the Galaxy Note features a proximity sensor.

The *proximity sensor* disables the touchscreen whenever the phone is in a confined space — or even pressed firmly against your cheek. You risk no danger that your phone might accidentally activate its touchscreen and suddenly dial Tibet.

- Though it's okay to let go of the phone when you're making a call, be careful not to touch the phone's Power Lock button (refer to Figure 1-2). Doing so may temporarily enable the touchscreen, which can hang up a call, mute the phone, or do any of a number of other undesirable things.

- You can always store your phone in one of a variety of handsome carrying case accessories, some of which come in fine Naugahyde or leatherette.

- Don't forget that the phone is in your pocket, especially in your coat or jacket. You might accidentally sit on the phone, or it can fly out when you take off your coat. The worst fate for any cell phone is to take a trip to the laundry. I'm sure that the Galaxy Note has nightmares about it.

Storing the phone

I recommend that you find a permanent place for your phone when you're not taking it with you. Make the spot consistent: on top of your desk or workstation, on the kitchen counter, on the nightstand — you get the idea. Phones are as prone to being misplaced as are your car keys and glasses. Consistency is the key to finding your phone.

Then again, your phone rings, so when you lose it, you can always have someone else call your cell phone to help you locate it.

- ✓ I keep my phone on my desk, next to my computer. Conveniently, I have the charger plugged into the computer so that the phone remains plugged in, connected, and charging when I'm not using it.
- ✓ Phones on coffee tables get buried under magazines and are often squished when rude people put their feet on the furniture.
- ✓ Avoid putting your phone in direct sunlight; heat is a bad thing for any electronic gizmo.
- ✓ Do not put your phone in the laundry (see the preceding section). See Chapter 23 for information on properly cleaning the phone.

2

On, Off, and Configuration

In This Chapter

▶ Turning on the phone

▶ Setting up your Galaxy Note

▶ Running AT&T Ready2Go setup

▶ Setting up accounts manually

▶ Locking the Galaxy Note

▶ Turning off your phone

Modern technology wastes no time in confusing you. Case in point: The Galaxy Note lacks an on-off switch. Unlike the common table lamp, the Galaxy Note has no switch to flip to turn on the phone. Likewise, it has no switch for turning off the phone. Instead, the job is handled by something called a Power Lock button, which serves several functions beyond turning the thing on or off.

See? What could be the most basic of operations turns out to be an ordeal that requires an entire chapter of explanation on turning the phone on, unlocking it, locking it, and turning it off. One button does all that. And if you haven't yet experienced the thrill of turning on your phone for the first time, that duty is covered here as well.

Hello!

Go back in time 40 years and ask someone whether they know how to turn on their telephone. They would probably reply that the phone is "on" all the time or that you have to lift the handset to make a call or answer. O, life was so simple then, but using a telephone was far more dull.

Saying "Hello" to your Galaxy Note involves more than lifting it to your nose. It's a process called *power up,* and this section explains how it works.

Turning on your phone

To turn on the Galaxy Note, press the Power Lock button for a second or two. The phone vibrates slightly as it starts, and you see the Samsung logo displayed on the touchscreen. After that, you can enjoy the start-up animation. It takes a few additional moments for the phone to complete the startup process.

Eventually, you see the main unlocking screen, shown in Figure 2-1. Unlock the phone by touching the screen and dragging your finger an inch or so in any direction, as illustrated in the figure. As you drag your finger outward, the Padlock icon animates by unlocking itself and you're granted access to the phone.

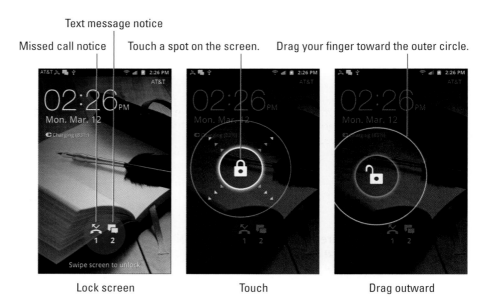

Text message notice

Missed call notice | Touch a spot on the screen. | Drag your finger toward the outer circle.

Lock screen   Touch   Drag outward

Figure 2-1: Unlocking the Galaxy Note.

You can touch the screen anywhere to unlock the phone. You don't necessarily need to touch it in the same spot indicated in Figure 2-1.

If you've configured extra security for your Galaxy Note, you might see one of three different types of lock screens, as illustrated in Figure 2-2. These screens appear in place of the standard locking screen, shown in Figure 2-1.

To work the various alternative locks, you must trace a pattern on the screen, type a PIN, or type a password, as shown in Figure 2-2. See Chapter 22 for details on applying and using these types of screen locks.

Place 911 call. Trace pattern.   Type PIN.   Type password. Display dialpad.

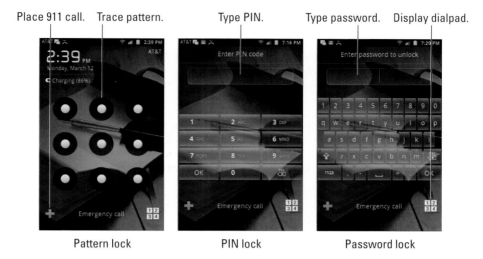

Pattern lock   PIN lock   Password lock

Figure 2-2: Alternative screen locks.

When you turn on your Galaxy Note for the first time, special start-up and configuration software runs. If the initial setup was completed at the Phone Store, you can now use your Galaxy Note. Otherwise, refer to the later section "Account Setup" to see how to work through the setup process.

If you've already set things up, you see the Home screen after you unlock the phone. Refer to Chapter 3 for information on what you can do at the Home screen.

- In Figure 2-1, the lock screen indicates that one call has been missed and two text messages await review.

- It's not necessary to unlock the phone for an incoming call. For information on receiving phone calls, see Chapter 5.

- Even if the phone has a security pattern, PIN, or password lock screen, you can still make emergency calls: Touch the red Plus button to dial 911, or touch the Dialpad button (refer to Figure 2-2) to dial an emergency number.

- The alternative screen locks may not show up if you lock and then quickly unlock the phone. That's because a time-out value is associated with their use. Refer to Chapter 22 for information on setting the time-out value. When this value isn't reached, the standard unlocking screen (shown in Figure 2-1) is used.

Unlocking the phone

Most of the time, you don't turn off your phone. Instead, you lock it. Either the Galaxy Note locks on its own, after a given period of inactivity, or you lock it by pressing the Power Lock button (covered later in this chapter).

When the phone is locked, it's still on and can receive calls, e-mail, and other notifications, but the touchscreen is turned off. You unlock the phone by pressing the Power Lock button. A simple, short press will do. Then work the locks as shown in Figures 2-1 and 2-2 and described in the preceding section.

- Touching the touchscreen when the screen is off doesn't unlock the phone.

- An incoming call doesn't unlock the phone, but information about the call is displayed on the touchscreen. See Chapter 5 for information on answering the phone.

- The Galaxy Note continues to play music while it's locked. See Chapter 16 for more information on using an Galaxy Note as a portable music player.

Account Setup

To get the most from your Galaxy Note, you need a Google account. If you have one, that's great. If you don't, it's easy — and free — to obtain one. See the nearby sidebar "Get yourself a Google account!" to get started.

Beyond the Google account, you probably have other Internet accounts, including various e-mail and social networking accounts. You can set them up for use with the Galaxy Note as well. The information in this section tells you how the account setup is done.

Setting up with AT&T Ready2Go

The easiest way to configure your Galaxy Note is to run the AT&T Ready2Go app. You may have already done so before leaving the Phone Store. If not, you can do so now.

The AT&T Ready2Go app works with your Galaxy Note and a computer connected to the Internet to help configure your phone. You'll fill in account information, contacts, and other configuration options on a web page using the computer. Then the AT&T mothership sends that information to your Galaxy Note, completing the setup process in one quick action.

Get yourself a Google account!

If you don't already have a Google account, run — don't walk or mince — to a computer and create your own, free Google account: Use the computer's web browser program to visit the main Google page, www.google.com. On that page, click the Sign In link. If you don't see it, you already have a Google account. You're done.

After you click the Sign In link, another page appears. Locate the link that lets you create a new account. At the time this book went to press, the link was titled Sign Up for a New Google Account, though it may change in the future. Continue heeding the directions on the screen until you've created your own Google account.

After your account is set up and configured. I recommend that you log off and then log back on to Google, to ensure that you did everything properly.

You can start the AT&T Ready2Go app in one of two ways:

- ✒ Touch the Applications icon found in the lower-right corner of the Home screen, and then choose the AT&T Ready2Go app from the Apps menu.

- ✒ Look for the Ready2Go notification icon, similar to the one shown in the margin. Pull down the notifications, and choose AT&T Ready2Go to run the app.

More information on using the Home screen and choosing notifications is found in Chapter 3. It's okay to read that information now and then come back here and complete the setup later.

After starting the AT&T Ready2Go app, follow these general steps to work through the process:

1. **Touch the Get Started button.**

2. **On your computer, visit the website listed on the phone.**

   The address I see is http://att.com/pair, though it may change in the future.

   A code also appears below the website address. You use the code in Step 3.

3. **On your computer, on the AT&T Ready2Go web page, type the code you see on your Galaxy Note.**

   Type the code using your computer. The code eventually synchronizes the information that you type on the web page with your Galaxy Note.

The remaining steps take place on your computer, but keep the phone handy, anyway.

4. Click the Submit button.

5. Type your Google Gmail account name and password.

6. Ensure that check marks appear by the options Sync Contacts and Sync Calendar and by any other items that may show up.

7. Click the Add Gmail Account button.

The web page thinks for a bit and eventually adds your Gmail account to a list of accounts on the right side of the screen.

8. Click the Next Step button.

The next step is to add your social networking accounts. On the web page, on the left side of the screen, I see options for Facebook, Twitter, and LinkedIn.

9. Type your Facebook login and password.

The login is usually your e-mail address.

If you don't have a Facebook account, you can choose another social networking site, or click the Next Step button to proceed.

10. Click the Add Account button.

11. Choose another social networking site, such as Twitter, from the left side of the screen, and repeat Steps 9 and 10 to add that account.

On my computer, I see an option for adding a LinkedIn account.

At this point, you're pretty much done with the configuration, and you can click the Jump to Finish button to wrap things up. Otherwise, you can continue to work through the steps, adding contacts or choosing wallpaper, for example — until you're finally bored and you click the Jump to Finish button out of exasperation.

The final screen summarizes all the steps you've taken.

12. Click the Set Up My Phone button.

As if by magic, the Internet communicates with your Galaxy Note and the changes you've specified are slapped down on the phone. Setup is complete.

13. On the phone, touch the Finish button.

The primary thing you're doing with the AT&T Ready2Go app is setting up your phone with a Google account. That account — specifically, your Google Gmail account — is the key to connecting the Galaxy Note with a host of services that Google offers for free on the Internet, as well as on your phone. Everything is nicely connected and synchronized — but only after you add your Google account.

Don't worry if you've skipped a step! You can, at any time, add or change accounts, add contacts, or change the wallpaper and other settings. This book describes all these items in later chapters; check the index for specific items.

Adding accounts the manual way

The AT&T Ready2Go app sets up all your Internet accounts on the Galaxy Note in one action. If you've skipped an account, or if you want to add one later, you can follow these steps at any time:

1. **Go to the Home screen.**

   The *Home* screen is the main screen on your phone. You can always get there by pressing the Home soft button, found at the bottom of the touchscreen.

2. **Press the Menu soft button.**

   The Menu soft button is found at the bottom of the touchscreen, right next to the Home soft button.

3. **Choose the Settings command.**

   The Settings command helps you access internal options, controls, and settings for configuring your Galaxy Note. This command is a popular place to visit while you read this book.

4. **Choose Accounts and Sync.**

   On the Accounts and Sync screen, under the Manage Accounts heading, is a list of accounts configured for your Galaxy Note. The list may be empty, or it may contain several accounts.

5. **Touch the Add Account button.**

   A list of accounts that you can add appears. The list varies, depending on which apps are installed on your phone.

6. **Choose an account to add.**

   For example, if you haven't yet set up your Google account, choose Google.

7. **Work through the steps on the screen to sign in to the account.**

   Typically, you type your username and password. The phone contacts the Internet and synchronizes your account information.

8. **If prompted, ensure that check marks appear by the all the Data & Synchronization options.**

   By placing check marks by all these items, you ensure that the phone completely synchronizes with all your account information.

9. **Touch the Finish button.**

10. **Touch the Finish Setup button.**

    You're done.

Press the Home soft button to return to the Home screen.

- ✐ The only accounts you can't configure using the Accounts and Sync screen are e-mail accounts. To set up your e-mail accounts, refer to Chapter 9.

- ✐ If you change an account password and forget to tell the phone about it, you see an alert notification, similar to the one shown in the margin. Pull down the notifications and choose Sign In Error for that specific account. Follow the directions on the screen to update your password.

- ✐ See Chapter 3 for more information about soft buttons, the Home screen, and the App menu.

Goodbye!

You can dismiss your Galaxy Note in one of several ways. The most popular way is to lock the phone. Another way is to turn off the phone. The most difficult way to dismiss the phone involves a vat of mayonnaise and a howitzer, but this book just doesn't have room enough to properly describe that method.

Locking the phone

To lock your Galaxy Note, press and release the Power Lock button. No matter what you're doing, the phone's touchscreen display turns off. The phone itself isn't off, but the touchscreen display goes dark and ignores your touches.

- ✐ Your Galaxy Note will probably spend most of its time locked.

- ✐ Locking the phone doesn't disconnect a phone call. In fact, it's safer to talk on the phone when it's locked because you eliminate the risk of accidentally touching anything on the screen.

- ✐ The Galaxy Note features a proximity sensor, which automatically locks the phone whenever its face is close to another object.

✓ Locking doesn't turn off the phone; you can still receive calls while the phone is locked.

   ✓ Any timers or alarms you've set are still scheduled while the phone is locked, and music continues to play. See Chapter 17 for information on setting timers and alarms; Chapter 16 covers playing music.

Controlling the automatic lock timeout

The Galaxy Note is configured to automatically lock itself after a given period of inactivity. You can control the time-out value to intervals between 15 seconds and 10 minutes. To confirm or change the time-out, obey these steps:

   1. **At the Home screen, press the Menu soft button.**

   2. **Choose Settings.**

   3. **Choose Display.**

   4. **Choose Screen Timeout.**

   5. **Choose a time-out value from the list that's provided.**

      The standard value is 1 minute.

   6. **Press the Home soft button to return to the Home screen.**

When you don't touch the screen, or when you aren't using the phone, the lock timer starts ticking. About ten seconds before the time-out value you've set (refer to Step 5), the touchscreen dims. Then the phone goes to sleep. If you touch the screen before then, the lock timer is reset.

Turning off the phone

To turn off your Galaxy Note, you must access the Phone Options menu, shown in Figure 2-3. Follow these steps:

Figure 2-3: The Phone Options menu.

1. **Press and hold the Power Lock button until the Phone Options menu appears.**

2. **Choose the Power Off item.**

   If you change your mind and don't want to turn off the phone, press the Back soft button to cancel.

3. **Touch the OK button to confirm.**

   You see some animation as the phone shuts itself off. Eventually, the touchscreen goes dark.

When the phone is turned off, it doesn't receive calls or trigger notifications or alarms. Incoming calls go to voice mail; see Chapter 7 for more information on voice mail.

Rule the Galaxy Note

In This Chapter

▶ Understanding the soft buttons
▶ Touching the touchscreen
▶ Changing the phone's volume
▶ Entering Vibrate mode or Silent mode
▶ Reorienting the phone
▶ Viewing Home screen panels
▶ Checking notifications
▶ Accessing Quick Actions
▶ Running applications and working widgets
▶ Reviewing recently used apps

I've looked and looked, and so far I count only two-and-a-half buttons on the Galaxy Note — the Power Lock button and the Volume button, which is only one physical button with an upper half and a lower half. Beyond that, the phone is utterly flat and devoid of buttons, knobs, switches, and dials. That begs the question: How do you control a phone whose main method of input is essentially a flat piece of glass?

Answer: You read this chapter, which explains the basic operations, methods, and features of the Samsung Galaxy Note smartphone.

Basic Operations

You probably messed around with your phone well before your eyes hit this page. That's fine: The urge to play with new technology can sometimes be unbearable. I'm certain that many a caveman set his hair ablaze learning to work with fire. Your exposure to the Galaxy Note need not be so dramatic or disfiguring. Simply read this section and you'll get the hang of things in no time.

Using the soft buttons

Below the touchscreen on your Galaxy Note dwell two to four buttons labeled with icons. They're *soft buttons,* and they perform specific functions no matter what you're doing on the phone. The soft buttons are, from left to right, Menu, Home, Back, and Search.

Menu

 Pressing the Menu soft button displays a pop-up menu, from which you can choose commands to control whichever app you're using. You can press the Menu soft button again to hide the pop-up menu. And if nothing happens when you press the Menu soft button, a pop-up menu isn't available.

Home

 Pressing the Home soft button displays the Home screen. In this way, it works like the "quit" command in a computer program, and it works no matter what you're doing on your phone.

When you're already viewing the Home screen, pressing the Home soft button returns you to the main (center) Home screen.

Pressing and holding the Home button displays a list of recently opened apps.

Back

 The Back soft button serves several purposes, all of which neatly fit under the concept of *back.* Press the soft button once to go back to a previous page, close a menu, close a window, or dismiss the onscreen keyboard, for example. I'm certain that the Back soft button is the one you'll press most often.

Search

 The Search soft button is your direct connection to the phone's powerful Search command. The Galaxy Note is, after all, a Google phone. Press the Search soft button once to summon the phone-and-web search command. Or press the Search soft button in a specific app, such as Contacts (the phone's address book), to search within that app.

See Chapter 8 for more information on your phone's address book app.

When you press and hold the Search soft button, you see the Voice Search app, which lets you command the phone with your voice. See Chapter 24 for more information on the Voice Search app.

Soft key enlightenment

All four soft buttons light up whenever you press one, which makes them easier to see. Whether you like them illuminated all the time or never, follow these steps:

1. **At the Home screen, press the Menu soft button.**

   See how they light up? Good.

2. **Choose Settings.**

3. **Choose Display.**

4. **Choose Touch Key Light Duration.**

   The Display screen refers to the soft buttons as *touch keys,* for some reason.

5. **Choose an option.**

   For example, choose Always On so that the buttons are always easy to see.

Keeping the soft key lights on all the time doesn't noticeably drain the battery.

When you lock the phone, the soft key lights turn off no matter which setting you've chosen.

Manipulating the touchscreen

The touchscreen works in combination with one or two of your fingers, or one of your fingers and the tip of your nose. Oh, why not be adventurous?

No matter how you touch it (and I do recommend fingers), you can use several touchscreen-manipulation techniques:

Touch: In this simple operation, you touch the screen. Generally, you're touching an object such as an app icon or button. You might also see the term *press* or *tap.*

Double-tap: Touch the screen in the same location twice. A double-tap can be used to zoom in on an image or a map or to zoom out. Because of the double-tap's dual nature, I recommend using the pinch and spread operations instead.

Long-press: Touch and hold part of the screen. Some operations, such as moving an icon on the Home screen, begin with the long-press.

Swipe: When you swipe, you start with your finger in one spot and then drag it to another spot. A swipe can move up, down, left, or right, and it can be fast or slow. A swipe, sometimes called a *flick,* can be used to slide something around on the screen or to move an object.

Pinch: A pinch involves two fingers, which start out separated and then are brought together. The pinch is used to zoom out on an image or a map.

Spread: In the opposite of a pinch, you start with your fingers together and then spread them. The spread is used to zoom in.

Rotate: Use two fingers to twist around a central point on the touchscreen, which has the effect of rotating an object on the screen. If you have trouble with this operation, imagine that you're turning the dial on a safe.

You cannot use the touchscreen while wearing gloves, unless they're gloves specially designed for using an electronic touchscreen, such as the gloves that Batman wears.

Setting the volume

The phone's volume control is found on the left side of the phone as it's facing you. Press the top part of the button to raise the volume. Press the bottom part of the button to lower the volume, as illustrated in Figure 3-1.

The volume control works for whatever noise the phone is making when you use it: When you're on a call, the volume control sets the level of the call. When you're listening to music or watching a video, the volume control sets the media volume.

The volume can be preset for the phone and for media, alarms, and notifications. See Chapter 22 for information.

"Silence your phone!"

You hear it all the time: "Please silence your cell phones." The quick way to obey this command on your Galaxy Note is to keep pressing the Volume Down button until the phone vibrates. What you're doing is setting the phone to Silent-and-Vibrate mode.

The phone can also be silenced from the Phone Options menu. Obey these steps:

1. **Press and hold the Power Lock button.**

   The Phone Options menu appears.

Volume Down

Volume Up   Onscreen volume display

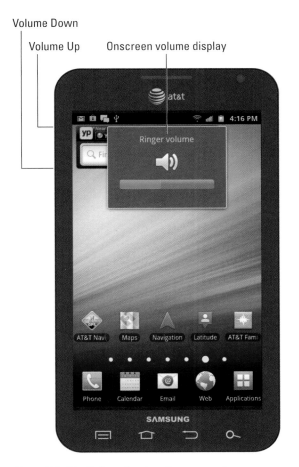

Figure 3-1: The Galaxy Note's volume control.

2. Choose the Silent Mode option.

The phone is silenced.

To make the phone noisy again, simply touch the Volume Up button.

When the phone is silenced, the Silenced icon appears on the status bar.

When the phone is in Vibrate mode, the Vibration icon appears on the status bar.

It's possible to silence the phone and not place it in Vibrate mode. Details are offered in Chapter 22.

Enjoying the accelerometer

An *accelerometer* is the gizmo that determines the Galaxy Note's orientation. Most often, the accelerometer comes into play when you move the phone from an upright position to a horizontal one, as illustrated in Figure 3-2.

Vertical orientation   Horizontal orientation

Figure 3-2: Vertical and horizontal orientations.

In Figure 3-2, the Web app is used to view a website in both vertical and horizontal locations. Often, websites are easier to view on a phone in horizontal orientation.

If the screen doesn't rotate, especially in the Web app, the Screen Rotation feature may be disabled on your Galaxy Note. See the later section "Using Quick Actions" for information on displaying Quick Actions. Choose the Screen Rotation Quick Action to reenable the feature.

Another way to employ the Galaxy Note's accelerometer is to activate the Motion feature. Follow these steps:

1. **At the Home screen, press the Menu soft button.**

2. **Choose Settings.**

3. **Choose Motion.**

   The Motions screen lets you control the Motion Activation services, as listed on the screen. The services let you control things that the Galaxy Note does by moving the phone.

4. **Place a check mark by the words *Motion Activation* to enable the feature.**

Four motions are available after Motion Activation is enabled:

Tilt to Zoom: Touch the screen with your thumbs and tilt the phone away or toward you to zoom in or out.

Pan to Edit: Touch an object on the screen, and shift the phone left or right to move the object to another screen.

Shake to Update: Shake the phone to scan it for available Bluetooth devices.

Turn Over to Mute: Flip the phone over on its face, and the sound is instantly silenced.

You can try out the motions by choosing one and then touching the Learn About menu item.

5. **Choose a motion to enable or disable that particular option, adjust sensitivity, or see a demo.**

The phone prompts you to try various motions when you start certain apps, such as the Web app. You can disable the prompt by placing a green check mark in the Do Not Ask Again box and then touching the Cancel button.

- You can orient the phone to the left or right, but rare is the app that orients itself when you twist the phone upside down.

- The Home screen stays in the vertical orientation unless you place the Galaxy Note into a desktop dock.

- See Chapter 10 for more information on using the Galaxy Note to browse the web.

- Most apps switch the orientation from portrait to landscape when you tilt the phone. A few apps, mostly games, are fixed to one orientation or another.

- See Chapter 19 for more information on Bluetooth.

- A useful application for demonstrating the phone's accelerometer is the game *Labyrinth*. It can be purchased at the Google Play Store, or a free version, *Labyrinth Lite,* can be downloaded. See Chapter 18 for more information on the Google Play Store.

Home Screen Chores

The center of activity on your Galaxy Note is the location called the *Home screen.* It's the first thing you see after unlocking your phone, it's where you're returned to when you quit an app, and it appears when you press the Home soft button. Knowing how to work the Home screen is the key to getting the most from your phone.

Examining the Home screen

The Galaxy Note Home screen is shown in Figure 3-3. It has several points of interest you need to know about. Here's the list, along with the names for those items as used throughout this book:

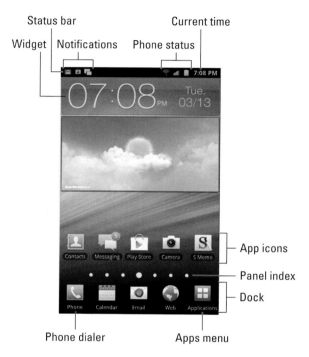

Figure 3-3: The Home screen.

Status bar: The top of the Home screen is a thin, informative strip that I call the *status bar*. It contains notification icons and status icons, plus the current time.

Notifications: These icons come and go, depending on what happens in your digital life. For example, a new notification icon appears whenever you receive a new e-mail message or have a pending appointment. The section "Reviewing notifications," later in this chapter, describes how to deal with notifications.

Phone status: Icons on the right end of the status bar represent the phone's current condition, such as the type of network it's connected to, signal strength, and battery status, as well as whether the speaker has been muted or a Wi-Fi network is connected, for example.

Widgets: These teensy programs can display information, let you control the phone, manipulate a phone feature, access a program, or do something purely amusing. You can read more about widgets in Chapter 22.

App icons: The meat of the meal on the Home screen plate is the app icon. Touching this icon runs its program, or *app*.

Panel index: These dots clue you in to which Home screen panel you're viewing. Touching a dot instantly zooms you to that panel. See the next section for more information on Home screen panels.

Dock: The bottom of every Home screen panel contains the same five icons. You can change the first four icons, but the Applications icon remains steady.

Phone: You use the Phone app to make calls. It's kind of a big deal.

Applications: Touching the Applications app displays the App menu, a paged list of all apps installed on your phone. The later section "All the Apps" describes how it works.

Specific directions for using these individual Home screen gizmos are found throughout this chapter.

- The Home screen is entirely customizable. You can add and remove icons from the Home screen, add widgets and shortcuts, and even change wallpaper images. See Chapter 22 for more information.

- Touching part of the Home screen that doesn't feature an icon or a control does nothing — unless you're using the *live wallpaper* feature. In that case, touching the screen changes the wallpaper in some way, depending on the wallpaper that's selected. You can read more about live wallpaper in Chapter 22.

Accessing the Home screen panels

The Home screen is six times wider than the one you see on the front of your Galaxy Note. The Home screen has left and right wings, three apiece, as shown in Figure 3-4. That's a total of seven Home screen panels.

To switch from one panel to the next, swipe the screen left or right. The Panel index (refer to Figure 3-3) tells you which panel you're viewing. You can touch any dot in the Panel index to instantly zoom to that panel; press the Home soft button to zoom to the center panel.

The number of Home screen panels, as well as their arrangement, can be changed. You can have anywhere from one to seven Home screen panels on the Galaxy Note. Chapter 24 describes how to add, remove, and rearrange the panels.

✔ To dismiss all notification icons, touch the Clear button, shown in Figure 3-6.

✔ When more notifications are present than can be shown on the status bar, you see the More Notifications icon displayed, as shown in the margin. The number on the icon indicates how many additional notifications are available.

✔ Dismissing notifications doesn't prevent them from appearing again later. For example, notifications to update your programs continue to appear, as do calendar reminders.

✔ Some programs, such as Facebook and Twitter, don't display notifications unless you're logged in. See Chapter 11.

✔ Notification icons appear on the screen when the phone is locked. You must unlock the phone before you can drag down the status bar to display notifications.

Using Quick Actions

Adorning the top of the notifications list are some buttons, as shown in Figure 3-6. These buttons, known as the *Quick Actions,* turn on or off certain common phone features: Wi-Fi network access, Bluetooth, GPS, Airplane mode, and the ability of the screen to reorient itself.

You access the Quick Actions by pulling down the notification list, as described in the preceding section. Touch a button to turn that Quick Action on or off; items that are on are displayed in green, such as Wi-Fi in Figure 3-6.

✔ There are more complicated ways to activate all the Quick Actions features, as described elsewhere in this book. But don't fret: I promise to remind you of the Quick Actions when the time comes.

✔ See Chapter 19 for information on Wi-Fi, Bluetooth, and GPS.

✔ Airplane mode is covered in Chapter 21.

✔ Screen rotation is mentioned earlier in this chapter, in the section "Enjoying the accelerometer."

Starting an app

It's cinchy to run an app on the Home screen: Touch its icon. The app starts.

✔ Not all apps appear on the Home screen, but all of them appear when you display the Apps menu. See the section "Browsing the Apps menu for apps," later in this chapter.

✔ When an app closes or you quit the app, you return to the Home screen.

✔ App is short for *application.*

Using a widget

A *widget* is a teensy program that "floats" over the Home screen, as shown earlier, in Figure 3-3. To use a widget, simply touch it. What happens after that depends on the widget.

For example, touching the Google Search widget displays the onscreen keyboard and lets you type, or dictate, something to search for on the Internet. A weather widget may display information about the current weather, and social networking widgets may display status updates or tweets, for example.

Information on these and other widgets appears elsewhere in this book. See Chapter 22 for information on working with widgets.

All the Apps

Your phone has far more apps than have been slapped down on the Home screen. The place to find those apps is the Apps menu.

Browsing the Apps menu for apps

To behold all apps installed on your Galaxy Note, touch the Applications icon, nestled in the lower-right corner of the Home screen. You see the Apps menu displayed, as shown in Figure 3-7.

Figure 3-7: The Apps menu screen.

As with the Home screen, you can have multiple App menu panels; swipe the screen left or right to hunt down additional apps. The panel index, illustrated in Figure 3-7, shows you how many panels are available and which one you're viewing.

To run an app, touch its icon. The app starts, taking over the screen and doing whatever magical thing the app does.

✔ When you can't find an app, remember to look on the Dock (refer to Figure 3-7). That Dock mirrors the Home screen Dock, with the exception of the Home icon where the Application icon would be. Touching the Home icon returns you to the Home screen.

✔ The Apps menu is entirely customizable. In Figure 3-7, you see Alphabetical Grid view. To change the view, touch the Menu soft button and choose the View Type command.

✔ Customizable Grid view allows you to edit and rearrange icons on the Apps menu. See Chapter 18.

✔ Apps menu folders can be created, as shown in Figure 3-7. Be sure to look into those folders for any apps you may be unable to find.

✔ When you need to find *all* apps, choose Alphabetical List view: Press the Menu soft button, choose View Type, and then choose Alphabetical List.

Reviewing recently used apps

If you're like me, you probably use the same apps over and over, on both your computer and your phone. You can easily access the list of recent programs on your Galaxy Note by pressing and holding the Home soft button. When you do, you see a list of the most recently accessed programs, as shown in Figure 3-8.

Figure 3-8: Recently opened apps.

Choose a recent app from the list to open that app again, or to return to the app if it's already open and running.

 To exit the list of recently used apps, press the Back soft button.

 ✔ You can press and hold the Home soft button in any application at any time to see the recently used apps list.

 ✔ See Chapter 24 for information on using the Task Manager.

 ✔ For programs you use all the time, consider creating shortcuts on the Home screen. Chapter 22 describes how to create shortcuts to apps as well as shortcuts to people and shortcuts to instant messaging and all sorts of fun stuff.

4

Text, Typing, and Writing

*O*ne of your duties on the Galaxy Note is typing text. Don't bother looking for the keyboard on your phone. It's not there. As a substitute, the *onscreen keyboard* appears. It can take on several different looks, but basically you type text on the touchscreen similarly to the way you type on a computer keyboard. Well, that and the Galaxy Note keyboard is flat. And tiny. And potentially maddening.

This chapter covers the typing chore on your Galaxy Note. Because the subject is writing text, the topic of text editing is also covered. Just to be a nice guy, I've tossed in information on input with the S Pen as well as the phone's amazing dictation feature. It's all here.

Keyboard Mania

O how I wish that the Galaxy Note had just one onscreen keyboard. It doesn't. Sure, when you're just starting out, you see one keyboard. And you can use only one keyboard at a time. But multiple keyboards are, in fact, available.

Yes, they did that just to confuse you.

Checking out the keyboard variations

Figure 4-1 illustrates the keyboard variations available on the Galaxy Note. Most of them have a wider version you can use by tilting the phone to landscape orientation, as shown in Figure 4-2.

Android keyboard

Samsung keyboard

Samsung 3x4 keyboard

Swype keyboard

Figure 4-1: Keyboard variations.

Android keyboard

Samsung keyboard

Swype keyboard

Figure 4-2: Keyboard variations, landscape orientation.

Here are the keyboard descriptions:

The Android keyboard: The stock keyboard, available to all Android phones. If you're familiar with using this keyboard, it's your best choice.

The Samsung keyboard: The keyboard that the phone normally uses, which is okay but not the best or only option.

The Samsung 3x4 keyboard: A modified, 9-key keyboard for folks who are used to typing on a phone keypad. Don't let the primitive nature of this keyboard fool you: It has the largest keys.

The Swype keyboard: It looks like a regular keyboard but helps you quickly type text without lifting a finger — literally.

All these onscreen keyboards, except for the Samsung 3x4, use the basic QWERTY layout that you're familiar with on a computer keyboard. See the later section "Typing on the 3x4 keyboard" for details on using this unique keyboard.

✔ See the later section "Using Swype to create text" for details on using the Swype keyboard.

✔ If you tire of typing or you suffer endless thumb cramps, you can dictate text to your phone. See the section "Jaw-Dropping Dictation," later in this chapter.

Selecting a different keyboard

To change keyboards, follow these steps:

1. **At the Home screen, press the Menu soft button.**
2. **Choose Settings.**
3. **Tap the Choose Language and Keyboard option.**
4. **Choose Select Input Method.**

   The three main keyboard varieties — Android, Samsung, and Swype — appear in the Select Input Method dialog box.
5. **Pick another keyboard from the list.**

To activate the Samsung 3x4 keyboard, follow Steps 1 through 3 in this list, but in Step 4 choose Samsung Keyboard and then Portrait Keyboard Types and then 3x4 Keyboard.

The change takes place immediately. Any app that uses the onscreen keyboard starts using the keyboard you selected in Step 5.

✔ You can also change keyboards on the fly in some instances: Long-press a chunk of text, and choose the Input Method command from the pop-up menu. From the next screen, select the keyboard you desire. (If you don't see the Input Method command, changing the keyboard isn't possible in that particular app.)

✔ The key layout on some keyboards changes depending on the app you're using and on what you're typing. For example, the Enter key may change to read *Next, Done,* or *Go.* You'd use the Next key to hop from one field to another.

Phone Typing

The onscreen keyboard appears whenever you need to type text. It happens more often than you think — when you compose e-mail, write a text message, type a web page address, or fill in a form, for example. This section offers tips and suggestions to make your phone typing task tolerable.

Typing on the Samsung and Android keyboards

The basic Android and Samsung onscreen keyboards work just as you'd expect: Touch the key you want, and that character appears in the program you're using. It's magic! A blinking cursor on the touchscreen shows where new text appears, which is similar to how text input works on your computer.

- Above all, *type slowly* until you get used to the keyboard.

- When you make a mistake, press the Delete key to back up and erase. The Delete key's icon is shown in the margin.

- People generally accept that typing on a phone isn't perfect. Don't sweat it if you make a few mistakes as you type e-mail or instant messages, though you should expect some curious replies about unintended typos.

- See the later section "Text Editing" for more details on editing your text.

- When you tire of typing, you can always touch the Microphone key on the keyboard to enter Dictation mode. See the section "Jaw-Dropping Dictation," later in this chapter.

Using Swype to create text

The key to using the Swype keyboard is to not lift your finger from the touchscreen. Start slowly; don't worry that the teenager sitting next to you is using Swype so fast that it looks like he's writing Chinese characters on his phone.

Your first task in Swype is to learn how to type simple, short words: Keep your finger on the touchscreen, and drag it over the letters in the word, such as the word *howdy,* shown in Figure 4-3. Lift your finger when you've completed the word, and the word appears in whichever app you're using.

Start here.

Figure 4-3: Swipe the word *howdy.*

Capital letters are typed by dragging your finger above the keyboard after touching the letter, as shown in Figure 4-4, where *Utah* is typed.

Start here.

Figure 4-4: Swiping a capital letter.

To create a double letter, such as the *oo* in *book*, you make a little loop on the letter you want to duplicate. In Figure 4-5, the word *spoon* is typed, using the double-letter trick.

Start here.

Swype key

Figure 4-5: Swiping double letters.

If Swype incorrectly guesses what you've typed, touch the proper word from the alternatives displayed just above the onscreen keyboard. That's the quickest way to fix a bad Swype swipe. Otherwise, you have to press the Delete key to back up and erase and then try again.

For more Swype typing tips, refer to the tutorial found by long-pressing the Swype key on the keyboard. (Refer to Figure 4-5.) Choose the How to Swype option to begin a tutorial.

✔ The Swype software interprets your intent as much as it interprets your accuracy. Even being *close to* the target letter is good enough — as long as you create the correct pattern over the keyboard, Swype usually displays the right word.

✔ Slow down and you'll get the hang of it.

Typing on the 3x4 keyboard

The 3x4 keyboard features two text-input methods:

XT9: It's perhaps the easiest way to type on a 10-key pad — simply touch the key with the letter you want, and the phone predicts what you're typing. (The XT9 method is in effect when the keyboard is first activated.) For example, typing *43356* generates *hello.* Further, you can choose the word that's generated from a list atop the keyboard, as shown in Figure 4-6.

Word suggestions

More suggestions

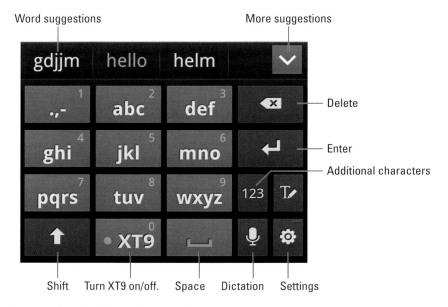

Delete

Enter

Additional characters

Shift   Turn XT9 on/off.   Space   Dictation   Settings

Figure 4-6: Using XT9 on the 3x4 keyboard.

Traditional: When XT9 is disabled, the 3x4 keyboard works the way that cell phone keyboards have traditionally worked: Touch a key to produce the first letter associated with the key. Touch the key again to produce the second letter. You disable XT9 by tapping the XT9 button. (Refer to Figure 4-6.)

For example, to produce the word *hello,* you type 4433555 (pause) 555666. Yes, it's awkward, but it's the way people typed on primitive cell phones for years. Some people are *used to* typing this way, which is why the traditional method is offered. I don't recommend using it.

XT9 comes from the T9 standard, where T9 stands for *Text on 9 keys.* I suppose that the X stands for something cool, like *extended* or *extra special* or *X-Men.*

Accessing special characters

You can type more characters on your Galaxy Note than appear on the keyboard. There are a few tricks you can try to access these additional characters.

The first trick is to locate the paging key. Touch that key, and the keyboard changes to show a new swath of keys.

 On the Android and Samsung keyboards, the paging key is labeled *?123*. On the Samsung 3x4 and Swype keyboards, it's labeled *123*. The Samsung keyboard's ?123 key is shown in the margin.

When additional symbol keys are available, look for the 123 key. Touching this key displays even more characters.

To switch back to the standard alphabetic keyboard, touch the ABC key.

 Another trick to access special characters is to long-press a key. Some keys, such as those found on the top row of the onscreen keyboard, feature tiny characters on them. For example, long-pressing the Q key produces the 1 character.

To produce an accented character, long-press its base key. For example, to type the à character, long-press the A key. You see a pop-up palette of character choices, as shown in Figure 4-7. Drag your finger to a character from the palette to insert that character into your text.

Figure 4-7: A pop-up character palette.

Extra characters are available in uppercase as well. To produce uppercase characters, touch the Shift key before you long-press a key on the onscreen keyboard.

Not every key sports a pop-up palette of special characters.

Choosing a word as you type

The Android and Swype keyboards help you type more efficiently by offering suggestions for words as you type. The suggestions appear above the onscreen keyboard, similar to the ones shown on the Android keyboard in Figure 4-8. On the Swype keyboard, you have to type more of the word to see more accurate suggestions.

Figure 4-8: Suggestions for typing *num*.

Choose a suggestion by touching it with your finger or by pressing the Space key to select the highlighted word. The word you choose appears instantly on the screen, saving you time (and potentially fixing your terrible spelling or typing — or both).

Text Editing

No one uses the Galaxy Note to compose a novel. Sure, maybe someone will try, but that's not what text editing on a phone is all about. No, it's more about fixing typos (if you bother) and juggling blocks of text. It's a feat that few perform on their cell phones, mostly because they haven't read this section on how it all works.

Moving the cursor

The first task in editing text is to move the *cursor,* that blinking, vertical line where text appears. By placing the cursor in the correct spot, you can then type, edit, or paste — or simply marvel that you were able to move the slender cursor using your stubby finger.

To move the cursor, touch the part of the text where you want the cursor to blink. If you're lucky, the cursor finds itself in the proper spot. If not, you have to do some adjusting.

 For precise cursor positioning, use the *cursor tab,* which appears when you touch text on your Galaxy Note. The cursor tab looks like a trapezoid, as shown in the margin. Drag that big tab around to specifically position the cursor.

When you touch the cursor tab, you see the pop-up text editing palette, as shown in Figure 4-9. Later sections describe what you can do with the buttons on the text editing palette.

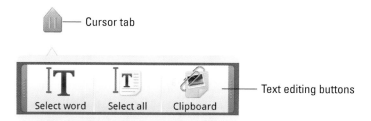

Figure 4-9: The text editing palette.

Selecting text

Selecting text on a phone works similarly to selecting text in a word processor, with the emphasis on the word *similarly*. As in a word processor, selected text appears highlighted on the touchscreen. You can then delete, cut, or copy the block of selected text.

Just to throw you, you can use several methods to select text on your Galaxy Note, as explained next.

Text selection with your finger on the touchscreen

To quickly select a word, tap your finger twice on the touchscreen. The word becomes highlighted — if you're lucky. Sometimes two words are highlighted, or sometimes part of a word is highlighted. I'll assume it's a bug that Samsung will fix. For now, though, I don't recommend selecting text by tapping your finger.

Text selection with the cursor tab menu

The fastest and most accurate way to select text is to summon the cursor tab, covered in the earlier section "Moving the cursor." Simply tap somewhere in the text. Then touch the cursor tab before it disappears. You see a pop-up palette, as shown earlier, in Figure 4-9.

Choose the Select Word command to select a single word. Choose Select All to select all text in the text box or editing area.

When you choose the Select Word option, you see highlighting similar to Figure 4-10. You can use the markers at the start and end of the highlighted text to extend the selection; drag a marker hither or thither using your finger.

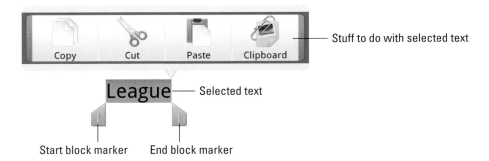

Figure 4-10: Selecting text.

Be quick with those start and end markers! If you don't manipulate them soon enough, they disappear and don't come back unless you reselect the text. Ditto for the button palette (refer to Figure 4-10); if you're not quick, it disappears as well.

Text selection using the Edit Text menu

A most-assured way to select text is to long-press it. When you do, the Edit Text menu appears, displaying two text-selecting options:

Select Word: Choose this option to select the word you long-pressed on the screen. You can then extend the selection as illustrated earlier, in Figure 4-10.

Select All: Choose this option to select all text, whether it's in the input box or you've been entering or editing it in the current application.

 To back out of the Edit Text menu, press the Back soft button.

You can cancel the selection of text by pressing the Back soft button.

Text selection on a web page

Selecting text on a web page works similarly to selecting text elsewhere on your Galaxy Note: Long-press a word to select that word. You can then extend the selection by dragging the start and end block markers, illustrated in Figure 4-10.

After extending the block, you see a pop-up palette with three buttons: Copy, Search, and Share. Touch the Copy button to copy text from the web page. See the next section for more information on copying text.

- The Search button on the pop-up palette is used to search for text only in the selected block.

- Use the Share button to copy the text and then send it off using another app on your phone. You can share text in a text message, by e-mail, on Facebook, and so on. The various Share options are discussed throughout this book.

- Refer to Chapter 10 for more information on surfing the web with your phone.

Cutting, copying, and pasting text

You can cut, copy, and paste text on your phone, just like in a word processor. Assuming that the text is selected, per the multitudinous options discussed in the preceding sections, you can follow these steps to cut or copy that chunk o' text:

1. **Choose the Cut or Copy command from the pop-up palette.**

   Refer to Figure 4-10 to see what the pop-up palette looks like.

    If the pop-up palette disappears, as it is wont to do, long-press the selected text. You see the Edit Text menu. Choose the Cut or Copy command from the menu.

2. **If necessary, start the app into which you want to paste text.**

3. **Touch the text box or text area where you want to paste the copied or cut text.**

4. **Move the cursor to the exact spot where the text will be pasted.**

5. **Long-press the text box or area.**

6. **Choose the Paste command.**

   The text you've cut or copied appears in the spot where the cursor was blinking.

The text you paste can be pasted again and again. Until you cut or copy additional text, you can use the Paste command to your heart's content.

✏ You can paste text only into locations where text is allowed. Odds are good that if you can type, or whenever you see the onscreen keyboard, you can paste text.

✏ The Paste command is also available on the pop-up palette. (Refer to Figure 4-10.) In that case, pasting replaces any selected text.

✏ You can use the Clipboard command to peruse previously cut or copied chunks of text. Scroll the list to find something to paste. The Clipboard command is found on the pop-up palette when text is selected.

S Pen Input

The S Pen lets you do more than draw mustaches on pictures. You can use it as a substitute for your finger — a much more precise substitute. You can use it for text input. You can even pull some handy shortcuts with the S Pen, all covered in this section.

✏ About the only thing you can't do with the S Pen is press the soft buttons on the front of the phone.

✏ See Chapter 17 for information on drawing mustaches on pictures with your Galaxy Note S Pen.

Text input with the S Pen

Yea verily, your phone has a *fifth* keyboard. It's the S Pen input pad, shown in Figure 4-11.

Show character keyboard.

Switch to numeric input mode.

Show keyboard.

Settings Dictation   Space   Delete   Enter/Return

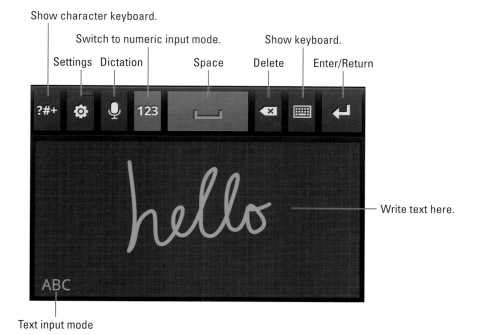

Write text here.

Text input mode

Figure 4-11: Writing text with the S Pen.

 The input pad is made available only from the Samsung keyboard: Touch the S Pen button, shown in the margin, to display it. Then you can create text by using the S Pen and your best grammar school cursive skills, as illustrated in Figure 4-11. The phone interprets the text you write and inserts it into a text box or wherever text is allowed.

✓ As with other keyboards, alternative suggestions and spellings appear above the input pad area. Tap a suggestion with the pen to insert it into the text.

✓ To draw a space, drag the pen from left to right. Or you can tap the Space button.

✓ Touch the 123 button to switch to numeric input mode. The input pad interprets text and numbers differently, so ensure that you're in the proper mode, as indicated in the lower-left corner of the screen. (Refer to Figure 4-11.)

Using various S Pen tricks

The S Pen works just like your finger on the touchscreen, though the pen is far more accurate. You can touch (tap) with the pen, drag, double-tap, and so on, just as you would with your finger.

The S Pen does several things when you press the S Pen button. Here are some common actions:

- **Drag down while pressing the S Pen button:** Go to the Home screen.
- **Drag up while pressing the S Pen button:** Display the app's menu.
- **Drag left while pressing the S Pen button:** Go back to the previous screen.
- **Double-tap while pressing the S Pen button:** Open the S Memo Lite app.
- **Long-press the screen while pressing the S Pen button:** Take a screen shot.

A *screen shot* is a captured image of what you see on the Galaxy Note touchscreen. After taking a screen shot, you see it previewed in the Gallery app, ready for editing. See Chapter 14 for more information on the Gallery app.

Screen shots are saved in the ScreenCapture album in the Gallery.

The S Pen has only one setting you can adjust, which determines whether you're using it with your right or left hand. Follow these steps to make the adjustment:

1. **At the Home screen, press the Menu soft button.**

   Or press the S Pen button and swipe up on the screen.

2. **Choose Settings.**

3. **Choose Pen Settings.**

4. **Choose Dominant Hand.**

5. **Choose Left Handed or Right Handed.**

   No, the pen has no Ambidextrous setting.

I can't tell the difference between the Right Handed and Left Handed settings, but I assume that *something* is different between them.

Jaw-Dropping Dictation

The Galaxy Note has the amazing ability to interpret your utterances as text. The Dictation feature can be used instead of typing to give control to your phone or to vent your frustrations.

Talking to your phone

The Dictation feature is available whenever you see the Microphone icon, similar to the one shown in the margin. To begin voice input, touch the icon. The Voice Input screen appears, as shown in Figure 4-12.

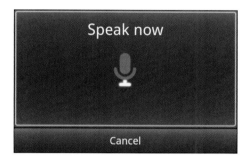

Figure 4-12: The voice input thing.

When you see the text *Speak Now,* speak directly at the phone.

As you speak, the Microphone icon (refer to Figure 4-12) flashes. The flashing doesn't mean that the phone is embarrassed by what you're saying. No, the flashing merely indicates that the phone is listening, detecting the volume of your voice.

After you stop talking, the phone digests what you've said. You see your voice input appear as a wavelike pattern on the screen. Eventually, the text you've spoken — or a close approximation of it — appears on the screen. It's magical, and sometimes comical.

- The first time you try to use Voice Input, you might see a description displayed. Touch the OK button to continue.
- The Dictation feature works only when voice input is allowed. Not every application features voice input as an option.

✔ The better your diction, the better the results. Try to speak only a sentence or less.

✔ You can edit your voice input just as you edit any text. See the section "Text Editing," earlier in this chapter.

✔ You have to "speak" punctuation to include it in your text. For example, you say, "I'm sorry comma James period" to have the phone produce the text *I'm sorry, James.*

✔ Common punctuation marks that you can dictate include the comma, period, exclamation point, question mark, and colon.

✔ Pause your speech before and after speaking punctuation.

✔ There's no way to dictate a capital letter, though you can say "period" to capitalize the first letter of the next word. (It's easier to edit your text and remove excess periods than to edit your text to capitalize.)

✔ Voice input may not function when no cellular data or Wi-Fi connection is available.

Uttering b**** words

The Galaxy Note features a voice censor. It replaces those naughty words you might utter, placing the word's first letter on the screen, followed by the appropriate number of asterisks.

For example, if *belch* were a blue word and you utter *belch* when dictating text, the Galaxy Note Dictation feature would place b**** on the screen rather than the word *belch.*

Yeah, I know: Silly. I mean S***.

The phone knows a lot of blue terms, including the infamous "Seven Words You Can Never Say on Television," but apparently the terms *crap* and *damn* are fine. Don't ask me how much time I spent researching this topic.

Part II
Phone Duties

The 5th Wave — By Rich Tennant

Cell Phones

"This model comes with a particularly useful function — a simulated static button for breaking out of long-winded conversations."

In this part . . .

*P*hone stores are full of interesting gizmos, such as smartphones, so named because they communicate with the Internet and sport features such as cameras and GPS, and dumbphones, which can't access the Internet. Oh, and the stores have tablets, none of which make phone calls.

Your Galaxy Note covers all the bases, which is why it's a unique and interesting device. At its core, however, it remains a phone. It can make and receive calls, place callers on hold, make conference calls, handle voice mail, and undertake all the basic phone duties.

Tom Corbett
213-555-1952
Space Academy, Polaris

❚❚ Hold   00:27

1
Voicemail

2
Jeremiah Goo

3
Coeur d'Alene

4
Jonah Gookin

5
+

6
+

7

8

9

Conference call
2 people

❚❚ Hold   00:53

Phone 101

Credit the Bell telephone company for its brilliant design. I've never seen a manual (or a book) on how to use the old landline telephone. When it rang, you picked up the handset and started talking. To make a call, you picked up the handset and dialed or punched in a number. It had neither an Enter key nor a Phone button. You heard either a dial tone or a busy signal, or you started talking. Life was simple.

Here in the 21st century, with a device as diverse as the Galaxy Note, making phone calls isn't quite so simple. Gone is the dial. Gone are the buttons. Present are a slew of options and settings that can potentially drive you nuts. To help fight any frustration, this chapter covers the basic tasks of placing and answering phone calls. Yes, it now takes a whole chapter to do that.

Voice call

Ronald Reagan
213-555-0206

I Just Called to Say . . .

The Phone Company had plenty of sayings, back when there was such a thing as *long distance*. They wanted you to make those calls because they made a lot of money from them. So they created slogans such as "Reach out and touch someone" and "It's the next best thing to being there."

Long distance is only a memory these days, but the basic reason for making a phone call remains. The methods have changed, however, which is why I wrote this section.

Making a phone call

To place a call on your Galaxy Note, heed these steps:

1. Touch the Phone app icon on the Home screen.

The Phone app is shown in Figure 5-1. If you don't see the keypad, touch the Keypad tab at the top of the screen, as illustrated in the figure.

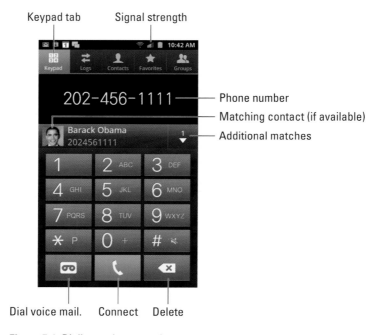

Figure 5-1: Dialing a phone number.

2. Type the number to call.

Use the keys on the keypad to type the number. If you make a mistake, touch the Delete button found in the lower-right corner, as shown in Figure 5-1, to back up and erase.

As you dial, you hear the traditional touch-tone sound as you input the number. If not, you can activate the touch-tones by opening the Settings app (found on the Apps menu), choosing Sound, and then placing a check mark by the Audible Touch Tones option.

Any contacts matching the number you dial appear on the screen. (Refer to Figure 5-1.) You can even type a contact's name using the keypad to scour your phone's address book. Choose a contact from the list to instantly display the number.

3. **Touch the green Phone button to make the call.**

   The phone doesn't make the call until you touch the green button.

   As the phone attempts to make the connection, two things happen:

   1. First, a Call in Progress notification icon appears on the status bar. The icon is a big clue that the phone is making a call or is actively connected.

   2. Second, the screen changes to show the number you dialed, similar to the one shown in Figure 5-2. When the recipient is on your Contacts list, the contact's name and photo (if available) may also appear, as shown in the figure.

   Even though the touchscreen is pretty, at this point you need to listen to the phone: Put it up to your ear and listen. If a headset is attached to the phone, you can listen using that device instead.

4. **When the person answers the phone, talk.**

   What you say is up to you, though it's good not to open your conversation with something like, "Remember how that tall tree was leaning toward your house?"

   Use the phone's Volume buttons (on the side of the device) to adjust the speaker volume during the call.

5. **To end the call, touch the red End Call button.**

   The phone disconnects. You hear a soft *beep*, which is the phone's signal that the call has ended. The Call in Progress notification goes away.

You can do other things while you're making a call: Just press the Home button to run an application, read old e-mail, check an appointment, or do whatever. Activities such as these don't disconnect you, though your cellular carrier may not allow you to do other things with the phone while you're on a call.

Phone call in progress

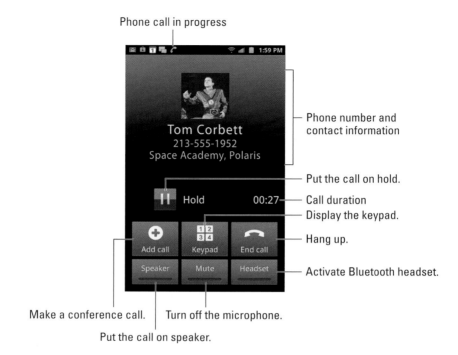

Phone number and contact information

Put the call on hold.

Call duration

Display the keypad.

Hang up.

Activate Bluetooth headset.

Make a conference call. | Turn off the microphone.

Put the call on speaker.

Figure 5-2: A successful call.

To return to a call after doing something else, swipe down the notifications at the top of the screen and touch the notification for the current call. You return to the Connected screen, similar to the one shown in Figure 5-2. Continue yapping. (See Chapter 3 for information on reviewing notifications.)

✔ If you're using earphones, you can press the phone's Power Lock button during the call to turn off the display and lock the phone. I recommend turning off the display so that you don't accidentally touch the Mute button or End Call button during the call.

✔ You can connect or remove the earphones at any time during a call. The call is neither disconnected nor interrupted when you do so.

✔ You can't accidentally mute or end a call when the phone is placed against your face; a sensor in the phone detects when it's close to something and the touchscreen is automatically disabled.

✔ Don't worry about the phone being too far away from your mouth; it picks up your voice just fine.

- To mute a call, touch the Mute button, shown in Figure 5-2. The Mute icon, similar to the one shown in the margin, appears as the phone's status (atop the touchscreen).

- Touch the Speaker button to be able to hold the phone at a distance to listen and talk, which allows you to let others listen and share in the conversation. The Speaker icon appears as the phone's status when the speaker is active.

- Don't hold the phone to your ear when the speaker is active.

- If you're wading through one of those nasty voice-mail systems, touch the Keypad button, shown in Figure 5-2, so that you can "Press 1 for English" when necessary.

- See Chapter 6 for information on using the Add Call and Hold buttons.

- The Headset button activates a Bluetooth headset only; it doesn't control a headset that you plug into the top of the phone.

- When using a Bluetooth headset, connect the headset *before* you make the call.

- Long-press the * key (refer to Figure 5-1) to insert a pause into the number. The pause appears as a comma, and it inserts a two-second wait when dialing.

- If you need to dial an international number, press and hold the 0 (zero) key until the plus-sign (+) character appears. Then input the rest of the international number. Refer to Chapter 21 for more information on making international calls.

- You hear an audio alert whenever the call is dropped or the other party hangs up. The disconnection can be confirmed by looking at the phone, which shows that the call has ended.

- You cannot place a phone call when the phone has no service; check the signal strength, as shown earlier, in Figure 5-1.

- You cannot place a phone call when the phone is in Airplane mode. See Chapter 21 for information.

- The Call in Progress notification icon (refer to Figure 5-2) is a useful thing. When you see this notification, it means that the phone is connected to another party. To return to the phone screen, swipe down the status bar and touch the phone call's notification. You can then press the End Call button to disconnect or put the phone to your face to see who's on the line.

Dialing a contact

The easiest way to call someone you know is to use your Galaxy Note's address book, summon their contact information, and dial them instantly. By keeping names, addresses, and phone numbers in a digital address book, you save wear and tear on your brain, freeing up gray matter for storing the latest celebrity gossip and social trends. Everybody wins!

To dial a contact stored in your phone's address book, obey these steps:

1. **On the Home screen, touch the Phone app icon.**

2. **Touch the Contacts tab at the top of the screen.**

   Figure 5-3 displays a sample of what the Contacts list might look like.

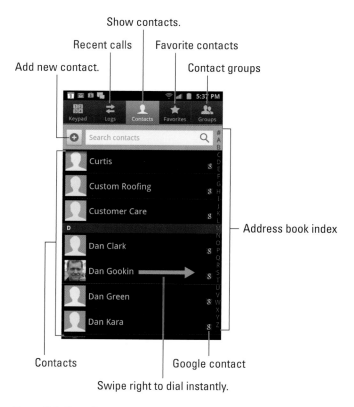

Show contacts.

Recent calls   Favorite contacts

Add new contact.   Contact groups

Address book index

Contacts   Google contact

Swipe right to dial instantly.

Figure 5-3: Perusing contacts.

3. **Scroll the list of contacts to find the person you want to call.**

   To rapidly scroll, you can swipe the list with your finger or use the index on the right side of the list, as shown in Figure 5-3.

4. **Touch the contact you want to call.**

5. **Touch the contact's phone number or the Phone icon by the phone number.**

   The contact is dialed immediately.

At this point, dialing proceeds as described earlier in this chapter.

   ✔ The Galaxy Note also has a Contacts app that you can open. It gets you to the same place — the Contacts tab in the Phone app — but it ensures that the Phone app always opens with the Contacts tab selected.

   ✔ The fastest way to dial a contact is to swipe the contact's entry to the right, as shown in Figure 5-3. You can skip Steps 3 and 4 in the preceding list: Swipe the name to the right to dial the primary number.

   ✔ Refer to Chapter 8 for information on setting a contact's primary number.

Phoning someone you call often

The Galaxy Note keeps track of all your calls — incoming, outgoing, and missed. The later section, "Perusing the call log" explains how to review these calls. For people you phone often, or those who phone you often, you can look in a special place: the Frequent Callers list.

To see your biggest fans, or people for whom you are their biggest fan, follow these steps:

1. **Touch the Phone app icon on the Home screen.**

2. **Touch the Favorites tab, found at the top of the window, as shown in Figure 5-3.**

   The Favorites tab lists contacts in the phone's address book whom you've flagged as being favorites. If you scroll down that list a tad, however, you see the people whom you frequently dialed. They're found under the Frequently Dialed heading.

3. **Choose an item from the Frequently Dialed list to see more information.**

   You see the last several calls made, received, or missed for that number. If the number is associated with a contact in the phone's address book, you see the contact's name and, if you've set one up, an image.

4. Touch the green Phone button to place the call.

> The phone dials the number.

Refer to Chapter 8 for information on how to make one of your contacts a favorite.

Ring, Ring, Ring

It's for you! Cell phones are truly personal. If your Galaxy Note rings, you can pretty much be assured that whoever is calling wants to talk with you. Okay, maybe they also want to talk with the "adult in the house," but most of the time an incoming call is an event. Someone cares enough to call.

Receiving a call

Several things can happen when you receive a phone call on your Galaxy Note:

- The phone rings or makes a noise signaling you to an incoming call.
- The phone vibrates.
- The touchscreen reveals information about the call, as shown in Figure 5-4.
- The panicked babysitter, eyes wide and out of breath, whispers that the killer is inside the house.

Thankfully, the last item in the list happens in horror movies. The other three possibilities, or a combination thereof, are your signals that you have an incoming call. A simple look at the touchscreen tells you more information, as illustrated in Figure 5-4.

To answer the incoming call, slide the green Answer button to the right. (Refer to Figure 5-4.) Then place the phone — or a headset, if one is attached — to your ear. Say "Hello" or, if you're in a grouchy mood, say "What?" loudly.

To dispense with the incoming call, slide the red Ignore button to the left. The phone stops ringing, and the call is banished into voice mail.

- You can slide the Answer or Ignore buttons outward in any direction, not just right or left.

✔ When you're already on the phone and another call comes in, you can touch the green Answer button to accept the call and place the current call on hold. See Chapter 6 for additional information on juggling multiple calls.

✔ The contact's picture, such as former President Reagan in Figure 5-4, appears only when you've assigned a picture to that contact. Otherwise, a generic icon shows up.

✔ If you're using a Bluetooth headset, you touch the control on the headset to answer your phone. See Chapter 19 for more information on using Bluetooth gizmos.

✔ The sound you hear when the phone rings is known as the *ringtone*. You can configure your phone to play a number of ringtones, depending on who is calling, or you can set a universal ringtone. Ringtones are covered in Chapter 6.

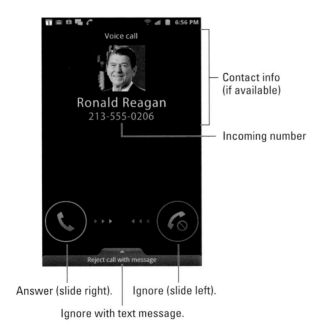

Answer (slide right).   Ignore (slide left).

Ignore with text message.

Figure 5-4: There's an incoming call.

Rejecting a call with a text message

I'm quite fond of the text-message rejection method. Rather than simply dismiss a call, you can use the tab at the bottom of the screen (refer to Figure 5-4) to display a list of text message replies, as shown in Figure 5-5. Choose one to send that text message to the caller, which I find far more polite than dismissing the call outright.

Add a new message.

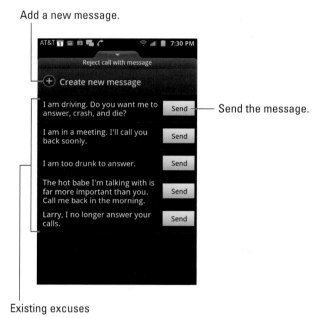

Send the message.

Existing excuses

Figure 5-5: Text-message rejection selection.

After you touch the Send button, the incoming call is dismissed. In a few cellular seconds, the person who called receives the indicated text message.

The messages shown in Figure 5-5 are ones I created myself. To change the standard dull messages provided on the Galaxy Note, heed these steps:

1. **At the Home screen, press the Menu soft button.**

2. **Choose Settings.**

3. **Choose Call.**

4. **Choose Set Reject Messages.**

   You see the list of messages on the Reject Messages screen.

5. **To create a new message, touch the Create button or choose an existing message to edit or replace it.**

   The device has slots for only six messages, so the Create button doesn't appear when you have six messages.

   Messages are edited like any text in the Galaxy Note. Refer to Chapter 4 for text editing information.

6. **Touch the Save button to save your text message rejection.**

Your new messages appear the next time you slide up the Reject Call with Message tab.

To delete a message, long-press it on the Reject Messages screen. Choose the Delete command. Touch the OK button to confirm.

    ✔ You can have a maximum of six text-message-rejection replies.

    ✔ Not every phone is a cell phone. Sending a text message to Aunt Cecilia's landline phone just won't work.

    ✔ See Chapter 9 for more information on text messages.

Dealing with a missed call

When you see the notification icon for a missed call looming at the top of the screen, it means that someone called and you didn't pick up. Fortunately, all the details are remembered for you.

To deal with a missed call, follow these steps:

1. **Display the notifications.**

   See Chapter 3 for details on how to deal with notifications.

2. **Touch the Missed Call notification.**

   You see details about the missed call. When the phone number matches someone on your Contacts list, you see the name displayed.

3. **Touch the green Phone button to return the call.**

The phone doesn't consider a call you've dismissed as being missed. To review all your calls — incoming, outgoing, dismissed, and missed — see the next section.

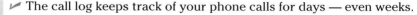

Perusing the call log

In addition to being a phone and a tablet, the Galaxy Note is a computer. As such, it keeps track of your phone calls in a handy database that you can quickly review. Your calls are found in the call log, which you can access by touching the Logs tab in the Phone app. (Refer to Figure 5-3.)

The Logs tab displays a list of calls you've made, received, and missed. Choose an item to see more information, such as the last several calls made, received, or missed for that number or contact. To dial that contact, touch the green Phone button.

✔ The call log keeps track of your phone calls for days — even weeks.

✔ Using the call log is a quick way to add a recent caller as a contact. Simply touch an item in the list, and touch the Create Contact button from the Details screen. See Chapter 8 for more information about creating contacts.

✔ To clear the call log list, press the Menu soft button and choose Delete. Place check marks by the entries you desire to remove, or place one check mark by the Select All item to remove everything. Touch the Delete button and then the OK button to confirm.

Super Phone Powers

In This Chapter

▶ Setting up speed dial
▶ Handling multiple incoming calls
▶ Setting up a conference call
▶ Configuring call forwarding options
▶ Banishing a contact to the reject list
▶ Changing the ringtone
▶ Assigning ringtones to your contacts

*Y*our Galaxy Tab is blessed with abilities far beyond those of a mere mortal phone. These features would have been scoffed at in the 1930s, ridiculed in the 1940s, met with blank stares in the 1960s, yearned for in the 1970s, and finally achieved in the 1980s, but at exorbitant monthly fees.

Today the fees are gone, but the features remain: speed dial, call waiting, call forwarding, three-way calling, and more. These bonus features are waiting, eager for you to use them. This chapter discusses these super phone abilities.

Über Speed-Dial

How fast can you dial a phone? Don't even try to attempt a new speed record. That's because the Galaxy Note comes with a Speed Dial feature that will put any of your attempts to shame.

Configure Speed Dial by following these steps:

1. **At the Home screen, start the Phone app.**

2. **If necessary, touch the Keypad tab to see the phone-dialing screen.**

3. **Press the Menu soft button.**

4. **Choose Speed Dial Setting.**

   The Speed Dial Settings screen appears, as shown in Figure 6-1. The Galaxy Note has nine potential speed dial numbers, though number 1 is already configured to dial voice mail, as shown in the figure.

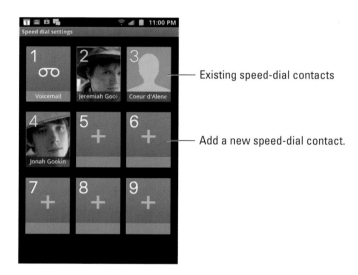

Existing speed-dial contacts

Add a new speed-dial contact.

Figure 6-1: Speed Dial setup.

5. **Touch a blank number.**

   Blank numbers have plus signs on them. (Refer to Figure 6-1.)

6. **Choose a contact to speed-dial.**

7. **Repeat Steps 5 and 6 to add more speed dial contacts.**

When you're done adding numbers, press either the Back or Home button to exit the Speed Dial Setup screen.

Using speed dial is simple: Long-press a number on the keypad to dial a contact. When you release your finger, the speed dial number is dialed.

To review your speed dial settings, follow Steps 1 through 4 in this section.

Captain Conference Call (and More!)

Psychologists, as well as other people in white lab coats, have determined that human beings can hold only one conversation at a time. Your Galaxy Note isn't under such limitations. It can handle as many as two calls with three different people. (For you folks in white lab coats, that's two other people and yourself, which totals three people.) The secret to performing this feat is divulged in this section.

Putting someone on hold

It's easy to place a call on hold, thanks to that big Hold button found on the In-Call screen and shown in the margin. Touch the Hold button and the person on the other line is "on hold."

To unhold the call, touch the Unhold button that replaces the Hold button and that's shown in the margin.

Receiving a call when you're on the phone

You're on the phone, chatting it up. Suddenly, someone else calls you. What happens next?

Your phone alerts you to the new call. The phone may vibrate or make a sound. Look at the front of the phone to see what's up and you'll see the standard incoming call screen. (Refer to Figure 5-4, in Chapter 5.)

You have three options:

Answer the call. Slide the green Answer button to answer the incoming call. The call you're already on is placed on hold.

Send the call directly to voice mail. Slide the red Ignore button. The incoming call is sent directly to voice mail.

Do nothing. The call eventually goes into voice mail.

When you choose to answer the call and the call you're on is placed on hold, you're actually on two calls at that time — but speaking with only one person. Keep reading in the next section.

Juggling two calls

After you answer a second call, as described in the preceding section, your phone is working with two calls at a time. In this particular situation, you can speak with only one person at a time; juggling two calls isn't the same as participating in a conference call.

The touchscreen displays information about both calls, as illustrated in Figure 6-2.

Current conversation

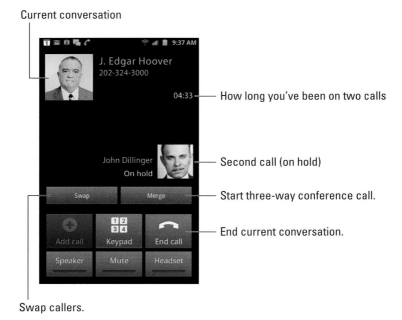

How long you've been on two calls

Second call (on hold)

Start three-way conference call.

End current conversation.

Swap callers.

Figure 6-2: Two calls at once.

You can do a few things while the phone is handling two calls:

Switch calls: To switch between callers, touch the Swap button that appears on the touchscreen. Every time you touch this button, the conversation moves to the other caller. The current person is then put on hold, as shown in Figure 6-2. (The current caller is on top.)

Merge calls: To combine both calls so that everyone is talking with each other (three people), touch the Merge button.

End: To end a call, touch the End Call button, just as you normally do. The current caller is disconnected, and you're left talking with the person who was on hold.

The number of different calls your phone can handle depends on your carrier. For AT&T, it's only two calls at a time. In this case, a third person who calls you either hears a busy signal or is sent directly to voice mail.

Making a conference call

Unlike someone interrupting a conversation with an incoming call, a *conference call* is one that you set out to make intentionally: You make one call and then *add* a second call. Touch a button on the phone's touchscreen, and then everyone is talking. Here's how it works:

1. **Phone the first person.**

2. **After your phone connects and you complete a few pleasantries, touch the Add Call button.**

   The first person is put on hold.

3. **Dial the second person.**

   You can use the keypad or choose the second person from the phone's address book or from a recent call from the call log.

   After you connect with the second person, the Galaxy Note touchscreen looks like it does when you're on two calls, as shown earlier, in Figure 6-2.

4. **Touch the Merge button.**

   The two calls are now joined: The touchscreen says *Conference Call,* as shown in Figure 6-3. Everyone you've dialed can talk to and hear everyone else.

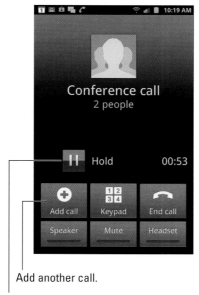

Add another call.

Place all calls on hold.

Figure 6-3: Multiple call mania!

5. **Touch the End Call button to end the conference call.**

All calls are disconnected.

When several people are in a room and want to participate in a call, you can always put the phone in Speaker mode: Touch the Speaker button.

Apparently, you can add a *fourth* conversation to the mix, as shown by the enabled Add Call button, in Figure 6-3. I've not tried this option to see whether it works.

Amazing Call Forwarding

Banishing an unwanted call is relatively easy on your Galaxy Note. You can forbid the phone from ringing by touching the Volume button. Or you can send the call scurrying off into voice mail by pressing the red Ignore button, as described in Chapter 5.

Other options exist for the special handling of incoming calls. They're the amazing forwarding options, described in this section.

Forwarding phone calls

Call forwarding is the process by which you reroute an incoming call. For example, you can send to your office all calls you receive while you're on vacation. Then you have the luxury of having your cell phone and still making calls but freely ignoring anyone who calls you.

To review the various call forwarding options, heed these steps:

1. **At the Home screen, press the Menu soft button.**

2. **Choose Settings.**

3. **Choose Call.**

4. **Choose Call Forwarding.**

You have several forwarding options:

Always Forward: All incoming calls are sent to the number you specify; your phone doesn't even ring. This option overrides all other forwarding options.

Forward When Busy: Calls are forwarded when you're on the phone and choose not to answer. This option is normally used to send a missed call to voice mail, though you can forward to any number.

Forward When Unanswered: Calls are forwarded when you choose not to answer the phone. Normally, the call is forwarded to your voice mail.

Forward When Unreached: Calls are forwarded when the phone is turned off or out of range or in Airplane mode. As with the two preceding settings, this option normally forwards calls to voice mail.

5. **Choose an option.**

6. **Set the forwarding number.**

   Or you can edit the number that already appears. For example, you can type your home number for the Forward When Unreached option so that your cell calls are redirected to your home when you're out of range.

7. **Touch the Enable button to confirm the forwarding number.**

The Call Forwarding status icon appears atop the touchscreen when you've activated a forwarding option.

To disable call forwarding, touch the Disable button when you're given the opportunity to type a forwarded phone number. (See Step 7 in the preceding list.)

Call forwarding affects Google Voice voice mail. Unanswered calls that you forward are handled by the forwarding number, not by Google Voice. Further, when you cancel call forwarding, you need to reenable Google Voice on your phone. See Chapter 7 for details.

Rejecting incoming calls

You can configure your phone to forward directly to voice mail any calls received from a specific contact. The phone never even rings. It's a helpful way to deal with a pest! Follow these steps:

1. **Touch the Applications icon on the Home screen.**

   The Apps menu appears.

2. **Open the Contacts app.**

3. **Ensure that the Contacts tab is chosen atop the screen.**

4. **Choose a contact.**

   Use your finger to scroll the list of contacts until you find the annoying person that you want to eternally banish to voice mail.

5. **Press the Menu soft button.**

6. **Choose More and then Add to Reject List.**

   The universal No symbol (or circle-backslash symbol) appears in blue next to the contact's phone number or numbers. All calls from the contact, no matter which of their phone numbers they use, are sent directly into voice mail.

To unbanish the contact, repeat these steps, but in Step 6 choose the command Remove from Reject List.

See Chapter 8 for more information on contacts; see Chapter 7 on voice mail.

Managing the rejected number list

You don't need to remember exactly which contacts have been added to the reject list. Further, it's possible to manually add numbers, even all numbers from a certain area code or prefix, because the Galaxy Note keeps track of your phone's rejected list in one handy spot.

To review or manage the reject list, follow these steps:

1. **At the Home screen, press the Menu soft button.**

2. **Choose Settings and then Call.**

3. **Chose Call Rejection.**

4. **Choose Auto Reject List.**

   You see a list of numbers and contacts you've slated for automatic rejection.

5. **Touch the Add button to manually add a number or group of numbers, or add or remove check marks to add or remove contacts from the list.**

   Touching a check mark box adds a check mark if one isn't there already, or it removes a check mark if one exists. To remove someone from the list, touch the check mark by their number. Or maybe remove only one number if they have multiple numbers on the reject list.

   If you want to reject all calls from unknown numbers — such as telemarketers or political calls — place a check mark by the item titled Unknown.

   Choosing the Add item displays a screen where you can type any number. To make the rejection list more inclusive, choose the Match Criteria item. You can reject all numbers starting with a certain area code or prefix, numbers that end in certain values, or numbers within numbers. Touch the Save button to manually add the number.

6. **Press the Back or Home soft buttons when you're done editing or perusing the list.**

This feature is one reason you might want to retain contact information for someone with whom you never want to have contact.

Incredible Ringtones

A *ringtone* is the sound your Galaxy Note makes when you have an incoming call. You may already know that. What you may not know is that you're not stuck with the preconfigured ringtone. You can change it to just about anything you want.

Choosing the phone's ringtone

To select a new ringtone for your phone, or to simply confirm which ringtone you're using already, follow these steps:

1. **At the Home screen, press the Menu soft button.**

2. **Choose Settings, and then choose Sound.**

3. **Choose Phone Ringtone.**

   If you have a ringtone application, you may see a menu that asks you which source to use for the phone's ringtone. Choose Android System.

4. **Choose a ringtone from the list that's displayed.**

   Scroll the list. Tap a ringtone to hear a preview.

5. **Touch OK to accept the new ringtone, or touch Cancel to keep the phone's ringtone as is.**

You can also set the ringtone used for notifications: In Step 3, choose Notification Ringtone rather than Phone Ringtone.

Text messaging ringtones are set from within the Messaging app. See Chapter 9.

 A free app at the Android Market, Zedge, has oodles of free ringtones available for preview and download, all shared by Android users around the world. See Chapter 18 for information about the Android Market and how to download and install apps such as Zedge on your phone.

Setting a contact's ringtone

Ringtones can be assigned by contact so that when your annoying friend Larry calls, you can have your phone yelp like a whiny puppy. Here's how to set a ringtone for a contact:

1. **Choose the Contacts app from the App menu screen.**

   Touch the Applications icon on the Home screen to see the App menu.

2. **From the list, choose the contact to which you want to assign a ringtone.**

3. **Touch the Edit button.**

4. **Choose Ringtone.**

   You may need to scroll down the list to find the Ringtone item.

   Three items are on the Ringtone menu:

   Default ringtone: The contact's ringtone is the phone's standard ringtone. See the preceding section.

   Select sound from My Files: Choose the contact's ringtone from sound files saved on your Galaxy Note.

   Phone ringtone: Choose a ringtone from the list of phone ringtones. The ringtone you choose sounds specifically for that contact.

5. **Choose a ringtone from the list.**

   For selecting a sound from My Files, you have to browse the folders on your Galaxy Note's storage system to look for sound files. For the Phone Ringtone option, you see the same list that's displayed for choosing the phone's ringtones, as described in the preceding section.

6. **Touch OK to assign the ringtone to the contact.**

Whenever the contact calls, the phone rings using the ringtone you've specified.

To remove a specific ringtone for a contact, repeat the steps in this section but choose Default Ringtone in Step 4. This choice sets the contact's ringtone to be the same as the phone's ringtone.

Voice Mail and Beyond

*Y*ou know the drill: "At the sound of the tone, please leave your message." Is it even necessary to ask any more? Can't the message simply say "Beep!"? Your astute friends would figure it out. Those not paying attention wouldn't leave a message, which is probably a good thing. Truly, phone message technology has come a long way from the humorous, disco-like messages on the answering machines of the 1980s.

Another thing that's changed since the 1980s is the terminology. It's *voice mail* now. It can be either two words or one word, depending on which editor is assigned to this book, but it still describes the same thing: The ability of your phone to record a message from a caller when you can't pick up or have somehow banished the incoming call.

Plain Old, Boring Carrier Voice Mail

The most basic, and most stupid, form of voice mail is the free voice mail service provided by your cell phone company. It's a standard feature with few frills and nothing that stands out differently, especially for your nifty Android phone.

Carrier voice mail picks up missed calls as well as those calls you thrust into voice mail. A notification icon, looking similar to the one shown in the margin, appears whenever a message has been left. You can use the notification to dial into your carrier's voice mail system, listen to your calls, and use the phone's dialpad to delete messages or repeat messages or use other features you probably don't know about because no one ever pays attention.

Setting up carrier voice mail

If you haven't yet done it, set up voice mail on your phone. I recommend doing so even if you plan to use another voice mail service, such as Google Voice. That's because carrier voice mail remains a valid and worthy fallback for when those other services don't work.

Your Galaxy Note comes preconfigured to use the My Carrier voice mail service, which is tied into your cellular provider. The cellular provider's voice mail number has also been preconfigured for you. You can check these items by opening the Settings app: Choose Call and then Voicemail Service.

To complete the carrier voice mail setup, you call into the service and set up your account. Follow these steps:

1. **Open the Phone app, found on the Home screen.**

2. **Ensure that the Keypad tab is selected.**

3. **Touch the Voicemail button.**

   The phone dials into the carrier's voice mail system. Because this is probably the first time you've called, you have to work through some initial setup.

4. **Work through the directions.**

   While you're responding to the cellular provider's cheerful robot, touch the Keypad button on the touchscreen. Also, touch the Speaker button. That way, you can hear the cheerful robot and respond by using the keypad.

5. **Set your name, a voice mail password, a greeting, and various other options as guided by your cellular provider's cheerful robot.**

   Just so that you remember the personal identification number (PIN) for your voice mail account, write it down on the following line:

   Your voice mail account PIN: _____

6. **Touch the End Call button when you tire of listening to the cheerful robot.**

I highly recommend that you choose a customized greeting for your voice mailbox. Callers who don't hear your voice sometimes don't leave messages because they mistakenly believe that they've dialed the wrong number.

Retrieving your messages

When you have voice mail pending, the New Voicemail notification icon appears on the status bar, as shown in the margin. You can either pull down this notification to connect to the voice mail service or dial into the voice mail service by using the Voicemail button on the Phone app's keypad.

After the voice mail service answers, you're asked to type your voice mail password. Touch the Keypad button to summon the keypad, and then type your password.

If you screw up while typing your password, touch the * key and start over.

The first unheard message is played automatically.

To delete the message you just heard, touch the 7 key. Touch the 7 key to delete a message at any time, or touch the * key to cancel message playback.

To hear a message again, touch the 4 key immediately after listening to the message.

Touching the * key disconnects you when you're done. Or you can just end the call.

If you don't delete a message, it stays in your voice mail inbox. You're prompted to delete the message the next time you dial into carrier voice mail.

Wonderful Google Voice

Perhaps the best option I've found for working your voice mail is something called *Google Voice*. It's more than just a voice mail system: You can use Google Voice to make phone calls in the United States, place cheap international calls, and perform other amazing feats. For the purposes of this section, the topic is using Google Voice as the Galaxy Note's voice mail system.

⮕ Even when you choose to use Google Voice, I still recommend setting up and configuring the boring carrier voice mail, as covered earlier in this chapter.

✔ You may need to reset Google Voice after using call forwarding. See Chapter 6 for more information on call forwarding, and see the section "Adding your phone to Google Voice," later in this chapter, for information on reestablishing Google Voice as your phone's voice mail service.

Configuring Google Voice

You need to create a Google Voice account on the Internet before you configure your Android phone for use with Google Voice. Start your adventure by visiting the Google Voice home page on the Internet: `http://voice.google.com`.

If necessary, sign in to your Google account. You use the same account name and password that you use to access your Gmail.

Your next task is to configure a Google Voice number to be used for your phone, as covered in the next section. Or, if you've just signed up for a Google Voice number, choose the options to use your existing cell phone number and select Google Voice Lite. This version sets you up with voice mail for your phone, which is the ultimate goal.

✔ If all you want is to use Google Voice as your voice mail service, choose the option that says Just Want Voicemail for Your Cell.

✔ Google Voice offers a host of features: international dialing, call forwarding, and other stuff I am not aware of and, honestly, am quite afraid of.

Adding your phone to Google Voice

After you have a Google Voice account, you add your phone number to the list of phone numbers registered for Google Voice. As in the preceding section, I recommend that you complete these steps on a computer connected to the Internet and keep your phone handy:

1. **Click the Gear icon in the upper-right corner of the Google Voice home page, and choose the Settings command from the menu.**

   The Settings command may change its location in a future update to the Google Voice web page. If so, the purpose of this step is to access the Settings screen, where you register phone numbers for use with Google Voice.

2. **Click the link Add Another Phone.**

3. **Work the steps to verify your phone for use with Google Voice.**

   Obey the directions on the web page.

4. **Click the Connect button to begin verifying your phone number.**

   Google Voice needs to phone your Galaxy Note.

5. **Answer the phone.**

   Use the keypad to type the code number you see on your computer's screen. After confirming the code number, you see your phone listed as a registered phone — but you're not done yet:

6. **Click the Activate Voicemail link.**

   You must activate your phone for it to work with Google Voice. It's the most important step!

7. **On your phone, dial the number you see on your computer screen.**

   If the call fails the first time, try again. And don't be concerned if you're dialing what looks to be an extremely odd phone number.

8. **On your computer screen, click the Done button.**

Your Galaxy Note is now registered for use with Google Voice.

Getting your Google Voice messages

Google Voice transcribes your voice mail messages, turning the audio from the voice mail into a text message you can read. The messages all show up eventually in your Gmail inbox, just as though someone sent you an e-mail rather than left you voice mail. It's a good way to deal with your messages, but not the best way.

The best way to handle Google Voice is to use the Voice app, available from the Google Play Store. Use either the QR code in the margin or the Play Store app to search for and install the Google Voice app. (See Chapter 18 for details on the Google Play Store.)

After the Google Voice app is installed, you have to work through some setup, which isn't difficult. Eventually, you see the app's main interface, which looks and works similarly to an e-mail program. You can review your messages or touch a message to read or play it, as illustrated in Figure 7-1.

Contact info (if available)

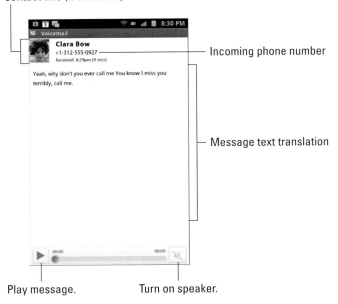

Incoming phone number

Message text translation

Play message.

Turn on speaker.

Figure 7-1: Voice mail with the Google Voice app.

When new Google Voice messages come in, you see the Google Voice notification icon appear, as shown in the margin. Pull down the notifications, and choose the Voicemail from *Whomever* item to read or listen to the message.

- ✔ With Google Voice installed, you see two notices for every voice mail message: one from Google Voice and another for the Gmail message that comes in.

- ✔ The Google Voice app works only after you activate Google Voice on your phone, as described in the preceding section.

- ✔ You can best listen to the message when using the Google Voice app. In Gmail, you see a transcript of the message, but you must touch the Play Message link to visit a web page and then listen to the message.

- ✔ The text translation feature in Google Voice is at times astonishingly accurate and at other times not so good.

- ✔ The text *Transcript Not Available* appears whenever Google Voice is unable to create a text message from your voice mail or the Google Voice service is temporarily unavailable.

Part III
Keep in Touch

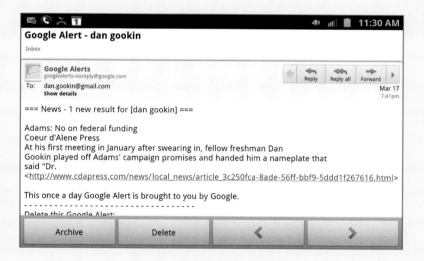

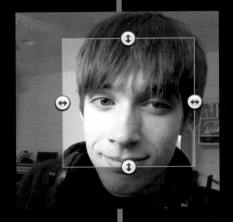

In this part . . .

1t's becoming more and more difficult to avoid keeping in touch with people. Not everyone, of course. You may know some people with whom you probably enjoy communicating. Then there are pests. At the dawn of the digital age, it's increasingly more difficult to avoid them. Consider the options they have: e-mail, text messaging, social networking, and antisocial networking, plus the holy grail of all communications — video chat.

This part of the book covers these methods of staying in touch with the people you know. For the people you know whom you'd rather avoid, this chapter has some suggestions, all of which are legal in most localities.

Today

SteveMartinToGo
8:05 PM
Feeling sleepy a bit early tonight.* *BASED ON THE INCREDIBLE TRUE STORY.

Kris Dengel Aylesworth
8:01 PM
Anna watching Princess and the Frog with Grandpa

👍 1 likes this   💬 1 comment

Brook Bassett
7:57 PM
A four poster bed is the best clothing dryer rack a girl could buy.

The People in Your Galaxy

1 felt embarrassed when a friend of mine (an older friend) gave me a gift. It was an address book. Actually, I believe it's called a *day planner* now. Whatever. I hear that people, once upon a time, jotted down the names and addresses of the people they knew. They'd add extra tidbits, such as birthdays. My day planner gift even had a spot for writing down an e-mail address. For that, I sadly had to shake my head.

There's really no longer a reason to write down address book information. That's because electronic gizmos such as your Galaxy Note are more than up to the task. It makes sense: The phone not only makes calls to your friends but can also send e-mail, navigate to their homes or offices, and perform plenty of other tricks. Day planner? Bah! You don't need one. Your phone is now your address book.

an Gookin

Don Barzini

Don Corleone

Don Luchesi

Don Stracci

The Digital Address Book

There are people in your phone. You'll find them in an app named Contacts. It's actually part of the Phone app, which is handy because you most often use your phone's address book when making a call. But that's not all you can do with the Contacts app.

Accessing the address book

To peruse your phone's address book, open the Contacts app. You may find a shortcut for this app on the Home screen, but you'll find the app for certain on the Apps menu. You can also view your contacts by touching the Contacts tab in the Phone app.

Figure 8-1 shows the Contacts app. Try to locate the items illustrated in the figure on your Galaxy Note's screen.

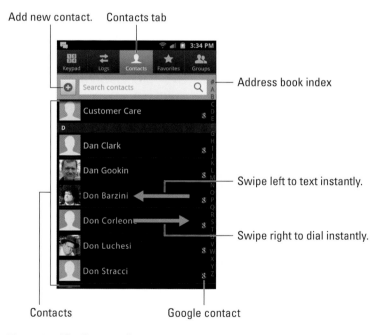

Figure 8-1: The Contacts list.

Scroll the list by swiping your finger. You can use the index on the right side of the screen (refer to Figure 8-1) to quickly scroll your Contacts list up and down or hop to a specific letter of the alphabet.

Viewing a contact's information

To do anything with a contact, you first have to choose it: Touch a contact's name on the screen, and you see more information, similar to what's shown in Figure 8-2.

Recent calls, texts, and e-mails

Social networking

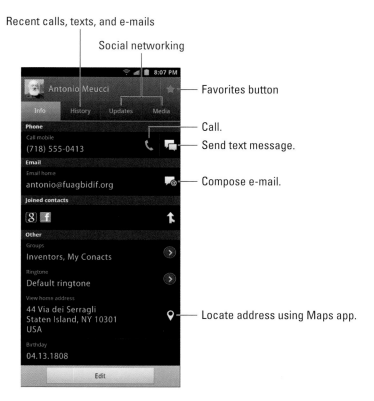

Favorites button

Call.

Send text message.

Compose e-mail.

Locate address using Maps app.

Figure 8-2: More detail about a contact.

You can do a multitude of things with the contact after it's displayed, as illustrated in Figure 8-2:

Make a phone call. To call the contact, touch one of the contact's phone entries, such as Home or Mobile. You touch the entry itself or touch the Phone icon by the entry.

Send a text message. Touch the Text Message icon, shown in Figure 8-2, to open the Messaging app and send the contact a message. See Chapter 9 for information about text messaging.

Compose an e-mail message. Touch the Email link to compose an e-mail message to the contact. When the contact has more than one e-mail address, you can choose to which one you want to send the message. Chapter 9 covers using e-mail on your phone.

View social networking info. To see the latest status updates for a contact, touch the Updates tab. The Media tab lists the contact's social networking pictures and videos. See Chapter 11 for additional information on social networking.

Locate your contact on a map. When the contact has a home or business address, you can touch the little doohickey next to the address, shown in Figure 8-2, to summon the Maps application. Refer to Chapter 13 to see all the fun stuff you can do with Maps.

Oh, and if you have birthday information therefore a contact, you can view it as well. Singing "Happy Birthday" is something you have to do on your own.

- ✔ When you're done viewing the contact, press the Back soft button.

- ✔ Information about your contacts is pulled from multiple sources: your Google account, the phone's storage, and your social networking sites. When you see duplicated information for a contact, it's probably because the information comes from two or more of those sources.

Sorting the address book

Your contacts are displayed in a certain order by the Contacts app. On my Galaxy Note, it's alphabetically by first name and first name first. You can change the order to whatever you like by following these steps:

1. **Start the Contacts app.**

2. **Press the Menu soft button.**

3. **Choose More and then Display Options.**

4. **Choose Sort By.**

5. **Select Given Name or Family Name to sort the list accordingly.**

   I prefer sorting by given (first) name.

6. **Choose Display Contact By.**

7. **Choose either Given Name First or Family Name First, which specifies how contacts are displayed in the list.**

   The way the name is displayed doesn't affect the sort order. So, if you choose Given Name First and Last Name as the sort order, you still see the list sorted by last name, even though the contacts' first name appears first.

8. **Touch the Done button.**

You see your changes right away in the Contacts app.

Some New Friends

Everyone makes friends in their own way. Sometimes, a shy smile does the trick, but I've found that having someone hand me a crisp $100 bill to be quite effective. No matter how you acquire new friends, the Contacts app is well equipped to help you add them.

There's no correlation between the number of contacts you have and the number of bestest friends you have — none at all.

Adding a contact from the call log

One of the quickest ways to bolster your Contacts list is to add people as they phone you — assuming that you've told them about your new phone number. After someone calls, you can use the call log to add the person to your phone's address book. Heed these steps:

1. **Open the Phone app.**

2. **Touch the Logs tab at the top of the screen.**

3. **Choose the phone number from the list of recent calls.**

4. **Touch the Create Contact button.**

   If the number belongs to an existing contact, touch the Update Existing button and choose the contact from the phone's address book.

5. **Choose your Google account as the location to store the new contact.**

   By choosing your Google account, you ensure that the contact's information is duplicated from your phone to your Google account on the Internet.

The Phone option keeps the contact stored on your Galaxy Note, and nowhere else. Ditto for the SIM option, which stores the contact's information on the phone's SIM card.

You can, optionally, place a green check mark by the setting Remember This Choice so that you're not prompted again.

6. **Fill in the contact's information.**

   Fill in as many blanks as you know about the caller: given name and family name, for example, and other information, if you know it. If you don't know any additional information, that's fine; just filling in the name helps clue you in to who is calling the next time that person calls (using the same number).

   I recommend that you add the area code prefix to the phone number, if it's not automatically added for you.

7. **Touch the Save button to create the new contact.**

You can merge duplicate contacts when you accidentally create a new contact where one already exists. See the later section "Joining contacts."

Creating a new contact from scratch

Sometimes, it's necessary to create a contact when you meet another human being in the real world. In that case, you have more information to input, and it starts like this:

1. **Open the Contacts app.**

   Ensure that the Contacts tab is chosen at the top of the screen.

2. **Touch the Add New Contact button.**

   Refer to Figure 8-1 for the button's location.

3. **If prompted, choose an account as the place to store the contact.**

   I recommend choosing Google.

4. **Fill in the information on the Create Contact screen as the contact begrudgingly gives you information.**

   Fill in the text fields with the information you know: the Given Name and Family Name fields, for example.

   To add a field, touch the green Plus button on the touchscreen. For example, when a contact has two phone numbers, use the green Plus button to add a second field.

Touch the gray button to the left of the phone number or the e-mail address to choose the location for that item, such as Home, Work, or Mobile.

Touch the More button at the bottom of the list to expand that area and add *even more* information!

5. Touch the Save button to complete editing and add the new contact.

You can also create new contacts by using your Gmail account on a computer. This option offers you the luxury of using a full-size keyboard and computer screen, though whenever you meet a contact face-to-face, creating the contact using your phone will have to suffice.

Importing contacts from your computer

Your computer's e-mail program is doubtless a useful repository of contacts you've built up over the years. You can export these contacts from your computer's e-mail program and then import them into your Galaxy Note. It's not the simplest thing to do, but it's a quick way to build up your phone's address book.

The key is to save or export your computer e-mail program's records in the *vCard* (.vcf) file format. These records can then be imported into the phone and read by the Contacts app. The method for exporting contacts varies depending on the e-mail program:

- **In the Windows Live Mail program,** choose Go⇨Contacts, and then choose File⇨Export⇨Business Card (.VCF) to export the contacts.

- **In Windows Mail,** choose File⇨Export⇨Windows Contacts, and then choose vCards (Folder of .VCF Files) from the Export Windows Contacts dialog box. Click the Export button.

- **On the Mac,** open the Address Book program, and choose File⇨Export⇨Export vCard.

After the vCard files are created, connect the phone to your computer and transfer the vCard files from your computer to the phone. Directions for making this type of transfer are found in Chapter 20.

After the vCard files have been copied to the phone, you need to import them into the Contacts app. Follow these steps:

1. In the Contacts app, press the Menu soft button.

2. Choose More and then Import/Export.

3. **Choose the command Import from SD Card.**

4. **Choose to save the contacts to your Google account.**

5. **If prompted, choose the option Import All vCard Files.**

6. **Touch the OK button.**

   Work through any additional steps, such as choosing an account type or touching the OK button when prompted.

The imported contacts are also synchronized to your Gmail account, which instantly creates a backup copy.

Mixing in social networking contacts

If you've configured your Galaxy Note using the AT&T Ready2Go app (as discussed in Chapter 2), your social networking accounts have already been added to the phone. The next step is to synchronize those accounts with the address book. Obey these steps:

1. **Start the Contacts app.**

2. **Ensure that the Contacts tab is chosen.**

   You'll find the Contacts tab at the top of the screen.

3. **Press the Menu soft button.**

4. **Choose More and then Accounts.**

   On the Accounts & Sync screen, you should find your social networking sites listed under the Manage Accounts heading.

5. **Touch the Sync button to the right of a social networking account.**

   If you don't see your social networking account in the list, touch the Add Account button to set it up. If that doesn't work, see Chapter 11 for information on adding specific social networking apps to your phone.

6. **Place green check marks in the boxes by the option Sync Contacts.**

   You can activate the other options as well, though synchronizing your social networking contacts is this section's topic.

7. **Touch the Sync Now button.**

8. **Press the Back soft button twice to return to your Contacts list.**

   Or press the Back button once and repeat steps 5 through 7 for additional social networking sites.

See Chapter 11 for more information on social networking with your Galaxy Note.

Finding a new contact by location

When you use the Maps application to locate a restaurant or cobbler or an all-night discount liquor outlet, you can quickly create a contact for that business based on its location. Here's how:

1. **Open the Maps app.**

   It's found on the Apps menu.

2. **Search for a location.**

   You can find oodles of information on using the Maps app in Chapter 13.

3. **Touch the location's cartoon bubble that appears on the map.**

   For example, in Figure 8-3, a sports bar has been found. Touching the cartoon bubble displays a window full of additional information.

You have to touch this (or a similar) cartoon bubble in Step 3.

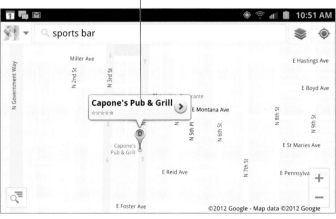

Figure 8-3: A business has been located.

4. **Scroll to the bottom of the location's information, and choose the command Add As a Contact.**

5. If prompted, choose in which account to store the contact.

I recommend choosing your Google account.

The information for the location is copied from the Maps app into the proper fields for the contact, including the address and phone number, plus other information (if available).

6. Touch the Save button.

The new contact is created.

Address Book Management

Nothing is more terrifying to cell phone owners than having to change phone numbers. They dread it more than having to move or having to change their Facebook status from In a Relationship to Single. I suppose that the dread comes from having to inform *everyone you know* of your new number and the burden that such a task places on your friends.

Well, fret not, gentle reader. Updates to your contacts happen frequently. Making changes is simple. That's because the Contact app features ample tools to ease the burden, plus some features that make your address book management duties less of a pain.

Making basic changes

To make minor touch-ups on any contact, start by locating and displaying the contact's information. Press the big Edit button that looms large at the bottom of the screen, as shown earlier, in Figure 8-2.

The contact's information is displayed, with all fields and options up for editing, modifying, or deleting: Change, add, or edit information by touching a field and typing. To add another phone number or e-mail address, touch the green Plus button to summon a new field. You remove some items by touching the red Minus button next to an item's field.

Certain information cannot be edited. For example, fields pulled in from social networking sites can be edited only by that account holder on the social networking site.

When you're done editing, touch the Save button.

Setting primary numbers

Some contacts have multiple phone numbers and e-mail addresses, probably more contacts than you would guess. I recommend that you set a primary number and e-mail address for these contacts. It's not a necessary step, but it makes things go faster when you need to phone, text, or e-mail that contact in the future.

To set a primary number, obey these steps:

1. **Summon the contact's information in the Contacts app.**

   Rather than edit the contact's information, you only have to look at it.

2. **Long-press the entry that you want to make the primary entry, such as the mobile phone number over the work or home number.**

3. **Choose the command Mark As Default.**

   The entry grows a blue check mark, which is your clue that the phone number or e-mail address is preferred.

4. **Repeat Steps 2 and 3 for the contact's e-mail address, if necessary.**

In technology lingo, the word *default* means "the main or primary value — the one that is automatically chosen."

Adding a picture to a contact

The simplest way to add a picture to one of your contacts is to have the image already stored in the phone. You can snap a picture and save it (covered in Chapter 14), grab a picture from the Internet (covered in Chapter 10), or use any image already stored in the phone's Gallery app (covered in Chapter 14). The image doesn't even have to be a picture of the contact — any image will do.

After the contact's photo, or any other suitable image, is stored on the phone, follow these steps to update the contact's information:

1. **Locate and display the contact's information.**

2. **Touch the Edit button at the bottom of the screen.**

3. **Touch the icon where the contact's picture would sit, or touch the existing picture assigned to the contact.**

   The icon shows a generic placeholder if no picture is assigned.

4. **Choose the Album option.**

   If you have other image management apps on your phone, you can instead choose the app's command from the list.

5. **Browse the Gallery to look for a suitable image.**

   See Chapter 14 for more information on using the Gallery.

6. **Touch the image you want to use for the contact.**

7. **Optionally, crop the image.**

   Drag the orange rectangle to include the portion of the image you want for the contact, as shown in Figure 8-4. Tap the rectangle's edges, and then drag it in or out to resize.

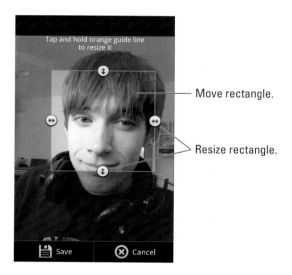

Figure 8-4: Cropping a contact's image.

8. **Touch the Save icon to set the contact's image.**

9. **Touch the Save button again to finish editing the contact.**

   The image is now assigned, and it appears whenever the contact is referenced on your phone.

 You can add pictures to contacts on your Google account by using any computer. Just visit your Gmail Contacts list to edit a contact. You can then add to that contact any picture stored on your computer. The picture is eventually synced with the same contact on your Android phone.

✓ Pictures can also be added by your Gmail friends and contacts when they add their own images to their accounts.

✓ You may also see pictures assigned to your contacts based on pictures supplied on Facebook or other social networking sites.

✓ Some images in the Gallery may not work for contact icons. For example, images synchronized with your online photo albums may be unavailable.

✓ To get rid of the existing contact's picture, in Step 4 choose the Remove Icon option.

Making a favorite

A *favorite* contact is someone you stay in touch with most often. The person doesn't have to be someone you like — just someone you (perhaps unfortunately) phone often, such as your parole officer.

The list of favorite contacts is kept on the Phone app's Favorites tab. The top part of the list shows contacts that you've flagged as favorites. Below that, you find the Frequently Dialed list, which contains contacts or phone numbers that you phone frequently but who are not (yet) favorites — ideal candidates for promotion to the Favorites list.

To add a contact to the Favorites list, display the contact's information and touch the Favorites button (the star) in the contact's upper-right corner, as shown earlier, in Figure 8-2. When the star is orange, the contact has been added to your list of favorites.

To remove a favorite, touch the contact's star again to remove its color. Removing a favorite doesn't delete the contact, but instead removes it from the Favorites list.

Contacts have no idea whether they're favorites, so don't believe that you're hurting anyone's feelings by not making them a favorite.

Creating a contact group

It's possible to corral contacts into groups, which makes it easier to send that group an e-mail or a text message. Heed these steps to create a contact group:

1. **Open the Contacts app.**

2. **Touch the Groups tab.**

3. **Press the Menu soft button, and choose the Create command.**

4. **Type a name for the group.**

   For example, type Friends Who Dislike Me.

5. **Set a ringtone for the group.**

   If anyone in the group phones you, the phone plays the ringtone you choose. For example, if you want a special ringtone for family members, you create a family group and assign the group a unique ringtone.

6. **Touch the Save button.**

   The group is created, but it's empty. The next step is to add members to the group.

7. **Choose the group from the list in the Groups tab.**

8. **Touch the Add Contacts button.**

   The button appears to the left of the Search Contacts text box, as shown in the margin.

   After touching the button, you see the full Contacts list displayed. Every contact has an empty check box to the left.

9. **Scroll your Contacts list, and place a green check mark by the names of people you want to add to the group.**

10. **Touch the Add button.**

    You see the group displayed, along with all its members.

To perform an action with the group, first choose it from the list of groups shown on the Groups tab. Press the Menu soft button, and choose Send Message or Send Email. Then follow along with the directions on the screen, as well as elsewhere in this book, for completing your group message or activity.

   ✔ To add members to an existing group, follow Steps 7 through 10.

   ✔ To remove someone from the group, display the group and long-press the contact you want to remove. Choose the Remove Member command from the pop-up menu.

   ✔ Delete a group by long-pressing the group's name on the screen. Choose the Delete command, and then choose Group Only.

Sharing a contact

You know Mark? I know Mark, too! Does he owe you money? Really? Me too! Would you like his contact information? Allow me to share it with you. Here's what I do:

1. **Open the Contacts app to display the Contacts list.**

2. **Long-press the contact you want to share.**

3. **Choose the Send Namecard Via command.**

   If you don't see the command, you've probably chosen a social networking contact, which cannot be shared. Otherwise you see the Complete Action Using menu, which displays a slew of methods for sharing the contact's information.

4. **If prompted, choose the items you want to share about the contact.**

   Touch a green check mark to select an item you want to share about the contact. Touch the OK button when you're done.

5. **Complete the action by using the app you selected: Email, Gmail, Bluetooth, Messaging, or whatever else might be displayed.**

   After you choose a method, the appropriate app appears for sharing the contact's name card.

Information about sharing by Email, Gmail, Text Messaging, or other options is explained elsewhere in this book.

What you're sending is a *vCard,* a common type of file used by databases and personal information software to exchange contact information. You can use the vCard, for example, to import information into your computer's e-mail program.

Joining contacts

Occasionally, you may notice that some people have duplicate entries in your Galaxy Note's address book, which simply means that the phone has pulled information about one person from several sources, such as Gmail and a social networking site, and the phone isn't smart enough to know that they are, in fact, the same person.

As a human who is smarter than your phone, you can fix this situation by following these steps:

1. **Open the Contacts app.**

2. **Choose someone who you know has duplicate contacts.**

   For example, if you have two Peter Griffins in your phone's address book, choose one of them — doesn't matter which.

3. **Choose Joined Contacts.**

   The Joined Contacts area shows the contact's sources, as illustrated in Figure 8-5. Touching this button displays the list of joined contacts.

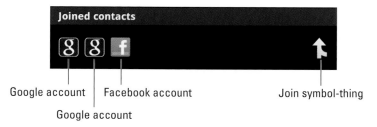

Figure 8-5: Joined contact information.

4. **At the Joined Contacts screen, touch the button named Join Another Contact.**

   The phone scans your contacts to cull potential matches. If you don't see any, choose Show All Contacts.

5. **Choose the matching contact.**

   You see all contact sources displayed on the Joined Contacts screen.

6. **Press the Back soft button to return to the contact's info screen.**

Having a *joined* contact means that all the information about a single person (or a business or whatever) is stored as one entry. No matter how many sources, the contact has only one address book entry.

Just as you can join two identical contacts, you can also split them. Follow Steps 1 through 3, but in Step 4 touch the red Minus button to the left of an account to separate it.

Removing a contact

Every so often, consider reviewing your phone's address book. Purge those folks whom you no longer recognize or remember. It's simple:

1. **Locate the contact in your phone's address book, and display the contact's information.**

2. **Press the Menu soft button, and choose the Delete command.**

3. **Touch OK to remove the contact from your phone.**

Because the Contacts list is synchronized with your Gmail contacts for your Google account, the contact is also removed there.

Removing a contact from your phone doesn't kill that person in real life.

9

Message for You!

In This Chapter

▶ Understanding messages and e-mail
▶ Configuring e-mail accounts
▶ Creating a text message
▶ Getting a text message
▶ Forwarding a text message
▶ Texting pictures, videos, and media items
▶ Reading your e-mail
▶ Sending an e-mail message
▶ Creating e-mail signatures

*Y*ou may view your Galaxy Note as a phone. This observation merely betrays your age. For young people, a device such as the Galaxy Note is primarily used to send and receive text messages. Yes, *text*. The telegraph may be long dead, but the youth of today rely on short quips of text far more than they rely on voice communications. My own kids talk on their cell phones for maybe 15 minutes a month and send thousands of text messages.

The Galaxy Note's ability to send messages isn't limited to texting. It also handles e-mail, which includes your Google Gmail account as well as your organization's e-mail, home e-mail, web-based e-mail — all of it. It's text on a phone — something that I'm sure Alexander Graham Bell never would have imagined.

Galaxy Note Messaging Overview

To master the text side of communications on your Galaxy Note, buy yourself a bright pink outfit, shave your head, and learn to speak Pengo.

Not really.

Several apps are used to perform text messaging and e-mail duties on the Galaxy Note. It also has multiple ways to configure e-mail accounts, if you haven't yet done so. This section helps solve the mysteries — no head shaving required.

Using the various messaging apps

Behold the three apps that are used to access your messages and e-mail on the Galaxy Note:

Messaging: The Messaging app is responsible for text messages. See the section "Life in Less Than 160 Characters," later in this chapter.

Gmail: For reading and composing Gmail, use the Gmail app. It hooks directly into your Google Gmail account. In fact, they're exact echoes of each other: The Gmail you receive on your computer is also received on your phone.

Email: For reading and composing all other types of e-mail, use the Email app. It's used to connect to non-Gmail electronic mail, such as the standard mail service provided by your ISP or a web-based e-mail system such as Yahoo! Mail or Windows Live mail.

 ✔ The Email app can be configured to handle multiple e-mail accounts, as described in the next section.

 ✔ Although you can use your phone's web browser to visit the Gmail website, you should use the Gmail app to pick up your Gmail.

 ✔ If you forget your Gmail password, visit this web address:

```
www.google.com/accounts/ForgotPasswd
```

Configuring e-mail accounts

Your Galaxy Note can handle your e-mail chores, but only if you've informed the phone of your e-mail accounts. I'm not talking about Gmail, which is handled by its own app. I'm referring to your other e-mail: web-based e-mail (such as Yahoo! or Hotmail) or your ISP's e-mail account or even the e-mail you use at work.

If you haven't yet run the Email app or configured the Galaxy Note to access your e-mail, read the next section. Otherwise, skip to the later section "Add more e-mail accounts."

Add the first e-mail account

If you corralled all your e-mail accounts and added them to the phone during setup, great! If not, you can add your web-based e-mail accounts, ISP, corporate and other accounts now by following these steps:

1. **Start the Email app.**

   The Galaxy Note may be preconfigured with the Email app on the Dock (at the bottom of the Home screen).

   If you see an inbox when you start the Email app, the inbox has already been initially configured. Skip to the next section, "Add more e-mail accounts."

2. **Type your e-mail account's address and password into the text boxes on the screen.**

3. **Touch the Next button.**

   The Galaxy Note contacts the e-mail service and attempts to configure your account automatically.

4. **Give the account a name.**

   The name of the service will work, though if you prefer another name (or if the phone guesses incorrectly), you can edit the name.

5. **Type your display name, which is your name as it appears in outgoing messages.**

   Often, the phone merely copies your e-mail account name into the Your Name field. Feel free to edit the name.

6. **Touch the Done button.**

   Your account is set up.

For some accounts, messages may be copied into the Galaxy Note and displayed on the screen. Refer to the later section "Reading an e-mail message" for information on using the Email app's inbox.

Add more e-mail accounts

When the Email app is already set up with one or more e-mail accounts, you can create additional accounts by following these steps:

1. **Touch the Accounts button at the top of the screen.**

   The Accounts button features the name of the current e-mail account, or it may say *All Inboxes.* In Figure 9-1, the button reads *Yahoo.*

   Accounts button   Folders button

   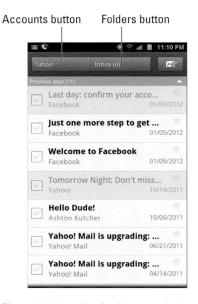

   Figure 9-1: Locating the Accounts button.

   Touching the Accounts button displays a summary of all your e-mail inboxes, plus a list of active accounts.

2. **Press the Menu soft button.**

3. **Choose Add Account.**

4. **Type your account's e-mail address.**

5. **Type the password for the account.**

6. **If you prefer to use this account to send e-mail from your Galaxy Note, place a check mark by the option Send Email from This Account by Default.**

7. **Touch the Next button.**

   In a few magical moments, the e-mail account is configured and added to the account list.

   If you goofed up the account name or password, you're warned: Try again.

8. **Give the account a name.**

   Touch the Account Name field to type a new name.

9. **Ensure that your own name is entered correctly.**

   The phone tries to guesses your name based on your e-mail address. Touch the Your Name field to change the text there. The name you type is used to identify who you are in outgoing messages.

10. **Touch the Done button.**

   The account is added, and you immediately see the account inbox.

Repeat the steps in this section to add more e-mail accounts. Your Galaxy Note can collect e-mail from just about anywhere you have an e-mail account.

Add an Exchange Server account

You need not worry that you and your Galaxy Note can wander too far from the clutches of your evil organization. It's entirely possible to get e-mail from a Microsoft Exchange Server, if that's what your outfit uses. Heed these steps, corporate drone:

1. **At the Home screen, press the Menu soft button.**

2. **Choose Settings, and then choose Accounts and Sync.**

3. **Touch the Add Account button.**

4. **Choose Microsoft Exchange ActiveSync.**

5. **Type your e-mail address (account name) and password.**

6. **Touch the Next button.**

   If you can't see the Next button, press the Back soft button to hide the onscreen keyboard.

7. **Touch the OK button after ignoring the warning.**

8. **Review the information in the Exchange Server Settings window.**

   You may need assistance in confirming that the fields are properly filled in, such as the server's domain name and the official name of the Exchange server. Only if the information is accurate can the phone be configured properly.

9. **Fill in information on the Account Options screen.**

   Your evil organization's IT professionals can assist you with the settings. I recommend that you offer them gifts of M&Ms or Doritos to appease them before asking.

10. **Touch the Next button.**

11. **Optionally, give the account a name.**

12. **Touch the Activate button to succumb to the demands of your organization's whims and gain access to the account.**

Your corporate e-mail now flows into the phone the same way as other e-mail does, and it's accessible from the Email app.

Life in Less Than 160 Characters

It's the most popular way for kids to communicate: Send a text message instead of calling. The messages are brief — fewer than 160 characters. But that's the way some people roll. And I admit that sending text messages is often quicker and easier than making phone calls. The messages are short, quick, and to the point.

On the Galaxy Note, the app that handles texting is Messaging. It can be found on the Home screen and on the Apps menu.

✔ Don't text while you're driving or while you're in a movie theater or in any other situation where it's awkward and inappropriate to be paying more attention to your phone than to your surroundings.

✔ Your cellular service plan may charge you per message for every text message you send. Some plans feature a given number of free (included) messages per month. Other plans, favored by teenagers (and their parents), feature unlimited texting.

✔ The process of sending and receiving text messages is commonly called *texting*.

✔ The nerdy term for text messaging is *SMS*, which stands for Short Message Service.

Messaging v. AT&T Messages

This book covers using the Messaging app to compose, send, and receive text messages. As an AT&T phone, the Galaxy Note also includes the text-messaging app AT&T Messages, which you can also use, though I don't specifically cover it.

When you choose a text messaging option, such as from the Share Via menu, you may be prompted to select either the AT&T Messages app or the Messaging app. My advice is to place a check mark by the Set As Default option and then choose the texting app you plan to use. I recommend Messaging.

Composing a text message

To send a short, pithy punch of prose to a fellow cell phone owner, follow these steps:

1. **Open the Messaging app.**

2. **If the app opens to a specific conversation, press the Back soft button to return to the main Messaging screen.**

   The main screen lists all your text message conversations.

3. **If you see the person you want to text listed as a conversation, touch that entry on the screen; otherwise, touch the Next Message button to compose a new text message.**

4. **Type the phone number or a contact's name into the Enter Recipient text box.**

   As you type, any matching contacts appear in a list; choose a contact to save yourself some typing time.

5. **You can, optionally, type the names of additional people to text, in which case the message is sent to everyone you specify.**

   Normally, you text only one person at a time.

6. **Touch the Tap to Enter Message field to type the text message.**

   Be brief. A text message has a 160-character limit. You can check the screen to see whether you're nearing the limit. (Refer to Figure 9-2.)

7. **Touch the Send button.**

   The message is sent instantly. Whether the contact replies instantly depends. When the person replies, you see the message displayed at the top of the screen.

8. **Read the reply.**

9. **Repeat Steps 6 through 8 as needed — or eternally, whichever comes first.**

There's no need to continually look at your phone while waiting for a text message. Whenever your contact chooses to reply, you see the message recorded as part of an ongoing conversation. See the next section.

✔ Quickly compose a text message to a contact by swiping that person's entry to the left in the Contacts app.

✔ When viewing a contact's information, you compose a text message to the contact by touching the Message icon, shown in the margin.

✔ You can send text messages only to cell phones. Aunt Jane cannot receive text messages on her landline that she's had since the 1960s.

✔ Continue a conversation at any time: Open the phone's texting app, peruse the list of existing conversations, and touch one to review what has been said or to pick up the conversation.

✔ Do not text and drive. Do not text and drive. Do not text and drive.

Contact or phone number

Unread text messages

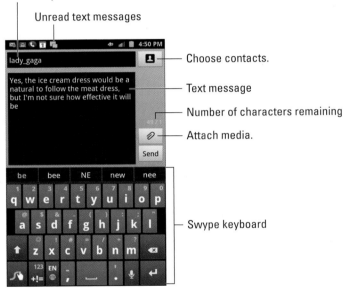

Choose contacts.

Text message

Number of characters remaining

Attach media.

Swype keyboard

Figure 9-2: Typing a text message.

Receiving a text message

Whenever a new text message arrives, you see the message appear briefly at the top of the phone's touchscreen. Then you see the New Text Message notification, similar to the one shown in the margin and in Figure 9-1.

To view the message, pull down the notifications, as described in Chapter 3. Touch the messaging notification, and that conversation window immediately opens.

When the message is sent to multiple people, you can reply to all of them by touching the Send to All button when composing your reply.

Forwarding a text message

Forwarding a text message isn't the same as forwarding e-mail. In fact, for forwarding information, e-mail has text messaging beaten by well over 160 characters.

When forwarding works as an option, your phone lets you forward only the information in a text messaging cartoon bubble, not the entire conversation. Here's how it works:

1. **If necessary, open a conversation in the Messaging app.**
2. **Long-press the text entry (the cartoon bubble) that you want to forward.**
3. **From the menu that appears, choose the command Forward.**

   From this point on, forwarding the message works the same way as sending a new message from scratch. (Refer to Figure 9-2.)
4. **Type the recipient's name (if the person is a contact) or phone number.**

   The text you're forwarding appears, already written, in the text field.
5. **Touch the Send button to forward the message.**

You can choose the Copy Message Text command in Step 3 to copy the text in the bubble and then paste it elsewhere on the Galaxy Note. See Chapter 4 for details on copying and pasting text on your Galaxy Note.

Attaching media to a text message

To show total disregard for its nickname, text messaging lets you send pictures, videos, music, or other types of media with the message. Doing so creates a *multimedia* message. The good news is that attaching media is simple. The better news is that you can use the same Text Messaging app to accomplish this task.

The trick works like this:

1. **Compose a message as you normally do, as described earlier in this chapter.**
2. **Touch the Attach button.**

   Refer to Figure 9-2 for its location; the button sports the traditional paperclip icon commonly used for attaching items to messages.

3. **Choose an item to attach from the Attach menu.**

A menu appears listing a whole slew of things you can stick into a text message. The variety depends on the apps installed on your phone, though traditionally the Pictures and Videos items are the most popular.

When you choose an option to create something (Take Picture, Capture Video, Record Audio), use the appropriate app on the Galaxy Note to create the instant attachment.

4. **Optionally, edit the media.**

For example, you might see a warning that the picture or video is too large. If so, obey the directions on the screen to make the attachment more suitable for a multimedia text message.

5. **Touch the Send button to send off the media.**

In just a few, short, cellular moments, the receiving party will enjoy your multimedia text message.

- An easier way to send a multimedia message is to start with the source, such as a picture or video stored on your phone. Use the Send Via command and choose Messaging to share the media item.

- Not every phone is capable of receiving multimedia messages. Rather than receive the media item, the recipient may be directed to a web page where the item can be viewed on the Internet.

- The official name for multimedia text messaging is *Multimedia Messaging Service*, which is abbreviated *MMS*.

Saving media from a text message

Any media you receive in a text message appears in a cartoon bubble. To save the media, such as a photograph, follow these steps:

1. **Long-press the media cartoon bubble in the text message conversation.**

2. **Choose Attached Items.**

3. **Place a check mark by the media item you want to save.**

The items are listed by filename, which can be confusing, especially when a single message contains multiple media items.

4. **Touch the Save button.**

The media is saved to the phone's internal storage or to the MicroSD card (if one is installed).

To view or hear the media, you must summon the appropriate app on your phone. The Gallery app is used to view visual media; use either the Music or Play Music app to listen to audio.

See Chapter 14 for details on using the Gallery app. Text message attachments are found in the Download folder.

Setting the text message ringtone

There's no reason that your Galaxy Note should sport the same boring ringtone notification when a new text message arrives. Spice things up a bit by following these steps:

1. **Open the Messaging app.**

2. **Ensure that you're viewing the main screen, which lists all your conversations.**

   If you're not viewing that screen, press the Back soft button.

3. **Press the Menu soft button.**

4. **Choose the Settings command.**

5. **Choose Select Ringtone.**

   The command is found at the bottom of the Settings screen.

6. **If prompted by the Complete Action Using menu, choose Android System.**

7. **Pluck a ringtone from the list.**

8. **Touch the OK button.**

To merely confirm the Messaging ringtone, work through these steps and choose the current ringtone in Step 7.

E-Mail on the Galaxy Note

Two apps on your phone deal with e-mail: the Gmail app and the Email app. They're both similar, handling the basic chores of e-mail: sending, receiving, forwarding, and otherwise mangling your electronic messages as best as can be done on a cell phone. This section goes over the basics.

Getting a new message

Every e-mail that floats into your Galaxy Note generates a notification. The notification icons differ, depending on the e-mail source. For example:

New Gmail messages produce the New Gmail notification, shown in the margin.

New e-mail messages generate the New Email notification. This notification appears for whatever e-mail accounts you've set up, including web-based e-mail accounts and evil corporate e-mail.

To deal with the new-message notification, drag down the notifications and choose the appropriate one. You're taken directly to your inbox to read the new message.

Reading an e-mail message

The way an e-mail message looks on your phone depends on whether you're using the Gmail app or the Email app. Figure 9-3 shows the Gmail interface; Figure 9-4 shows the Email app's message-reading interface.

Figure 9-3: Reading a Gmail message on your phone.

Newer messages   Reply All   Delete message.

Older messages   Reply   Forward   Display boring information.

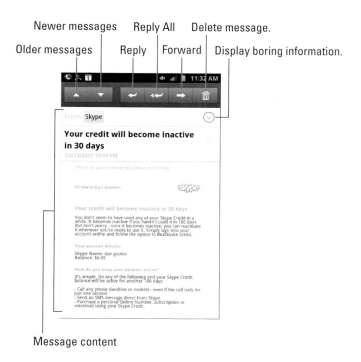

Message content

Figure 9-4: Reading an e-mail message.

Browse messages by touching the arrow buttons at the bottom of the message screen. The buttons may point left and right, as shown in Figure 9-3, but they can point up or down instead. This difference was created merely to confuse you.

Replying to the message works similarly to composing a new message in the Gmail and Email programs. Refer to the next section.

Composing a new e-mail missive

If you're familiar with creating e-mail on a computer, doing so on a phone isn't that much different. You use the Gmail app to compose new Gmail messages, and the Email app composes messages for whatever other e-mail services you use. The interface on both apps is similar, as shown in Figure 9-5.

Save a draft copy.

Send.

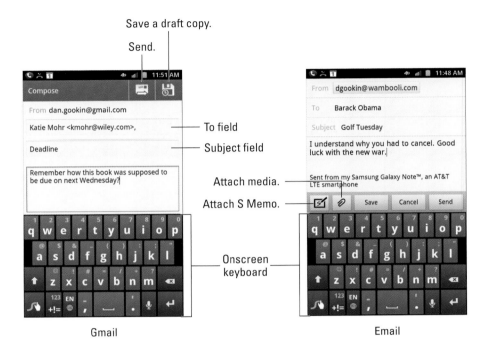

To field

Subject field

Attach media.

Attach S Memo.

Onscreen keyboard

Gmail

Email

Figure 9-5: Writing a new e-mail message.

Here's how to create an e-mail message using your phone:

1. **Start an e-mail app, either Gmail or Email.**

   You may also be able to compose a new message from the universal Inbox app, as shown earlier, in Figure 9-1.

2. **In the Gmail app, press the Menu soft button and choose Compose; in the Email app, touch the New Message button.**

   A new message screen appears, looking similar to Figure 9-5 but with none of the fields filled in.

3. **If necessary, touch the To field to select it.**

4. **Type the first few letters of a contact name, and then choose a matching contact from the list that's displayed.**

   You can also send a message to any valid e-mail address not found in your Contacts list by typing the address.

5. **Type a subject.**

6. **Type the message.**

7. **Touch the Send button to instantly deliver your e-epistle.**

   In Gmail, you can touch the Save Draft button and the message is stored in the Drafts folder. You can open this folder to reedit the message. Touch Send to send it.

Copies of the messages you send in the Email app are stored in the Sent mailbox. If you're using Gmail, copies are saved in your Gmail account, which is accessed from your phone or from any computer connected to the Internet.

Refer to Figure 9-1 for the location of the Folders button in the Email app.

Changing your e-mail signature

I compel you to join me in the fight against boring e-mail signatures. Arm yourself and your Galaxy Note by heeding the directions in this section.

In the Gmail app, follow these steps:

1. **Press the Menu soft button.**

2. **Choose More and then Settings.**

3. **Choose your account (your e-mail address).**

4. **Choose Signature.**

5. **Type a new signature, or edit the old one.**

6. **Touch the OK button.**

In the Email app, follow these steps:

1. **Choose the account to which you want to apply a signature.**

   Select an account by touching the Accounts button. (Refer to Figure 9-1.) A specific account must be listed; it cannot say *All Inboxes*.

2. **Press the Menu soft button.**

3. **Choose More and then Account Settings.**

4. **Choose Signature.**

5. **Create a new signature, or edit the old one.**

   My Galaxy Note originally had this signature:

   ```
   Sent from my Samsung Galaxy Note™, an AT&T LTE
   smartphone.
   ```

Don't be a dork and use this signature. Create something clever and new, such as this one:

```
Sent from my Galaxy Note, which is much bigger and
better than your stupid cell phone.
```

6. **Touch the OK button.**

Repeat these steps for all accounts in the Email app. Every account can have its own signature, so changing one doesn't change them all.

Review Chapter 4 for information on copying and pasting text on your Galaxy Note.

The signature you specify appears at the bottom of every e-mail message sent from the phone. The signature is automatically inserted any time you create a new message, as shown in Figure 9-5.

10

It's a World Wide Web We Weave

1 can be honest: The web was not designed to be viewed on a cell phone. Even when using the Galaxy Note, with its lovely and large screen, the web experience isn't exactly what it's intended. It's like watching a wide-screen movie on TV or peeking through a fence at a nudist colony. The visual experience isn't quite as fulfilling as intended.

You probably know the web well. Browsing the web on your Galaxy Note works similarly to how it works on your computer. This chapter highlights the basics of the web on your phone and describes useful ways to make the visual experience more rewarding — like having a chain link fence around the nudist colony.

   ✔ The Galaxy Note has apps for Gmail, social network-ing (Facebook, Twitter, and others), YouTube, and potentially other popular locations or activities on the web. I highly recommend using these applications on the phone over visiting their websites using the phone's Web app.

> ✔ If possible, activate the phone's Wi-Fi connection before you venture out on the web. See Chapter 19 for more information on Wi-Fi.

Web Web Web

The web adventure begins with the appropriately named Web app, found on the Dock on the Home screen.

When you first open the Web app, you're taken to the home page. Figure 10-1 shows the Yahoo! website, which is the home screen that's preconfigured for your Galaxy Note (on the AT&T network). You can reset the home page to something else, as described later in this chapter.

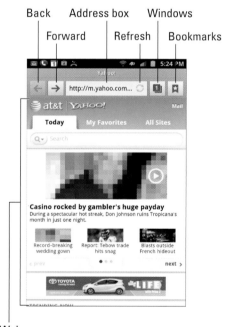

Web page

Figure 10-1: The Web app beholds the Yahoo! home page.

Because your cell phone screen isn't a full desktop screen, not every web page looks good on it. Here are a few tricks you can use:

- Pan the web page by dragging your finger across the touchscreen. You can pan up, down, left, and right.

- Many websites are smart enough to display mobile versions of their pages. Text is automatically formatted for the phone's screen.

- Pinch the screen to zoom out, or spread two fingers to zoom in. (Not every screen can be magnified by zooming in or out.)

- Tilt the phone to its side to read a web page in Landscape mode. Then you can spread or double-tap the touchscreen to make teensy text more readable.

Visiting a web page

To visit a web page, type its address in the Address box. (Refer to Figure 10-1.) You can also type a search word, if you don't know the exact address of a web page. Touch the Go button by the Address bar to search the web or visit a specific web page.

If you don't see the Address box, swipe your finger so that you can see the top of the window, where the Address box lurks.

You click links on a page by using your finger on the touchscreen: Touch a link to "click" it and visit another page on the web.

- To reload a web page, touch the Refresh icon found in the Address box. Refreshing updates a website that changes often, and the command can also be used to reload a web page that may not have completely loaded the first time.

- To stop a web page from loading, touch the Stop (X) button that replaces the Refresh icon in the Address box.

- You can use the S Pen to click links on a web page. You may find doing so to be far more accurate than trying to stab at links using your plump fingers.

Browsing back and forth

The basic navigation tools you need for browsing the web are found atop the Web app's window, shown in Figure 10-1.

To return to a previous web page, touch the Back button next to the Address bar or press the Back soft button.

To go forward, or to return to the page you were on before you used the Back button, touch the Forward button next to the Address bar.

To review the long-term history of your web browsing adventures, touch the Bookmarks button. On the Bookmarks screen, touch the History tab atop the screen. Previous places you've visited are organized chronologically. To view a page you visited weeks or months ago, choose it from the History list.

To clear the History list, press the Menu soft button while viewing the list, and choose the Clear History command.

Working with bookmarks

Bookmarks are the electronic breadcrumbs you drop as you wander the web. Need to revisit a website? Look up its bookmark. This advice assumes, of course, that you bother to create (I prefer *drop*) a bookmark when you first visit the site. Here's how it works:

1. **Visit the web page you want to bookmark.**

2. **Press the Menu soft button.**

3. **Choose the Add Bookmark command.**

4. **If necessary, edit the bookmark name.**

   The bookmark is given the web page name, which might be kind of long. I usually edit the name to fit beneath the thumbnail square.

5. **Optionally, choose a folder.**

   I don't mess with folders, so keeping the bookmarks in the Home folder is fine.

6. **Touch OK.**

   The bookmark is created and added to the list of bookmarks.

To use a bookmark, touch the Bookmarks button next to the Address bar atop the Web app's screen. (Refer to Figure 10-1.) Choose a bookmark thumbnail from the list to visit its website.

⮡ A good way to add bookmarks is use the Most Visited tab: Touch the Bookmarks button to view the Bookmarks screen, and then touch the Most Visited tab. This screen lists the web pages you frequent. To add one of these pages, long-press it and choose the Add Bookmark command.

- Remove a bookmark by long-pressing its thumbnail on the Bookmarks screen. Choose the Delete Bookmark command. Touch the OK button to confirm.

- Bookmarked websites can also be placed on the Home screen: Long-press the bookmark thumbnail, and choose the command Add Shortcut to Home Screen.

- You can obtain the MyBookmarks app at the Google Play Store. The app can import your Internet Explorer, Firefox, and Chrome bookmarks from your Windows computer into your Android phone. See Chapter 18 for more information on the Play Store.

- Refer to Chapter 4 for information on editing text.

Managing multiple web page windows

The Web app sports more than one window, so you can have multiple web pages open at a time. You can summon another window in one of several ways:

- **To open a link in another window,** long-press the link and choose the command Open in New Window from the menu that appears.

- **To open a bookmark in a new window,** long-press the bookmark and choose the Open in New Window command.

- **To open a blank browser window,** press the Menu soft button and choose New Window.

You switch between windows by pressing the Window button found atop the Web app's screen. (Refer to Figure 10-1.) Swipe the window thumbnails left and right to browse between them, as shown in Figure 10-2.

To switch to an open window, choose it from the list. You can close a window by touching the Minus (–) button to the right of the window's name.

New windows open using the home page that's set for the Web app. See the section "Setting a home page," later in this chapter, for information.

✔ The Downloads app can be used to review all items downloaded from the Internet to your phone. It even lists items received via e-mail or text message. You can find the Downloads app on the Apps menu.

Downloading a file

When a link opens a document on a web page, such as a Microsoft Word document or an Adobe Acrobat (PDF) file, you can download that information to your phone. Simply long-press the download link, and choose the Save Link command from the menu that appears.

You can view the link by referring to the Downloads screen. See the next section.

Reviewing your downloads

You can view downloaded information by perusing the Downloads screen. Summon this screen while using the Web app by pressing the Menu soft button and choosing More and then Downloads.

The Downloads screen presents a list of downloaded items, organized by date. To view the download, you have to choose an item. The phone then starts the appropriate app to view the item so that you can see it displayed on the touchscreen.

Well, of course, some of the things you can download, you cannot view. When this happens, you see an appropriately rude error message.

You can quickly review any download by choosing the Download notification.

Sharing links

If your goal is to share a web page with a friend, share only the link, and don't download anything. Follow these steps:

1. **Long-press a link to the page you want to share.**

2. **From the menu, choose the Share Link command.**

3. **Choose a method to share from the Share Via menu.**

   The variety of choices depends on the apps installed on your phone.

4. **Complete the action by using the app or sharing method you've selected.**

   Specific directions for the various apps are found throughout this book.

To share the page you're currently looking at, long-press the page's address on the Address bar. From the pop-up menu, choose the Share Page command.

Master the Web App

More options and settings and controls exist for the Web app than for just about every other app on your Galaxy Note. It's complex. Rather than bore you with every dang doodle detail, I thought I'd present only a few of the options worthy of your attention.

Setting a home page

The *home page* is the first page you see when you start the Web app, and it's the first page that's loaded when you fire up a new window. To set your home page, heed these directions in the Web app:

1. **Browse to the page that you want to set as the home page.**

2. **Press the Menu soft button.**

3. **Choose Settings.**

   A massive list of options and settings appears. Don't let it frighten you.

4. **Choose Set Home Page.**

5. **Touch the Use Current Page button.**

   Because you obeyed Step 1, you don't need to type the web page's address.

6. **Touch OK.**

   The home page is set.

If you want your home page to be blank, and not set to any particular web page, set the name of the home page (in Step 5) to about:blank. That's the word *about,* a colon, and then the word *blank,* with no period at the end and no spaces in the middle. I prefer a blank home page because it's the fastest web page to load. It's also the web page with the most accurate information.

Changing the way the web looks

You can do a few things to improve the way the web looks on your phone. First and foremost, don't forget that you can orient the phone horizontally to see the wide view of any web page.

From the Settings screen, you can also adjust the text size used to display a web page. Heed these steps while using the Web app:

1. **Press the Menu soft button.**

2. **Choose Settings.**

3. **Choose Default Zoom.**

4. **Choose Far for tiny text, Close for larger text, and Medium for somewhere in the middle.**

   For example, try Large or Huge.

5. **Press the Back soft button to return to the web.**

I don't make any age-related comments about text size at this time, and especially at this point in my life.

Setting privacy and security options

With regard to security, my advice is always to be smart and think before doing anything questionable or tempting on the web. Use common sense. One of the most effective ways that the Bad Guys win is by using *human engineering* to try to trick you into doing something you normally wouldn't do, such as click a link to see a cute animation or a racy picture of a celebrity or politician. As long as you use your noggin, you should be safe.

As far as the phone's settings go, most of its security options are already enabled for you, including the blocking of pop-up windows (which normally spew ads).

If web page cookies concern you, you can clear them from the Settings window. Follow Steps 1 and 2 in the earlier section "Changing the way the web looks," and choose the option Clear All Cookie Data. Touch the OK button to confirm.

You can also choose the command Clear Form Data to remove any memorized information you may have typed on a web page.

Remove the check mark from Remember Form Data. This setting prevents any characters you've input into a text field from being summoned automatically by someone who may steal your phone.

You might be concerned about various warnings regarding location data. What they mean is that the phone can take advantage of your location on Planet Earth (using the phone's GPS, or global satellite positioning system) to help locate businesses and people near you. I see no security problem in leaving this feature on, though you can disable location services from the Web app's Settings screen: Remove the check mark by Enable Location. You can also choose the item Clear Location Access to wipe out any information saved in the phone and used by certain web pages.

See the earlier section "Browsing back and forth" for steps to clear your web browsing history.

11

Social Networking

In This Chapter

▶ Adding social networking accounts

▶ Configuring synchronization

▶ Exploring the Social Hub

▶ Updating your status

▶ Using the Facebook app

▶ Setting up a Twitter client

▶ Accessing other social networking sites

*I*n a world where people proclaim to value their privacy, not a single aspect of the human existence doesn't find itself broadcast to the universe via the technology of social networking. It makes sense, too. After all, you and I dwell in a culture where the most desired goal of today's youth is not to be successful or rich or popular or the best of anything. No, the driving force behind our culture is the desire to be famous. Social networking is the perfect match to fill that want.

And that's the end of my rant.

If you desire to achieve fame via the pathway of social networking, your Galaxy Note is more than up to the task. Even if you're only curious or you want to stare, agape, at the antics of others, social networking is a useful tool. You can keep in touch, tell others what you're doing, and, yes, potentially become famous using your Galaxy Note and the fine suggestions I offer in this chapter.

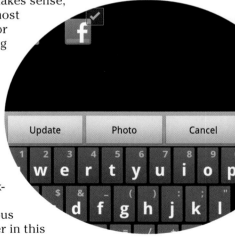

Get Social

The point of social networking is to be social. The benefit to being on the Internet is that you don't have to wear proper social clothing. This section provides an overview of the social networking experience on your Galaxy Note.

If you're new to the social networking thing, I recommend first setting up your social networking accounts on the web — preferably, using a computer. This way, you have a full screen and keyboard to help you create the accounts and get things configured. Though you can add new accounts using your phone, I find it more convenient to first use a computer.

Adding social networking accounts

If you've run through the Galaxy Note's setup process, obeying the directions on the phone or my instructions in Chapter 2, your phone should be all set up and ready to go for social networking. You can stop reading this section and enjoy a doughnut.

If you haven't yet configured social networking on your Galaxy Note, you can follow these steps at any time to do so:

1. **At the Home screen, press the Menu soft button.**

2. **Choose Settings.**

3. **Choose Accounts and Sync.**

   The Accounts and Sync screen appears, as shown in Figure 11-1. It lists all the accounts you've set up on your Galaxy Note, displayed under the Manage Accounts heading.

4. **Touch the Add Account button.**

5. **Choose your social networking site from the list of accounts.**

   Only three social networking opportunities are available: Facebook, Twitter, and LinkedIn. Additional social networking opportunities are made using other, specific apps, as covered throughout this chapter.

6. **Succumb, if you're prompted to agree to the terms.**

   Place a green check mark in the box, and touch the Agree button.

7. **Work through the account setup.**

   You may see some screens to read, so you have to touch the Next button a lot. Eventually, you type your login information (user ID or e-mail address) and your password for the social networking site.

App set up for synchronization

App needs to be set up for synchronization.

Accounts set up on this phone

Figure 11-1: Your social networking accounts.

8. **Touch the Log In button to connect.**

9. **Configure any synchronization options.**

   Place a green check mark by the various options to ensure that the phone stays up-to-date with all your digital social activities.

10. **Touch the Done button.**

    The account is now added to the Galaxy Note's inventory. Access to the social networking site is provided via the Social Hub app, covered later in this chapter.

To configure additional social networking sites, repeat these steps — specifically, steps 5 through 10.

✔ The Galaxy Note lets you set up accounts for Facebook, Twitter, and LinkedIn using the directions in this section.

✔ The accounts you can configure are used in the Social Hub app. You can also add individual Facebook, Twitter, Linked In, and other social networking apps to your phone. They must be configured individually, as covered elsewhere in this chapter.

Synchronizing accounts

To make your social networking accounts truly useful, you must ensure that they're configured to synchronize your information. Confirm that everything is set up properly by obeying these steps:

1. **At the Home screen, press the Menu soft button.**

2. **Choose Settings and then Accounts and Sync.**

   Peruse your accounts as listed in the Manage Accounts area, shown earlier in Figure 11-1.

3. **Touch the Sync button to the right of the account name.**

   The General Settings screen for that account appears.

4. **Place a check mark by every item that you want to synchronize between your social networking account and the Galaxy Note.**

   The number and variety of items depends on the service. Common items to synchronize include contacts, messages, and calendars.

   If you choose to sync the Picasa Web Albums associated with your Google account, those images show up in the Gallery app. See Chapter 14.

5. **Press the Back soft button when you're done.**

6. **Repeat Steps 3 and 4 for all your accounts.**

The account's General Settings screen is also the place to go when you want to remove an account from your phone: Touch the Remove Account button, and then touch the Remove Account button again to delete the account.

Exploring the social networking apps

You can use several apps on your Galaxy Note to sate your social networking desires. The primary one you use is Social Hub. It's the app that your social networking accounts are hooked into. (Refer to the preceding sections.)

Another app, Latitude, is used in conjunction with your Google account, the Maps app, and other social networking services to tell people where you are.

Additional social networking apps can be acquired from the Google Play Store. See the later section "Various Social Networking Apps" for the variety.

Your Digital Social Life

The Galaxy Note comes with a central location for serving some, if not all, of your social networking desires. This app, called Social Hub, is a great place to start exploring your digital social life, if you have one.

Finding out what's happening

The Social Hub app displays information on one of two screens, as shown in Figure 11-2. The Feeds tab contains status updates, tweets, and whatever LinkedIn calls its news items. The Messages tab displays items meant directly for you.

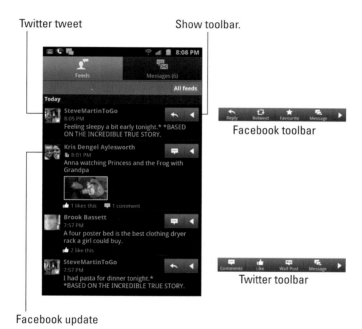

Figure 11-2: Social networking updates.

You can use the toolbar associated with a feed item to do more things with the feed, as shown in Figure 11-2. The toolbar is the easy way to Like an item or to reply to it or retweet it.

Touching an entry displays more details, such as comments, links, or images. If you want to make a comment on a Facebook post, for example, you have to touch the post to see the details. To express your opinion, type your comment in the text box that's provided.

Setting your status

There's no point in doing the social networking thing if you're not going to be social. When you use Social Hub, sharing the most intimate details of your life with the entire online universe is as simple as it can be potentially career-ending.

To set your status in the Social Hub app, heed these steps:

1. **Ensure that the Feeds tab is selected.**

2. **Press the Menu soft button.**

3. **Choose Status Update.**

   The Status Update screen appears, as shown in Figure 11-3.

Number of characters remaining (for Twitter)

Status update

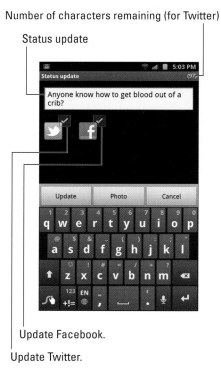

Update Facebook.

Update Twitter.

Figure 11-3: Updating your status.

4. **Type your status or tweet.**

5. **Choose which services you want to update.**

   In Figure 11-3, both Twitter and Facebook are selected.

6. **Touch the Update button.**

   And now everyone knows.

To cancel the message, touch the Cancel button in Step 6. Touch the OK button to confirm.

✓ When posting to Facebook, your status explains that you've posted using a mobile device. This text is a clue to others that you've used your phone to set your status.

✓ You have only 140 characters to write your Twitter tweets. Use the character counter (refer to Figure 11-3) to see how many characters remain.

✓ You can use the Photo button (refer to Figure 11-3) to share images already stored on the phone or to take a picture right there on the spot.

✓ It's also possible to share information with social networking sites by using the various Share Via menus found attached to many of the phone's apps.

✓ There's no way to unpost a status using the Social Hub app. For that kind of magic, I recommend visiting the social networking site on a computer.

Various Social Networking Apps

The Social Hub app works okay for general social networking. When you need to get your hands dirty and you want to enjoy all the features you're familiar with on a computer, I recommend getting a specific social networking app.

Using the Facebook app

The Facebook for Android app is the best way to enjoy the Facebook experience on your Galaxy Note. That's great news. Even better news is that Facebook for Android comes preinstalled on your phone.

The first time you run the Facebook for Android app, you have to log in to your Facebook account. (Before that, you may have to update the app; follow the directions on the screen.) The reason you have to log in is that the Facebook for Android app is separate from the Social Hub app. It knows nothing of any accounts you may have already configured for the phone.

The main Facebook app screen is shown in Figure 11-4. You can use this interface to do most of the Facebooky things you can do on the web, including upload a photo or keep your status up-to-date wherever you go with your phone.

Facebooky things to do

Notification

News Feed and updates   Comment/Like

Figure 11-4: Facebook on your phone.

Set your Facebook status by touching the Status button, illustrated in Figure 11-4.

To take a picture with the Facebook app, touch the Camera icon, which appears below the text box where you type your status. You get to decide whether to upload a picture you've already taken from the Gallery or choose the Capture a Photo command to take a picture immediately.

After you take the picture, touch the Done button. Add a caption, and then touch the Upload button to send the picture to Facebook.

✔ Choose the News Feed item to see status updates, newly added photos, and other information from your Facebook friends.

✔ Choose Photos to review your Facebook photo albums.

✔ Choose Profile to review your personal Facebook page, your status updates, and whatever else you're wasting your time doing on Facebook.

✔ To return to the main Facebook screen from another area, press the Back soft button.

✔ To sign out of Facebook on your phone, touch the Menu soft button when viewing the main Facebook screen and choose the Logout command. Touch the Yes button to confirm.

Tweeting to other twits

The Twitter social networking site proves the hypothesis that everyone will be famous on the Internet for 140 characters or fewer.

Like Facebook, Twitter is used to share your existence with others or simply to follow what others are up to or thinking. It sates some people's craving for attention and provides the bricks that pave the road to fame — or so I believe. I'm not a big Twitter fan, but your phone is capable of letting you tweet from wherever you are.

The Twitter application provides an excellent interface to many Twitter tasks. You can search for the app at the Google Play Store or use your phone to scan the QR code, shown in the margin. Chapter 18 offers more information on installing new apps on your phone.

After installing the app, sign in. You eventually see the Twitter app's main interface, where you can read tweets from the people you're following.

To tweet, touch the New Tweet icon, shown in the margin. Use the New Tweet screen to send text, upload an image from the Gallery, or take a new picture.

✔ They say that of all the people who have accounts on Twitter, only a small portion of them actively use the service.

✔ A message posted on Twitter is a *tweet*.

✔ You can post messages on Twitter or follow others who post messages.

Exploring other social networking opportunities

The web is brimming with new social networking phenomenon. My guess is that each of them is trying to dethrone Facebook as the king of the social networking sites. Good luck with that.

Despite the fact that Facebook and Twitter capture a lot of media attention, other popular social networking sites are out there, such as

- ✔ Foursquare
- ✔ Google+
- ✔ MySpace
- ✔ Tumblr

These sites may have special apps you can install on your phone. Check the Google Play Store for details, as described in Chapter 18.

As with Facebook and Twitter, you should always configure an account by using a computer and then set up options on your phone.

After adding some social networking apps, you may see them appear on various Share menus found on several apps. Use the Share menus to share media files with your online social networking pals.

I See What You're Doing There

Back in the 1960s, it was called the *picture phone.* Just like the flying car, its introduction to the world was only a few years off. Definitely, you would know that the future had arrived when you would make a video phone call. Well, the future has arrived, but you probably don't have a picture phone in your house. Or do you?

The Galaxy Note comes with a front-facing camera. Bingo. There's your picture phone. Armed with the proper app, you can make video calls. It's ready, and it's happening right now. Unfortunately, you still have to wait a while for that flying car.

Me: I thought I saw you the other day

Elvis: It probably wasn't me

Me: No. I'm sure it was you

Elvis: Seriously. It wasn't me! Go away!

compose | Send

Google Talk . . . and See

The Galaxy Note ships with two video chat apps — Google Talk and Qik Lite. Both do the job of helping you to chat, but of the two, Google Talk is easier to configure and most likely offers you the widest possible array of people with whom to chat. Therefore, this section covers using Google Talk as your phone's primary video chat app. But there's more to Google Talk than seeing your friends.

✔ Google Talk is available on the Internet, found on the main Gmail page. If your computer has a camera, you can activate the video chat feature for your computer as well as for your phone.

✔ Google Talk started out as an extension of Gmail on the Internet, primarily as a way to instantly text-chat with Google friends. Eventually, they added video chat, and, lo, after all these years, video chat is now available on your Galaxy Note as well as on the variety of other Android mobile devices.

Using Google Talk

Get started with Google Talk by starting the Talk app on your phone. Like all apps, it can be found on the Apps menu. If you find yourself using it often, consider placing a shortcut to the Talk app on the Home screen; for details, see the section in Chapter 24 about creating direct-dial and direct-text shortcuts.

When you start the Talk app the first time, you're prompted to sign in using your Google account: Touch the Sign In button. I'm sure that they could have made the setup more painful than that, but they didn't.

After signing in, you see the main Talk screen, shown in Figure 12-1. Your Google contacts who have activated Google Talk, either on their computers or on mobile Android gizmos, are shown along with whether they're available to chat.

There are three things you can do with your friends while using the Talk app: text-chat, voice-chat, or video-chat. But before you do any of these things, you need to get some friends.

✔ Set your status by touching your account name at the top of the list, shown in Figure 12-1. You can also set a status message and determine whether you're available for voice chat or video chat.

✔ To sign out of Google Talk, press the Menu soft button and choose the Sign Out command.

Inviting friends to Google Talk

Yeah, it happens: You have no friends. Well, at least you have no friends showing up on the Friends list in the Talk app. This problem can easily be fixed by heeding these steps in the Talk app:

1. **Press the Menu soft button.**
2. **Choose the Add Friend command.**

3. **Type your friend's name or e-mail address.**

   As you type, matches from your phone's address book appear in a list. Choose a friend from the list to instantly stuff that address into the text box.

4. **Touch the Send Invitation button.**

Available for video chat

Available for text chat

Touch to set your status.

Away, but video possible

Friends list   Away

Figure 12-1: Google Talk.

The best way for your pal to receive the invitation is to be using either a mobile device running the Talk app or a computer with the Gmail web page open. After receiving the invitation, the friend finds it listed in their Friends list; Google Talk invitations have the heading *Chat Invitation.*

Your friends can be on a computer or mobile device to use Google Talk; it doesn't matter which. But they must have a camera available to video-chat.

Typing at your friends

The most basic form of communications using the Talk app is the *text chat,* or typing at another person, which is probably one of the oldest forms of communications on the Internet. It's also the most tedious, so I'll be brief.

Text chatting starts when you touch a contact's name on the Friends list. Type a message, as shown in Figure 12-2. Touch the Send button to send your comment.

Current chat friend

Google Talk notification

Enter video chat.

Type text message.   Send message.

Figure 12-2: Text chatting.

You type, they type, and so on until you get tired or die or the phone runs out of battery juice.

When you're done talking, press the Menu soft button and choose the Friends List command to return to the main Talk screen. (Refer to Figure 12-1.) You can either choose another friend from the list and chat or press the Home soft button to do something else with your phone.

Resume any conversation by choosing the same contact from the Friends list.

Talking and video chat

Elevate the conversation a notch by touching the Voice or Video button on the right side of the text chat window. (Refer to Figure 12-2.) The Camera icon, shown in the figure, indicates that video chat is available; the Microphone icon, that voice chat (not video) is available; the dot, text chat only.

When you start a voice or video chat, your friend receives a pop-up invite and a Talk notification, similar to the one shown in Figure 12-3. Touch the Accept button to begin talking.

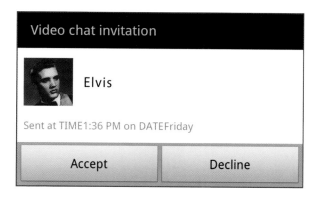

Figure 12-3: A video chat invite.

Figure 12-4 shows a video chat in progress. The person with whom you're communicating appears in the big window, and you're in the smaller window. With the connection made and the invite accepted, you can begin enjoying video chat.

Enter text chat.

Mute the microphone.

Switch cameras.   End video chat.

Person you're calling

You

Figure 12-4: Video chat with Google Talk.

The controls atop the screen may vanish after a second; touch the screen to see the controls again.

To end the conversation, touch the X (Close) button. Well, say "Goodbye" first, and then touch the X button.

- ✔ You must be connected to a Wi-Fi network to initiate a video chat.

- ✔ Using the fast 4G signal for video chat consumes mass quantities of your monthly data allotment. My advice: Switch to Wi-Fi.

- ✔ When you're nude or you simply don't want to video-chat, touch the Decline button in the video chat invite. Then choose that contact, and reply with a text or voice message instead.

- ✔ You can disable incoming voice and video chats by deselecting the Allow Video and Voice Chats option on your Talk account's Status screen: At the main Talk screen, touch your account in the Friends list. (Refer to Figure 12-1.)

✔ Your phone's front-facing camera is at the top, near the speaker, to the right. If you want to make eye contact, look directly into the camera. (Keep in mind that you cannot then see the other person.)

Connect with Skype

The popular Skype app is used the world over as a free way to make Internet phone calls and, relevant to this chapter, conduct video chats. Plus, if you're willing to pony up money, you can make inexpensive calls to phones around the world.

Obtaining a Skype account

Get started with Skype by creating an account. I recommend visiting www.skype.com on a computer, where you can enjoy the full screen and keyboard.

At the Skype website, click the Join Skype button, or, if the page has been updated since this book went to press, find and click a similarly labeled button or link. Succumb to the website's directions to sign up with your own Skype account.

After you have a Skype account, the next step is to obtain a copy of the Skype app for your Galaxy Note, as covered in the next section.

✔ As with other web services, you create a Skype name to identify your user account. It's the name you use to identify yourself to others who use Skype.

✔ To use Skype to place calls to phones or to dial internationally, you simply stuff some cash into your account. Log in to the Skype website, and follow the directions for getting Skype Credit.

✔ There's no charge for using Skype to chat with other Skype users. As long as you know the other party's Skype name, connecting and chatting are simple operations. See the later section "Chatting with another Skype user."

✔ Be careful not to confuse Skype with Swype. *Swype* is a keyboard variation that's available for your Galaxy Note. (Refer to Chapter 4.) *Skype* is an Internet communications tool.

Getting Skype for your phone

The Galaxy Note doesn't come preinstalled with the Skype app (though it may, in the future). To obtain a copy at the Google Play Store, use the AT&T Code Scanner app to scan the QR code in the margin, or see Chapter 18 for directions on finding the app in the Google Play Store.

After installing the Skype app, follow these steps to get started:

1. **Start the Skype app.**

2. **Read the initial, informational screens.**

   You can't make emergency calls using Skype. Use the Phone app for that instead. Duh.

3. **Sign in using your Skype account name and password.**

4. **Touch the Sign In button.**

   You may be asked to accept the terms of agreement; do so. A tour may be presented that previews how Skype works. Feel free to skip the tour.

One important question that you're asked when you first run the Skype app on your phone is whether you want to synchronize your contacts. I recommend choosing the preset option, Sync with Existing Contacts. Touch the Continue button.

The main Skype screen is shown in Figure 12-5. Pressing the Contacts button lists the people and phone numbers you've connected with on Skype. The later section "Building your Skype Contacts list" describes how to get more contacts than just Skype Test Call.

The Skype app stays active the entire time your phone is on. If you desire to sign out of Skype, follow these steps:

1. **Touch the Profile button on the Skype app's main screen.**

   Refer to Figure 12-5.

2. **Press the Menu soft button.**

3. **Choose Sign Out.**

4. **Touch the Yes button.**

The next time you run the app, you're prompted to sign back in to Skype.

To quickly access Skype, touch the Skype notification, shown in the margin.

Building your Skype Contacts list

Text, voice, and video chats on Skype are free over the Internet. If you can use a Wi-Fi connection, you can chat without exceeding your cellular plan's data quota. Before you can talk, however, you need to connect with another Skype user.

Yes, the other person must have a Skype account. Further, the person must agree to your request to become a Skype contact.

Skype notification

Set your mood.　Set your status icon.

Message waiting

Skypey things to do

Figure 12-5: The main Skype screen.

The Skype app can scan your phone's address book for any potential Skype subscribers you may have missed. The operation can take some time — like, over an hour — though the wait is worth it. To find your friends on Skype, follow these steps:

1. **Touch the Contacts button on the Skype app's main screen.**

2. **Press the Menu soft button.**

3. **Choose Search Address Book.**

   You most likely already have a gaggle of contacts in your phone. The Skype app can scour that list and discover which ones are already on Skype.

4. **Touch the Continue button.**

   This operation can take some time. (I'm serious — more than an hour.) Be patient.

You can snooze the phone while Skype is plowing through the address book.

Eventually, you see a list of Skype contacts that the Skype app has found in your Contacts list.

5. Touch the Continue button.

6. Remove the check marks by the contacts you don't want to add.

The Skype app lists all contacts it found who have Skype accounts. If you add these contacts (see Step 7), a Skype request is sent to each one. If you don't want to send a request to someone in the list, remove the check mark by that contact's name.

Be sure to check the list of accounts that Skype finds! It searches for matching text, not for individuals, so random and unusual Skype contacts will doubtlessly show up in the list, especially ones who list multiple Skype names; look for `Customer Care` and `noreply`, and be sure to remove them.

7. Touch the Add button.

8. Type an introductory message.

The contact has to approve you as a Skype buddy, so make the message sound important but not urgent, wanting but not desperate.

9. Touch the Add Contacts button.

Contacts are added to the Contacts tab, but they sport the question mark status until they agree to accept your Skype invitation.

If scanning the phone's address book doesn't do the job, you can try searching for a specific contact:

1. Touch the Contacts button on the Skype app's main screen.

2. Press the Menu soft button.

3. Choose Add Contacts.

4. Type a name or phone number.

5. To start the search, touch the Search button next to the text field.

6. Scroll the list of results to find the exact person you're looking for.

If your friend has a common name, the list is quite extensive. You can use city information to help narrow the list, but not every Skype user specifies a current city. The Skype username may also help you identify specific people.

7. **Touch an entry to add it to your Contacts list.**

   You see a full-page description for the contact, where you can choose to call the person, chat on Skype, or add them to your Contacts list.

8. **Touch the Add button.**

No matter how you add people to your list, you see the Question Mark icon as their status until they agree to accept your request.

- ✔ You can always e-mail people you know and ask them whether they're on Skype.

- ✔ Some people may not use Skype often, so it takes a while for them to respond to your friend request.

- ✔ If you accidentally add unusual Skype contacts, my advice is to delete them. To remove a contact, long-press the contact's name in the list and choose the Remove Contact command from the pop-up menu.

- ✔ You can block a contact by long-pressing the entry and choosing the Block Contact command from the pop-up menu.

- ✔ If the Skype app crashes during a contact-searching operation, you've likely collected bogus Skype contacts. It happens. A good way to get out of this situation is to use the Skype program on a computer to clean up and remove unwanted contacts. You may also need to uninstall and then reinstall the Skype app. See Chapter 18 for information on uninstalling apps.

Chatting with another Skype user

To text-chat, choose a Skype user from the Contacts list. (Refer to Figure 12-5 for the Contacts icon location.) You see a screen with more detailed information about the contact. Choose the option Send IM, where *IM* stands for *instant message*. As long as your Skype friend is online and eager, you'll be text-chatting in no time.

- ✔ The Skype Chat notification, shown in the margin, appears whenever someone wants to chat with you. It's handy to see, especially when you may have switched from the Skype app to do something else on your phone. Choose this notification to get into the conversation.

- ✔ To stop chatting, press the Back soft button. The conversation remains in the Skype app, even after the other person has disconnected.

- ✔ Old chats stored in the Skype app are accessed from the Recent icon button. (Refer to Figure 12-5.)

- ✔ For the chat to work, the other user must be online and available.

Using Skype for voice and video chat

Typing is so 19th century, so why bother? When you tire of typing at your Skype buddies, you can have them "pick up the phone" and start a voice or video chat. Follow these steps:

1. **Touch the Contacts icon on the Skype app's main screen.**

    Refer to Figure 12-5.

2. **Choose a contact.**

    Chatting works best when the contact is available: Look for a green check mark icon by the contact's name.

3. **Choose Video Call from the Actions tab on the contact's information screen.**

    If prompted, choose the contact's Skype account, not the phone number. You can't place a Skype phone call unless you have Skype Credit. Even then, it's probably cheap (or free) to make a regular call using your phone instead of Skype.

    In a few Internet seconds, the other person picks up and you're speaking with each other.

4. **Talk.**

    Blah-blah-blah. There's no time limit, though Internet connection problems may inadvertently hang you up.

To disconnect the call, touch the red End Call button.

When someone calls you on Skype, touch the Audio button to answer as a voice-only call; touch the Video button (if it's available) to answer using video. Touch Decline to dismiss the call, especially when it's someone who annoys you.

- Incoming Skype calls wake up the phone when it's locked, just as any phone call would.

- Voice and video chat on Skype are free over the Internet. When you use a Wi-Fi connection, you can chat without using your cellular plan's data minutes.

- You can chat with any user on your Skype Contacts list, by using a mobile device, a computer, or any other gizmo on which Skype is installed.

- Video chat is available on only a handful of cell phones that have front-facing cameras but that are also allowed to video-chat. Not every cell phone with a front-facing camera has video chat available. (Blame the cellular provider.)

- ✔ Video chat may be available only over a Wi-Fi or 4G connection.

- ✔ Calling a real phone — cellular, landline, or international — with Skype is possible only when you have Skype Credit. See Chapter 21.

- ✔ If you plan to use Skype a lot, get a good headset.

- ✔ It's impossible to tell whether someone has dismissed a Skype call or simply didn't answer. And there's no Skype voice mail so that you can leave a message.

Part IV
Incredible Tasks and Amazing Feats

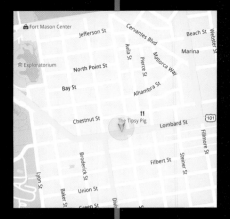

In this part . . .

The potential of your Galaxy Note has yet to be realized. Beyond being a modern communications device, it can be used as a shim to prop up a wobbly table, as a doorstop, or as a paperweight.

I'm kidding.

Seriously, the Galaxy Note is so much more than a phone that I had to concoct this lengthy part of the book just to cover the basics of what else it's capable of doing. It can be your map, your guide, your camera, your video recorder, your portable music player, your day planner, your game machine — and countless other handy things. This part of the book only scratches the surface.

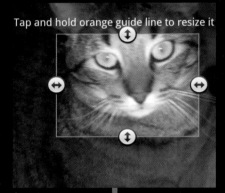

Tap and hold orange guide line to resize it

13

There's a Map for That

In This Chapter

▶ Exploring your world with Maps
▶ Adding layers to the map
▶ Finding your location
▶ Sharing your location
▶ Searching for places
▶ Finding someone or something
▶ Using the Galaxy Note as a navigator

*A*fter searching for a few minutes, Alan finally found Susan. "Are you all right?" he asked.

"Fine," she said, getting to her feet and dusting herself off. "If Dr. Cornelius ever expects the general public to adopt teleportation, he had better iron out the kinks."

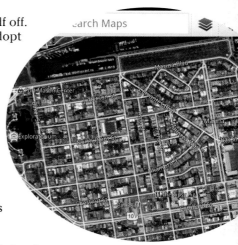

Alan thought for a moment. "Speaking of Cornelius," he began, "where is the beloved professor? For that matter, where is a Mexican restaurant? I need tacos."

Susan deftly pulled out her Galaxy Note. In a flash, she summoned the Maps app and quickly located a nearby taco stand.

"Cornelius can wait," muttered Alan. "I need my tacos now!"

"I'm just glad that I've read Chapter 13 in Dan Gookin's book, *Samsung Galaxy Note For Dummies,* published by John Wiley & Sons," Susan said. "Otherwise, we'd be wandering aimlessly and yearning for tacos."

Behold the Map

It's one of the most amazing apps on your phone. The Maps app charts the entire country. It plots out freeways, highways, roads, streets, avenues, drives, bike paths, addresses, businesses, and points of interest.

Using the Maps app

Start the Maps app by choosing it from the Apps menu, or you may find a shortcut to the Maps app lurking on a Home screen panel. If you're starting the app for the first time or if it has been updated recently, you can read its What's New screen; touch the OK button to continue.

The Galaxy Note communicates with global positioning system, or GPS, satellites to hone in on your current location. (See the later sidebar "Activate your locations!") Your location is shown on the map, similar to the one you see in Figure 13-1. The position is accurate to within a given range, as shown by the location-in-a-blue-circle on the map.

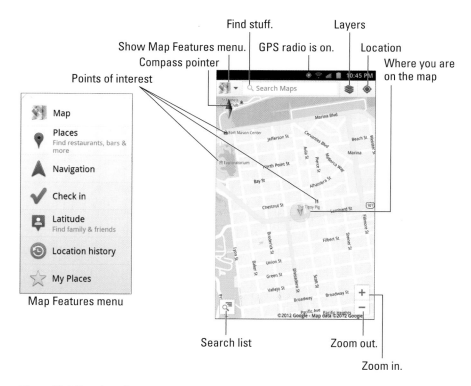

Figure 13-1: Your location on a map.

Here are some fun things you can do when viewing the basic street map:

Zoom in: To make the map larger (to move it closer), touch the Zoom In button, double-tap the screen, or spread your fingers on the touchscreen.

Zoom out: To make the map smaller (to see more), touch the Zoom Out button, or pinch your fingers on the touchscreen.

Pan and scroll: To see what's to the left or right, or at the top or bottom, of the map, drag your finger on the touchscreen; the map scrolls in the direction you drag your finger.

Rotate: Using two fingers, rotate the map clockwise or counterclockwise. Touch the compass pointer (shown earlier, in Figure 13-1) to reorient the map with north at the top of the screen.

Perspective: Tap the Location button to switch to Perspective view, where the map is shown at an angle. Touch the Location button again (though now it's the Perspective button) to return to flat-map view or, if that doesn't work, touch the compass pointer.

The closer you zoom in to the map, the more detail you see, such as street names, address block numbers, and businesses and other sites — but no tiny people.

✔ Touching the Map Features Menu button displays a menu full of interesting things you can do with the Maps app, as shown in Figure 13-1. Several of these items are covered elsewhere in this chapter.

✔ The blue triangle (refer to Figure 13-1) shows in which general direction the phone is pointing.

✔ When the phone's direction is unavailable, you see a blue dot as your location on the map.

✔ When all you want is a virtual compass, similar to the one you lost as a kid, you can get the Compass app from the Google Play Store. See Chapter 18 for more information about the Play Store.

✔ Perspective view can be entered for only your current location.

Adding layers

You add details from the Maps app by applying layers: A *layer* can enhance the map's visual appearance, provide more information, or add other fun features to the basic street map, such as Satellite view, shown in Figure 13-2.

Layers button   Main roads

Your location

Figure 13-2: The satellite layer.

The key to accessing layers is to touch the Layers button, illustrated in Figure 13-2. Choose an option from the Layers menu to add that information to the Map app's display.

You can add another layer by choosing it from the Layers menu, but keep in mind that some layers obscure others. For example, the terrain layer overlays the satellite layer so that you see only the terrain layer.

To remove a layer, choose it from the Layers menu; any active layer appears with a green check mark to its right. To return to Street view, remove all layers.

✔ Most of the features found on the Layers menu originated in the Google Labs. To see new features that may be added to the Maps app, visit the Labs by pressing the Menu soft button in the Maps app. Choose Settings and then Labs to pore over potential new features.

✔ The phone warns you whenever various applications access its Location feature. The warning is nothing serious — it's just letting you know that an app is accessing the phone's physical location. Some folks may view this action as an invasion of privacy; hence the warnings. I see no issue with letting the phone know where you are, but I understand that not everyone feels that way. If you'd rather not share location information, simply decline access when prompted.

Activate your locations!

The Maps app works best when you activate all the phone's location technology. Activation may have been done when you first configured the Galaxy Note using the AT&T Ready2Go program. (Refer to Chapter 2.) Even so, I recommend that you confirm activation of the location settings: From the Home screen, press the Menu soft button and choose Settings. Then choose Location and Security. On the Location and Security Settings screen, in the My Location area, ensure that green check marks appear by all items in the following list:

Use Wireless Networks: Allows software access to your location using Google technology. Specifically, the phone checks for nearby Wi-Fi networks and uses that data to hone your position.

Use GPS Satellites: Allows your phone to access the global positioning system (GPS) satellites, though it's not that accurate. That's why you need to activate the Wireless Network service to fully use your phone's location abilities.

Use Sensor Aiding: Allows the phone to better determine your location indoors, but only if you point the phone in the direction you're moving.

See Chapter 19 for information on activating the Galaxy Note's Wi-Fi setting.

How to Find Yourself

Allow me to save you tons of time and buckets of money. You don't need a self-help course. You don't need to climb a mountain, visit a head shrink, discover your inner beauty, or fight demons from your childhood. Seriously, you're a good person, so you can understand that my references to "finding yourself" mean that you'll use the Maps app on your Galaxy Note to discover exactly where you are.

Finding out where you are

The Maps app shows your location as a blue dot or compass arrow on the screen. But *where* is that? I mean, if you need to phone a tow truck, you can't just say, "I'm the blue triangle on the orange slab by the green thing."

Well, you *can* say that, but it probably won't do any good.

To find your current street address, or any street address, long-press a location on the Maps screen. Up pops a bubble, similar to the one shown in Figure 13-3, that gives your approximate address.

If you touch the address bubble (refer to Figure 13-3), you see a screen full of interesting things you can do, as shown in Figure 13-4.

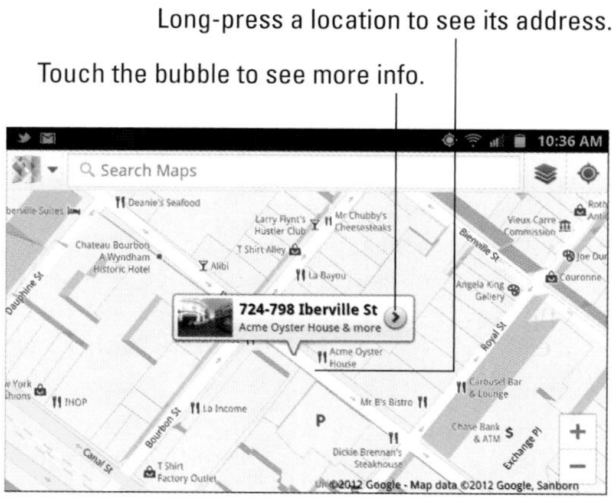

Long-press a location to see its address.
Touch the bubble to see more info.
10:36 AM
Search Maps
724-798 Iberville St
Acme Oyster House & more
©2012 Google - Map data ©2012 Google, Sanborn

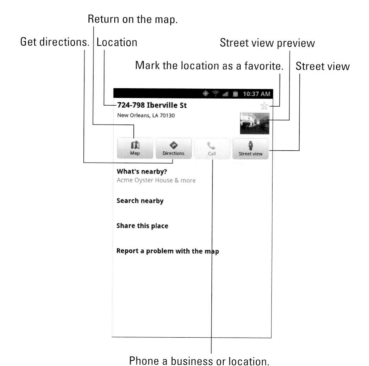

Figure 13-3: Finding an address.

Return on the map.
Get directions.
Location
Street view preview
Mark the location as a favorite.
Street view
10:37 AM
724-798 Iberville St
New Orleans, LA 70130
Map
Directions
Call
Street view
What's nearby?
Acme Oyster House & more
Search nearby
Share this place
Report a problem with the map
Phone a business or location.

Figure 13-4: Things to do when you find a location.

The What's Nearby command displays a list of nearby businesses or points of interest, some of them shown on the screen (refer to Figure 13-4) and others available by touching the What's Nearby command.

Choose the Search Nearby item to use the Search command to locate businesses, people, or points of interest near the given location.

What's *really* fun to play with is the Street View command. Choosing this option displays the location from a 360-degree perspective. In Street view, you can browse a locale, pan and tilt, or zoom in on details to familiarize yourself with an area, for example — whether you're familiarizing yourself with a location or planning a burglary.

Helping others find your location

You can use the Messaging app to send your current location to a friend. If your pal has a phone with smarts similar to your Galaxy Note's, they can use the coordinates to get directions to your location. Maybe they'll even bring tacos!

To send your current location in a text message, obey these steps:

1. **Open the Maps app and find your current location.**

   Specific directions are found in the preceding section.

2. **Long-press the blue arrow on the map.**

3. **Touch the My Location bubble.**

   A descriptive screen appears, similar to the one in Figure 13-4.

4. **Choose the command Send Location to Others.**

5. **Choose Messaging to send a text message.**

   You can also choose Gmail or Email, though when you're desperate for tacos, a text message seems a more logical choice.

   The Messaging app opens and prompts you to input a contact name or phone number. The message text contains the time and date and your approximate street address. A link to the location on the map is also included.

6. **Enter the name of the person to whom you want to send your location.**

7. **Touch the Send button.**

A recipient who receives the text message can touch the link to open your location in the Maps app. When the location appears, the recipient can follow my advice in the later section "How to Get There" to reach your location. Don't loan them this book, either; have them buy their own copy. And bring tacos. Thanks.

- ✔ It may seem that you can send your current location by using the Attach button in the Messaging app and then choosing the Location option. This procedure merely sends a picture of your location on the map, not the actual coordinates.

- ✔ Refer to Chapter 9 for information on text messaging and the Messaging app.

How to Find Other Things

Just as you can search the Internet with Google, you can search the real world using the Maps app. The app may not help you find love, wealth, or fame, but it most certainly can help you locate the best tacos in town.

Looking for a specific address

To locate an address, type it into the Search box; for example:

```
1600 Pennsylvania Ave., Washington, D.C. 20006
```

Touch the Search button to the right of the Search box, and that location is then shown on the map. The next step is getting directions, which you can read about in the later section "How to Get There."

- ✔ You don't need to type the entire address. Oftentimes, all you need is the street number and street name and then either the city name or zip code.

- ✔ If you omit the city name or zip code, the Maps app looks for the closest matching address near the location currently shown on the screen.

Finding a business, restaurant, or point of interest

You may not know an address, but you know when you crave sushi or bulgogi or perhaps the exotic flavors of Nepal. Maybe you need a hotel or a gas station or you have to find a place that removes tattoos. To find a business entity or a point of interest, type its name in the Search box; for example:

```
Sports bar
```

This command flags taverns and community watering holes on the current Maps screen or nearby.

Or you can be specific and look for businesses near a certain location by specifying the city name, district, or zip code, such as

```
Tacos 92123
```

After typing this command and touching the Search button, you see a smattering of taco stands and restaurants found in my old neighborhood in San Diego, similar to the ones shown in Figure 13-5.

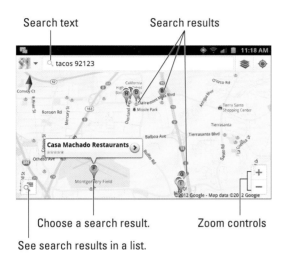

Figure 13-5: Search results for tacos in San Diego.

To see more information about a result, touch its cartoon bubble, such as the one for Casa Machado, shown in Figure 13-5. The screen that appears offers more information, plus perhaps even a web address and phone number. You can touch the Get Directions button (refer to Figure 13-4) to get directions; see the later section "How to Get There."

🖛 Every letter or dot on the screen represents a search result. (Refer to Figure 13-5.)

🖛 Use the Zoom controls or spread your fingers to zoom in to the map.

🖛 You can create a contact for the location, keeping it as part of your Contacts list: After touching the location balloon, scroll down the information screen and choose the command Add As a Contact. The contact is created using data that's known about the business, including its location and phone number and even a web page address — if that information is available.

Searching for interesting places

Maybe you don't know what you're looking for. Maybe you're like my teenage sons, who stand in front of the open refrigerator, waiting for the sandwich fairy to hand them a snack. The Maps app features a sort of I-don't-know-what-I-want-but-I-want-something fairy. It's the Places command.

Touch the Map Feature button (refer to Figure 13-1), and choose the Places command to see the Places screen. It shows categories of places near you: restaurants, coffee shops, bars, hotels, attractions, and more. Touch an item to see matching locations in your vicinity.

The Galaxy Note also has the Places app, found on the Apps menu, which takes you directly to the Places screen.

Locating one of your contacts

You can hone in on where your contacts are located by using the Maps app. This trick works when you've specified an address for the contact — either home or work or another location. If so, your phone can easily help you find that location or even give you directions.

The secret to finding a contact's location is the little icon by the contact's address. The icon looks like the standard "Here it is" pushpin icon that's used in the Maps app and shown in the margin. Anytime you see this icon or a similar one, you can touch it to view that location by using the Maps app.

How to Get There

Finding something is only half the job. The other half is getting there. Thanks to its various direction and navigation features, the Maps app stands at the ready to be your copilot. It's like having a backseat driver, but one who knows where they're going and — *bonus* — who has a Mute option.

Asking for directions

One command associated with location displays in the Maps app is Get Directions. Here's how to use it:

1. **Touch a location's cartoon bubble that's displayed by an address, a contact, or a business or from the result of a map search.**

2. **Touch the Directions button.**

   You see the Directions screen, shown in Figure 13-6. The information is already filled out, including your current location (shown as My Location in the figure) as the starting point.

Choose a new starting location or destination.

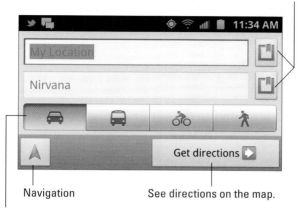

Figure 13-6: Going from here to there.

3. **Choose a method of transportation.**

The four methods are car, public transportation, bicycle, and walking, as shown in Figure 13-6.

4. **Touch the Get Direction button.**

You see a map with a blue line detailing your journey. Use the Zoom controls to make the map larger, if necessary.

5. **Follow the blue line.**

If you'd rather see a list of directions, touch the Directions List button on the map after you see the map with the blue line on it.

You can switch back to Map view (with the blue line) by pressing the Back soft button.

✔ The Maps app alerts you to any toll roads on the specified route. As you travel, you can choose alternative, non-toll routes, if they're available. You're prompted to switch routes during navigation; see the next section.

✔ You may not get perfect directions from the Maps app, but for places you've never visited, it's a useful tool.

✔ To receive vocal directions, touch the Navigation button (refer to Figure 13-6) or read the next section.

Navigating to your destination

Maps and lists of directions are so 20th century. I don't know why anyone would bother, especially when your Galaxy Note features a digital copilot, in the form of voice navigation.

To use navigation, choose the Navigation option from any list of directions. Or touch the Navigation button, as shown earlier, in Figure 13-6. You can also enter the Navigation app directly by choosing it from the Map Features menu (refer to Figure 13-1) or opening the Navigation app found on the Apps menu screen. Yes, sometimes it seems like you need navigation directions merely to find the Navigation feature.

If you're prompted to choose between AT&T Navigator and Navigation, choose Navigation. It's the Google app, whereas AT&T Navigator was installed by your cellular provider. Oh, and be sure to place a check mark by the option Set As Default so that the phone never again bothers you with that question.

In Navigation mode, your phone displays an interactive map that shows your current location and turn-by-turn directions for reaching your destination. A digital voice tells you how far to go and when to turn, for example, and gives you other nagging advice, such as to sit up, be nice to other drivers, refrain from spitting out the window, and call your mother once in a while.

After choosing Navigation, sit back and have the phone dictate your directions. You can either listen or simply glance at the phone for an update of where you're heading.

To stop the navigation, press the Menu soft button and choose the Exit Navigation command.

- ✔ To remove the navigation route from the screen, exit Navigation mode: Press the Menu soft button, and choose the Exit Navigation command.

- ✔ The phone stays in Navigation mode until you exit. The Navigation notification can be seen atop the touchscreen in Navigation mode.

- ✔ When you tire of hearing the navigation voice, press the Menu soft button and choose the Mute command.

- ✔ I refer to the navigation voice as *Gertrude*.

- ✔ You can press the Menu soft button while navigating and choose Route Info to see an overview of your journey.

- ✒ When viewing the Route Info screen, touch the Gears button to see a handy pop-up menu. From this menu, you can choose options to modify the route so that you avoid highways or toll roads, for example.

- ✒ The neat thing about Navigation is that whenever you screw up, a new course is immediately calculated.

- ✒ In Navigation mode, your phone consumes a lot of battery power. I highly recommend that you plug the phone into your car's power adapter ("cigarette lighter") for the duration of the trip.

14

Everyone Say "Cheese"

A phone without a camera is like a hair dryer without a cheese grater. I suppose it was the shrinking of digital cameras and cell phones that caused the two technologies to mingle. They had room!

So, into your cell phone walked the camera. It's a good combination: Oftentimes, picture-taking opportunities arise and no camera is available, but you always have your cell phone. So whenever you spy a UFO, Bigfoot, or your father-in-law actually picking up the dinner bill, you can snap a picture. You can even send it out to posterity over the Internet.

Smile for the Camera App

A camera snob will tell you that no true camera has a ringtone. You know what? He's correct: Phones don't make the best cameras. Regardless, your phone has a camera. Why not make the best of it?

Understanding the Camera app

To use your phone as a camera, you need to do two things. First, you must hold the phone away from your face. That's because the phone has no viewfinder. Nope, the image preview shows up on the touchscreen.

The second thing you need to do is run the Camera app, which is found on the Home screen or, like every other app on the phone, on the Apps menu.

Figure 14-1 shows the Camera app's main screen, though the buttons you see on the left may be different. These buttons are customizable, as described in the later sidebar "Make your own shortcuts."

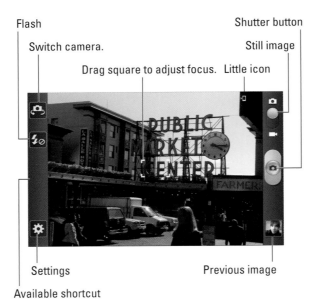

Figure 14-1: The Galaxy Note as a camera.

Here are some things to look for on your phone's Camera app screen:

Camera button: This button switches the Camera app between Still and Video modes. In Figure 14-1, the button is shown in the position for still images.

Shutter button: Touch this button to snap the picture.

Previous image: You can touch the tiny preview of the previous image to review that image in Full Screen mode, share the image, delete the image, or do a number of thrilling things.

Switch camera: Touch this button to switch between the front- and back-facing cameras. How can you tell which is which? When you see yourself, the front-facing camera is active.

Flash: Use this button to set the rear camera's flash mode. (The front camera has no flash.)

Available shortcut: Assign functions to the left side of the Camera app's screen, as described in the sidebar, "Make your own shortcuts."

Settings: Touch this button to display a pop-up menu of options for the Camera app.

Focus square: Drag around this graphical square to change the camera's focus.

The zoom is controlled by touching the phone's Volume buttons. You can zoom in or out by touching the Up Volume or Down Volume button. Or, after you initially touch the Volume button, you can drag the sliding control on the screen to zoom in or out.

- The Camera app can also be used in vertical orientation. The icons on the screen reorient themselves as you turn the camera.

- The Galaxy Note's camera uses *digital* zoom, where the image is magnified using software — as opposed to an *optical* zoom, which is done by adjusting the camera's lens.

- Little icons appear atop the screen indicating which settings you've made. One of those icons, indicating that images are being saved to the MicroSD card, is shown in Figure 14-1.

- The Camera app is also used to shoot video. See Chapter 15.

Snapping a picture

To take a picture, first ensure that the Camera app is in Camera mode. The slide switch should be by the Camera icon, as illustrated Figure 14-1, in the upper-right corner of the screen.

After confirming that the phone is in picture-taking mode, point the camera at the subject. Touch the Shutter button. (Refer to Figure 14-1.) After you touch the Shutter button, the camera will focus, you may hear a mechanical shutter sound play, and the flash may go off. You're ready to take the next picture.

To preview the image you just snapped, touch the little icon that appears on the screen, shown in Figure 14-1 in the lower-right corner.

- The camera focuses automatically, though you can drag the focus square around the touchscreen to specifically adjust the focus.

✔ You can take as many pictures with your phone as you like, as long as you don't run out of storage for them on the phone's internal storage or MicroSD card.

 ✔ If your pictures appear blurry, ensure that the camera lens on the back of the phone isn't dirty.

 ✔ Use the Gallery app to preview and manage your pictures. See the later section "Where Your Photos Lurk" for more information about the Gallery.

Deleting an image immediately after you take it

Sometimes you just can't wait to delete an image. Either an annoyed person is standing next to you, begging that the photo be deleted or you're just not happy and you feel the urge to smash into digital shards the picture you just took. Hastily follow these steps:

1. **Touch the image preview that appears at the bottom of the screen. (Refer to Figure 14-1.)**

   After touching the preview, you see the full-screen image.

2. **Press the Menu soft button and choose the Delete command.**

3. **Touch the OK button to confirm.**

   The image has been banished to bit hell.

4. **Press the Back soft button to return to the Camera app.**

If these steps don't do the job, remember that you can always delete (and manage) your images by using the Gallery app. See the later section "Deleting one or more images."

Make your own shortcuts

The icons that appear along the left side of the screen in Figure 14-1 are shortcuts. They give you quick access to camera features such as Switch Camera, Flash, and Settings, as shown in the figure. The panel on the left has spaces for adding two more shortcuts, if you like.

To add a shortcut, touch the Settings button and choose the Edit Shortcuts command. Drag a shortcut icon from the palette to the edge of the screen. You can drag to one of four positions. If you drag to a shortcut position that already has an icon, the two icons are swapped. You can also drag an icon from a shortcut position back to the palette, in which case the shortcut slot is blank.

All Camera app features are available by scrolling the Settings menu, though having some available as shortcuts can be handy. Various sections in this chapter offer tips on adding handy shortcut items, such as the GPS Tag in the section, "Setting the image's location."

Setting the flash

Three flash settings are controlled by the Camera app. Table 14-1 lists them, along with icons used to represent the settings.

Table 14-1		Galaxy Note Camera Flash Settings
Setting	*Icon*	*Description*
Off		The flash never activates, even in low-light situations.
On		The flash always activates.
Auto Flash		The flash activates during low-light situations, but not when it's bright outside.

To change or check the flash setting, touch the Settings button, shown earlier, in Figure 14-1. Choose Flash and then the setting you want. If the Flash shortcut button appears on the screen (refer to the figure), you can choose the flash setting from the button's menu.

A good time to turn on the flash is when you're taking pictures of people or objects in front of something bright, such as little Barbara holding her favorite cat in front of a nuclear explosion.

Changing the image resolution

A lot of technobabble is involved in describing digital photography and image resolution. Suffice it to say that the higher the resolution, the more detail in the image. You need that detail only when editing an image or when enlarging it for printing. Otherwise, fussing over image resolution is rather pointless.

To set the image resolution in the Camera app, touch the Settings button and choose the Resolution command. You may have to scroll down a ways to find it.

You can set six resolutions, ranging from 8MP, the highest and most detailed, to 0.3MP, the lowest resolution. The letter *W* prefixed to the resolution indicates that the setting uses the widescreen format.

Press the Back soft button to dismiss the Settings menu after choosing a new resolution.

- ✏ Image resolution is set *before* you snap the picture.

- ✏ For sending e-mail or posting to a social networking site, lower resolutions are fine. I'd choose 2.4MP or 3.2MP.

- ✏ For family portraits or images you want to print and enlarge, use 8MP.

- ✏ Text messages should use the lowest resolution, 0.3MP, which is 640-by-480 pixels.

- ✏ The front-facing camera has a fixed resolution of 1600-by-1200 pixels, which is about 2MP.

- ✏ MP stands for *megapixel,* a measurement of the amount of information stored in an image. One megapixel is approximately 1 million *pixels,* or individual dots that comprise an image.

Doing a self-portrait

Who needs to pay a ton of money for a mirror when you have the Galaxy Note? Well, forget the mirror. Instead, think about taking all those self-shots without having to second-guess whether the camera is pointed at your face.

To take your own mug shot, start the Camera app and touch the Switch Camera button, shown earlier, in Figure 14-1. When you see yourself on the screen, you're doing it properly.

Smile. Click. You got it.

Touch the Switch Camera button again to direct the phone to use the main camera again.

Shooting a panoramic image

A *panorama* is a wide shot, like a landscape, a beautiful vista, or a family photograph where everyone should seriously lose some weight. You can take a picture as wide as you like using the Camera app, if you switch the camera into Panorama mode. Obey these steps:

1. **Start the Camera app.**

2. **Touch the Settings button.**

3. **Choose Shooting Mode.**

4. **Choose Panorama from the Shooting Mode menu.**

5. **Hold your arms steady.**

6. **Touch the Shutter button.**

7. **Pivot slightly to your right (or left or up or down, but you must continue in the same direction).**

   As you move the camera, a green frame appears, helping you line up the next shot.

8. **Continue pivoting as subsequent shots are taken.**

   The shots are snapped automatically.

9. **Touch the Shutter button to end the panorama.**

   If you don't, the panorama ends by itself after taking the eighth shot. You can use the progress bar at the bottom of the screen to clue you in to how many shots remain.

The Camera app sticks the different shots together, creating a panoramic image.

To restore the Camera app to normal operating mode, repeat Steps 1 through 4, but choose Single Shot in Step 4.

The camera automatically captures the panoramic shot. You touch the Shutter button only when you're done.

Setting the image's location

The Galaxy Note not only takes a picture but also tracks where you're located on Planet Earth when you take the picture — if you've enabled that option. The feature is GPS Tag, and here's how to ensure that it's on:

1. **While using the Camera app, touch the Settings button.**

2. **Ensure that the GPS Tag option is set to On.**

   If not, choose the GPS Tag item and then touch the On menu item.

3. **Press the Back soft button to close the various menus.**

When the GPS Tag setting is enabled, you see the GPS icon appear atop the Camera app's screen.

Not everyone is comfortable with having the phone record a picture's location, so you can turn off this option. Just repeat these steps, but in Step 2, choose the Off command.

See the later section "Viewing an image's location on the map" for information on how to use the GPS Tag feature.

Where Your Photos Lurk

The pictures and videos you take with your phone don't completely vanish after you click the Shutter button. Though you can preview a previously shot picture or video, the place you go to look at the entire gamut of visual media is the app named Gallery.

Visiting the Gallery app

You can start the Gallery app by locating its icon on the Apps menu. Images (and videos) stored in the Gallery are organized into piles or albums, as shown in Figure 14-2.

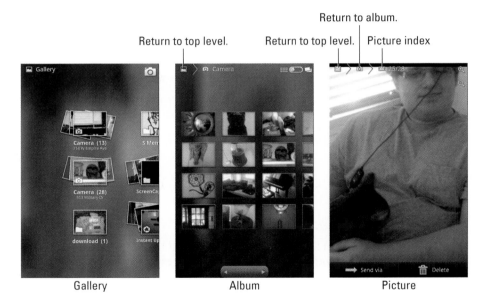

Return to album.

Return to top level.　　Return to top level.　Picture index

Gallery　　　　　　Album　　　　　　Picture

Figure 14-2: The Gallery app.

Choosing a pile displays a grid of thumbnail images. Touch a thumbnail to see the full-screen image, as shown in the figure.

✔ Press the Back soft button to back out of viewing an image and return to the album. Likewise, press the Back soft button to return to the main Gallery Library screen after you're done viewing an album.

✔ Albums from online photo-sharing sites also show up in the Gallery, as long as you've configured the Galaxy Note with your photo sharing account. Google's photo-sharing service, Picasa Web, is one service that Galaxy Note can link to. Picasa Web albums are flagged by a special icon in the Gallery.

Viewing an image's location on the map

When an image has been GPS-tagged, you can use the Gallery app to preview not only that image but also the location where the image was taken. Follow these steps in the Gallery app:

1. Touch the image so that you can view it in Full-Screen mode.

2. Press the Menu soft button.

3. Choose More and then Show on Map.

If you don't see the Show on Map command, the image lacks a GPS tag. Otherwise, the Maps app opens and shows you the spot where the image was taken.

Press the Back soft button to return to the image in the Gallery app.

See Chapter 13 for more information on the Maps app.

Editing images

The best tool for image editing is a computer amply equipped with photo editing software, such as Photoshop or one of its inexpensive alternatives. Even so, it's possible to use the Gallery app to perform some minor photo surgery. Two popular tasks are cropping and rotating.

Crop an image

Cropping is the process of removing a portion of an image to bring the focus to a specific part of the image and cut out the rest, as shown in Figure 14-3.

Drag the cropping box.

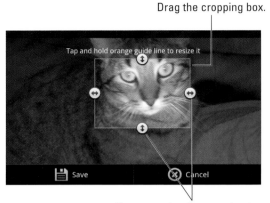

Drag to resize the cropping box.

Figure 14-3: Cropping an image.

Here are the steps required to crop an image using the Gallery app:

1. **Open the Gallery app, and display the image you want to crop.**

2. **Press the Menu soft button.**

3. **Choose More and then Crop.**

4. **Use the onscreen controls to crop the image.**

   Refer to Figure 14-3 for help with using the onscreen controls, though the controls you see on your screen may be subtly different.

5. **Touch the Save button to crop the image.**

   The image's size and content are changed immediately.

There's no way to undo a crop.

Rotate an image

To rotate an image clockwise or counterclockwise, follow these steps:

1. **Display the image in the Gallery app.**

2. **Press the Menu soft button, and then choose More.**

3. **Choose Rotate Left to rotate the image counterclockwise 90 degrees, or choose Rotate Right to rotate the image clockwise 90 degrees.**

   The image is rotated immediately. There's no confirmation, warning, or opportunity to save, though you can undo the rotation by simply rotating it in the other direction.

Not every image can be rotated, such as images synchronized from web albums and social networking sites.

Deleting one or more images

Pruning an image from the Gallery is simple:

1. **Summon the full-screen image in the Gallery app.**

2. **Choose the Delete command from the onscreen menu.**

   If the onscreen menu doesn't appear, tap the touchscreen.

3. **Choose the Confirm Deletions option from the menu.**

   The image is gone.

There's no way to use the phone to undelete an image you've zapped from the Gallery.

To delete a swath of images at one time, summon an album where you can see a bunch of thumbnails. Heed these steps:

1. **Press the Menu soft button.**

   The images in the album grow little check mark boxes, as shown in Figure 14-4.

Selected images

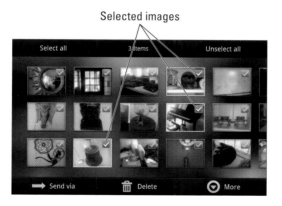

Figure 14-4: Selecting images for decimation.

2. **Touch the images you want to remove.**

   Selected images have little check marks by them. (Refer to Figure 14-4.) Or you can use the Select All item to select all images in the album.

3. **Touch the Delete button.**

4. **Choose Confirm Deletions to zap away all the images.**

This mass extinction event cannot be undone.

✔ To cancel your selections, choose the Unselect All command, illustrated in Figure 14-4.

✔ You can also remove albums by repeating these steps at the main Gallery screen.

✔ It's also possible to rotate a gang of images: In Step 3, choose More and then Rotate Left or Rotate Right. The horde of selected images is rotated in a single action.

Sharing images

Images don't need to be bottled up inside your phone. Nope — you can take advantage of the Send Via and Share Via commands to liberate your images, setting them free on the Internet for others to enjoy.

You can share multiple images by selecting them as a group. Refer to the preceding section for group selection information. (When a group of images is selected, you find the Share Via command on the More menu.)

Send Via

The Send Via command sends your image by using e-mail or text messaging or by beaming the image to another device using the Wi-Fi network or a Bluetooth connection.

Access the Send Via command by looking at an image full-screen in the Gallery app. Touch the screen to see the Send Via command, similar to the one shown in Figure 14-2. Options available on the Send Via menu include:

Bluetooth: The image is sent (uploaded) to a Bluetooth device, such as a computer or printer. See Chapter 19 for information on Bluetooth devices and how to print images stored on your Galaxy Note using a Bluetooth printer.

Email and Gmail: Choosing Email or Gmail for sharing sends the media file from your phone as a message attachment. Fill in the To, Subject, and Message text boxes as necessary. Touch the Send button to send the media.

Text Messaging: Media can be attached to a text message, which then becomes the famous MMS, or multimedia message, that I write about in Chapter 9.

Wi-Fi: Choose a shared Wi-Fi Direct resource to share the image, such as a digital picture frame or Wi-Fi Direct printer.

Additional options may appear on the Send Via menu, depending on the various apps installed on your phone.

Share Via

The Share Via command offers up the image on a social networking site, on an image-sharing site, on devices connected to your Galaxy Note for media sharing, or via other image-sharing apps on the phone.

To see the Share Via command, press the Menu soft button while viewing an image. Here are some of the options you may find on the Share Via menu:

AllShare: The AllShare command allows you to view the image(s) you select on another device, such as a computer or an HDMI monitor. The other device must be configured for media sharing.

Picasa: The Picasa photo sharing site is one of those free services you get with your Google account. Choose this option to upload a photo to your Picasa account: Type a caption, choose an online album, and then touch the Upload button.

S Memo: The image opens in the S Memo editor, where you can use the S Pen to doodle and then save the image or send it on from there. See Chapter 17 for more information on the S Memo app.

Social Hub: You can share the image on your social networking sites (Facebook, Twitter, LinkedIn) by choosing this option. See Chapter 11 for information on the Social Hub.

Additional options may appear on the menu, depending on which apps you have on the phone. For example, if you've installed the Facebook for Android app, a Facebook item appears on the menu.

Viva Video

*T*he image you capture using your Galaxy Note need not be stationary. Just as the phone can snap still images, it can capture video. You can record all sorts of events — birthdays, sporting events, plane crashes — and store them on the phone or share them elsewhere. And when you grow bored of your own stuff, you can enjoy videos on YouTube or rent movies and TV shows. It all happens using your phone, as described in this chapter.

Your Phone's Video Studio

The first video cameras came out decades ago. They were bulky, they required heavy batteries, and they recorded images on something called *video tape*. Those days are long gone, because you can now use your lightweight Galaxy Note and its deliciously large screen to record all the video you desire.

Well, okay: You're limited by the phone's storage capacity, but at least the technicians have freed you from the bondage of video tape.

Recording video

The Galaxy Note uses the same Camera app whether it's taking still images or recording video. The secret is to switch the Camera app to Video mode, as shown in Figure 15-1. Once in that mode, the screen changes to offer you video controls and to prepare you to record events as they happen.

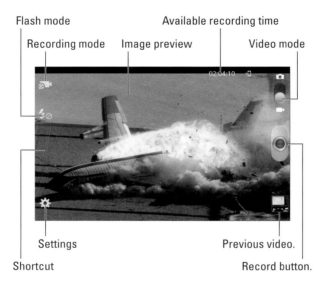

Flash mode   Available recording time

Recording mode   Image preview   Video mode

Settings   Previous video.

Shortcut   Record button.

Figure 15-1: The Galaxy Note recording video.

Start shooting the video by pressing the Record button, as illustrated in Figure 15-1. A red dot appears on the screen, by the elapsed recording time, which is one indication that you're recording video.

To stop recording, touch the Record button again.

- ✔ Hold the phone steady! The camera still works when you whip around the phone, but wild gyrations render the video unwatchable.

- ✔ The video's duration depends on its resolution (see the next section) and on the storage available on your phone. The maximum recording time is shown on the screen before you shoot. (Refer to Figure 15-1.) While you record, the elapsed time appears.

- ✔ Use the phone's volume buttons to zoom: Volume Up zooms in, Volume Down zooms out. Additionally, an onscreen control appears, which you can manipulate to zoom in or out.

✔ To delete a video after you shoot it, touch the Previous Video button. When the video appears, touch the Delete button. Touch the OK button to confirm.

✔ Recorded video is saved in the phone's storage, either internal storage or the MicroSD card. To select one or the other, touch the Settings button and choose Storage. Select the Phone option for internal storage, or Memory Card to store video on the MicroSD card. The time shown on the screen is affected by the amount of available storage at whichever location is chosen.

Making a video message

Maybe you don't want to record that UFO landing in the park. Perhaps you want to record your reaction to it and send that video to a friend. Despite your questionable priorities, here are the steps to accomplish such a thing:

1. **Switch the Camera app to Video Recording mode.**

2. **Touch the Settings button.**

3. **Choose Recording Mode and then Limit for MMS.**

   The size of the preview image shrinks, as does the video format. You can now record a message in a format that's compatible with a text message or an e-mail attachment.

4. **Record your video.**

5. **Touch the Previous Video button to watch your masterpiece.**

6. **Touch the Share button.**

   If you don't see the Share button, touch the screen and it appears.

7. **Choose a method to share, such as Email, Gmail, or Messaging.**

8. **Continue composing your message.**

   Refer to Chapter 9 for specifics on using the Email, Gmail, and Messaging apps.

Be sure to switch the recording mode back to Normal when you're done: Work through Steps 1 through 3, but choose Normal from the Recording Mode menu.

You can use the Recording Mode shortcut button on the screen to quickly access the Recording Mode menu. Refer to Figure 15-1.

To use the front-facing camera to record yourself, choose Self-Recording from the Recording Mode menu. You also have to adjust the image's resolution if you plan to attach your missive to an e-mail or text message. See the later section "Setting video quality" for directions.

Shedding some light on your subject

You don't need a flash for recording video, but occasionally you need a little more light. You can manually turn on the Galaxy Note's LED flash to help: Touch the Settings icon, choose Flash, and then choose On. The LED on the phone's rear turns on when you start recording a video.

An easier way is to touch the Flash Mode shortcut button, as illustrated in Figure 15-1. Choose On or Off from the menu. The icon used for the Flash Mode shortcut button tells you whether the LED is on or off. In Figure 15-1, it's off.

Turning on the LED light consumes a hefty portion of the phone's battery power. Use it sparingly.

Setting video quality

There's no reason to record all your videos at the highest quality setting. Unless you're shooting something that you plan to edit or broadcast or you're fortunate enough to have oodles of storage on your Galaxy Note, there's no point. Most of the videos you plan to upload to Facebook or attach to an e-mail message don't need all that high definition.

To set the video quality, touch the Settings icon and choose Resolution. (You may have to scroll down the Settings menu to find the option.) The Resolution menu lists several settings for video quality:

1920x1080: The highest-quality setting is best suited for video you plan to show on a large-format TV or computer monitor. It's useful for video editing or for showing important events, such as alien invasions. This format is also known as 1080i.

1280x720: The second-highest-quality setting is a good choice if you need to record longer but still want high quality. This standard setting is also known as 720i.

720x480: This option, known as the DVD setting, has good quality for shooting video when you don't know where the video will be shown.

640x480: This setting, good for quality Internet video, doesn't enlarge well. It's known as the VGA setting.

320x240: This setting, also known as the QVGA setting, is designed for use with video attachments in text messaging.

176x144: The lowest setting, with the crummiest quality, is ideal for MMS or other attachments where quality is the last thing you care about.

Check the video quality *before* you shoot! Especially if you know where the video will be shown (on the Internet, on a TV, or in an MMS message), set the quality first.

The front-facing camera has only one video setting, which cannot be changed: 640x480.

Manage Your Videos

As with still images you take using the Camera app, the videos you record can be viewed by using the Gallery app. It's found on the Apps menu. Unlike still images, the number of things you can do with videos in the Gallery app is limited. For example, the Gallery app has no commands for editing video, though video-editing apps are available at the Google Play Store. See Chapter 18.

Viewing your videos

To pore over your videos, open the Gallery app, found on the Apps menu. The Gallery's main screen shows images and videos, organized by album. You find your videos in the Camera album, which contains all the still images and videos taken with your phone.

 Videos appear in the album with the Play icon superimposed over the Thumbnail icon, as shown in margin. To view a full-screen video, touch its thumbnail preview. The controls, shown in Figure 15-2, eventually disappear. If so, touch the screen to see them again.

Figure 15-2: Watching a video.

Touch the Play button to play the video. After doing so, the Play button changes to the Pause button. You can drag the slider (refer to Figure 15-2) to "scrub" the video forward or backward.

After viewing the video, you return to the video's album in the Gallery app.

You can also use the Play Movies app to view your videos. Unlike the Gallery app, the Play Movies app shows only videos stored on the phone (no images). The app also shows any rentals you may have purchased at the Google Play Store. See the later section "Watching videos with Google Play."

Deleting a video

To delete a video from the Gallery, display the album containing the video. Long-press the video, and then choose the Delete command. Choose Confirm Delete to remove the video.

When you long-press a video in the Gallery, you select it. A green check mark appears on the video's thumbnail. You can touch other videos (or images) to select them for deletion as well: Touch the Delete command, and then choose Confirm Delete to zap the group to bit hell.

There's no way to undelete an image you've removed from the Gallery.

The YouTube Experience

YouTube is the Internet phenomenon that proves Andy Warhol right: In the future, everyone will be famous for 15 minutes. Or, in the case of YouTube, everyone will be famous on the Internet for the duration of a 10-minute video. That's because *YouTube* is *the* place on the Internet for anyone and everyone to share their video creations.

Watching a YouTube video

To view the mayhem on YouTube, start the YouTube app, which is found on one of the Home screen panels as well as on the Apps menu. The main YouTube screen is depicted in Figure 15-3.

Get information.

Upload a video.

Touch a video to watch it.

Figure 15-3: YouTube.

To view a video, touch its name or icon in the list.

 To search for a video, press the Search soft button while using the YouTube app. Type or dictate whatever you want to search for, and then peruse the results.

Turn the phone to Landscape mode to view a video in Full-Screen mode. You can touch the screen to see the onscreen video controls.

✔ Use the YouTube app to view YouTube videos rather than use the Web app to visit the YouTube website.

> ✔ Because you have a Google account, you also have a YouTube account. I recommend that you log in to your YouTube account when using the YouTube app: Press the Menu soft button, and choose the command My Channel. Log in, if necessary. Otherwise, you see your account information, your videos, and any video subscriptions.
>
> ✔ Not all YouTube videos can be viewed on mobile devices.

Uploading a video to YouTube

The best way to share video you've shot using your Galaxy Note is to upload it to YouTube. You can upload it straight to your YouTube account. You can use the YouTube app on your phone to upload videos to the Internet, where everyone can see them and make rude comments upon them. Here's how:

1. **Activate the phone's Wi-Fi.**

   The best way to upload a video is to turn on the Wi-Fi connection. You can use the 4G signal, if available, though you see a warning about data usage surcharges, which is a distinct possibility when you upload a video. My advice: Use Wi-Fi.

   See Chapter 19 for information on how to turn on the Wi-Fi connection.

2. **Start the YouTube app.**

3. **Touch the Upload button.**

   Refer to Figure 15-3. If you don't see the button, press the Menu soft button and choose My Channel.

   The Gallery app opens, showing only those albums in which videos are stored.

4. **Open an album, and then choose a video to upload.**

5. **Touch the OK button if you're prompted with a warning message about data surcharges.**

6. **Fill in the blanks to describe the video.**

   For example, you can type the video's title and description, select privacy options, and assign any tags to help others find the video.

7. **Touch the Upload button.**

   You can view the progress of the video being uploaded on your account screen in YouTube.

After your video has been fully uploaded, you can view it on your channel page in the YouTube app. Ensure that you've selected the Uploads tab, shown earlier, in Figure 15-3.

Videos to Buy and Rent

It will be some time before anyone shoots the next *Citizen Kane* using a cell phone. Don't despair: It could be you! Or maybe you'll find enough video entertainment using the YouTube app. When these resources dry up, you can turn to Hollywood and view the latest blockbusters, classics, and even plain old TV right on your phone.

Watching videos with Google Play

The Google Play Store is a great place to get bonus goodies for your Galaxy Note. Those goodies include more apps, books, music, and videos.

Here are the general steps you take to rent and view a video on your phone:

1. **Activate the Galaxy Note's Wi-Fi connection.**

   You don't want to incur any data overages while you watch the movie. See Chapter 19 for details on activating Wi-Fi.

2. **Open the Play Store app.**

3. **Choose the Movies category.**

   All movies are rentals.

4. **Browse or search for a movie.**

5. **Touch the movie's Rent button, which also lists the rental price.**

   You're not charged for touching the Rent button. Instead, you see more details, such as the rental terms. Typically, you have 30 days to watch the film, but once you start watching, you can pause and resume — or watch it over and over — during a single 24-hour period.

6. **Choose a payment method.**

   If you don't yet have an account set up at Google Checkout, you can configure one by touching the Add Payment Method button. Otherwise, choose your Google Checkout credit card, as shown on the screen.

7. **Touch the Accept & Buy button to rent the movie.**

8. **Touch the Play button to view the movie.**

   The movie is viewed by using the Play Movies app. The app opens automatically, though it may need updating before you can view your film.

The move is *streamed* to your phone, which means that it's sent as you watch it. Therefore, I highly recommend that you plug your phone into a power source when you're watching the video.

The Video app may eventually change its name to *Play Movies*.

Using other video viewing apps

There are several additional ways to watch professional videos and movies on your Galaxy Note. Beyond the Google Play Store's selection, you can peruse three additional apps that come with your phone for your movie watching pleasure:

Live TV: Though the app is named Live TV, its full name is AT&T U-verse Live TV. As the name implies, you use this app to view live (broadcast) TV. It's not free, though you get a 7-day free trial. The biggest downside, however, is that you must use your cellular data connection to view the programs. Unless you have an unlimited data plan, I highly recommend avoiding this app.

Movies: AT&T's Movies app is similar to the Google Play Store in that you can rent movies to watch, and the prices are quite reasonable. They even offer free deals every so often, so it's worth checking out.

Samsung Media Hub: Not only does AT&T throw in extra software that you don't have to use, but Samsung gets into the act as well. Samsung Media Hub lets you rent *and buy* movies and TV shows for viewing on a Samsung gizmo such as the Galaxy Note. The videos you buy are tied into your Samsung media account, which means that they can be made available on other Samsung mobile devices as well.

Beyond these apps, included on your phone, other apps are available at the Google Play Store, where you can rent, buy, or preview videos. See Chapter 18 for information on visiting the Google Play Store and searching for apps.

Listen to the Music

Musicians can be expensive. Years back, I would hire a band to follow me around and play music. The band had to be versatile: classic, jazz, show tunes, rock, no country. So you can imagine the money I've saved since I discovered that my Galaxy Note also serves as a portable music player. Not only that, but the phone is lighter and eats a lot less than the musicians.

Just to confuse you, *two* music-playing apps are on your phone. The first is *Music Player*, the traditional music app found on just about every Android phone. Then there's the newer *Google Play Music* app, which is Google's own music player. Because the Play Music app is more versatile, this chapter covers it.

Your Top 40

In addition to being a phone (and everything else), the Galaxy Note serves well as your portable music player. Wherever you go with your phone, which is probably everywhere, you can carry along, and enjoy, all your favorite tunes. The experience is even more enjoyable when you read the information in this section, which explains how it all works.

Browsing your music library

The music stored on your phone is accessed and played by using a music-playing app. Both apps that come with the Galaxy Note — Play Music and the Music Player — can access your music library, including all the music you've obtained and stored on the phone, though only the Play Music app can access music you've purchased at the Google Play Store.

Figure 16-1 shows the Play Music app in Album view. The number and variety of albums you see depends on how cool you are, but also on whether you've obtained any music for your phone. See the later section "The Hits Just Keep On Coming" for details.

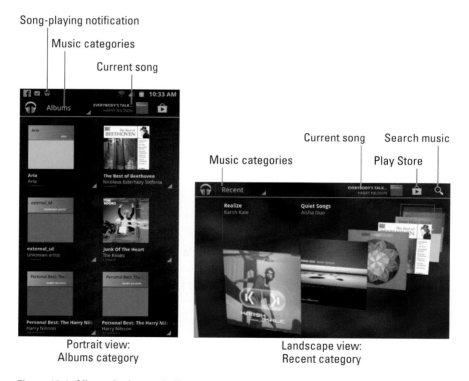

Song-playing notification
Music categories
Current song

Current song   Search music
Music categories   Play Store

Portrait view:
Albums category

Landscape view:
Recent category

Figure 16-1: Albums in the music library.

The Play Music app organizes by category the music stored on your phone, which is chosen from the Music Categories menu, as shown in Figure 16-1:

Recent: Only those albums or songs last copied to or purchased for the phone are listed.

Albums: Songs are organized by album. Choose an album to list its songs.

Artists: Songs are listed by recording artist or group. Choose this category, and then choose an artist to see their albums. Choosing an album displays the songs for that album. Some artists may have only one song, not in any particular album.

Songs: All songs are listed alphabetically.

Playlists: Only songs you've organized into playlists are listed by their playlist names. Choose a playlist name to view songs organized in that playlist. The section "Music Organization," later in this chapter, discusses playlists.

Genres: Tunes are organized by theme, such as classical, rock, or irritating. Not every phone may have this category.

These categories are merely ways to organize the music — ways to make tunes easier to find when you may know an artist's name but not an album title or when you may want to hear a song but you don't know who recorded it.

- ✔ While browsing your music, you can use the Play Music icon, found in the upper-left corner of the screen, to return to the top level of the Music app. You can also press the Back soft button to back out of a subcategory.

- ✔ Any song that's playing appears on the screen, as shown earlier, in Figure 16-1. Touch that song's button to pause or resume the tune.

- ✔ Music is stored on your phone's internal storage as well as on the MicroSD card.

- ✔ The size of the phone's storage limits the total amount of music you can keep on your phone. Also, consider that pictures and videos stored on your phone horn in on some of the space that can be used for music.

- ✔ See the later section "The Hits Just Keep On Coming" for information on getting music into your phone.

- ✔ Album artwork generally appears on imported music as well as on music you purchase online. If an album has no artwork, it cannot be manually added or updated (at least, not by using the Play Music app).

- ✔ When your phone is unable to recognize an artist, it uses the title *Unknown Artist*. This happens with music you copy manually to the phone. Music that you purchase, or import or synchronize with a computer, generally retains the artist and album information. (Well, the information is retained as long as it was supplied on the original source.)

Playing a tune

To listen to music on your phone, you first find a song in the Music app's library, as described in the preceding section. Then you touch the song title. The song plays on its own screen, similar to the one shown in Figure 16-2.

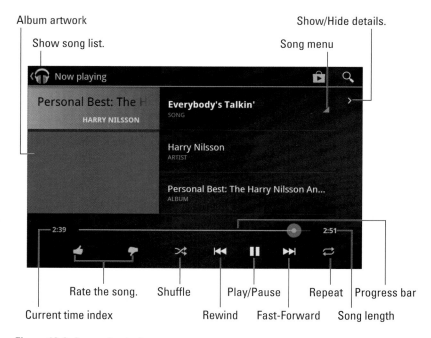

Figure 16-2: A song is playing.

While the song is playing, you're free to do anything else with the phone. In fact, the song continues to play even if the phone goes to sleep.

After the song is done playing, the next song in the list plays. Touch the Show Song List button (in the upper-left corner of Figure 16-2) to review the songs in the list.

The next song doesn't play if you have activated the Shuffle button. In this case, the phone randomizes the songs in the list, so who knows which one is next?

The next song also may not play if you have the Repeat option on: The three repeat settings are listed in Table 16-1, along with the shuffle settings. To change a setting, simply touch either the Shuffle or Repeat button. When you don't see these options, touch the Show Details button, illustrated in Figure 16-2.

Table 16-1		The Shuffle and Repeat Button Icons
Icon	*Setting*	*What Happens When You Touch the Icon*
	Shuffle Is Off	Songs play one after the other.
	Shuffle Is On	Songs are played in random order.
	Repeat Is Off	Song don't repeat.
	Repeat All Songs	All songs in the list play over and over.
	Repeat Current Song	The same song plays over and over.

To stop the song from playing, touch the Pause button. (Refer to Figure 16-2.)

 When music plays on the phone, a notification icon appears, similar to the one shown in the margin. Use this notification to quickly summon the Play Music app, to see which song is playing or to pause the song.

- ✔ Volume is set by using the Volume switch on the side of the phone: Up is louder; Down is quieter.

- ✔ Determining which song plays next depends on how you chose the song that's playing. If you choose a song by artist, all songs from that artist play, one after the other. When you choose a song by album, that album plays. Choosing a song from the entire song list causes all songs in the phone to play.

- ✔ To choose which songs play after one another, create a playlist. See the section "Music Organization," later in this chapter.

- ✔ After the last song in the list plays, the phone stops playing songs — unless the Repeat option is on, in which case the song or list plays again.

The Hits Just Keep On Coming

Odds are good that your Galaxy Note came with no music preinstalled. It may have: Some resellers may have preinstalled a smattering of tunes, which merely lets you know how out of touch they are musically. Regardless, you can add music to your phone in a number of ways, as covered in this section.

Borrowing music from your computer

It may seem odd, but when you look for music in the 21st century, you look to your computer, not to a stereo system. Even the once ubiquitous stack of CDs or shelf full of albums is now replaced by the humble PC. So why not purloin a few of the tunes stored there and copy them to your phone? Here's how it works:

1. **Connect the phone to the PC.**

   Specific phone-computer connection information is found in Chapter 20.

2. **On your PC, start Windows Media Player.**

   You can use most any media program, or "jukebox." These steps are specific to Windows Media Player, though they're similar to the steps you take in any media-playing program.

   If you see a device window for your phone in Windows 7, choose the item Manage Media on Your Device.

3. **If necessary, click the Sync tab in Windows Media Player.**

   Figure 16-3 shows your phone (known as SGH-I717, for some reason) in the Sync list on the right side of Windows Media Player. When two SGHI717 items show up, one represents the phone's internal storage, and the other represents storage on the MicroSD card. The items may even be labeled Card and Phone, as shown in the figure.

4. **Drag to the Sync area the music you want to transfer to your phone. (Refer to Figure 16-3.)**

5. **Click the Start Sync button to transfer the music.**

6. **Close Windows Media Player when you're done with the transfer.**

   Or keep it open — whatever.

7. **Unmount your phone from the PC's storage system.**

   Refer to Chapter 20 for specific unmounting instructions.

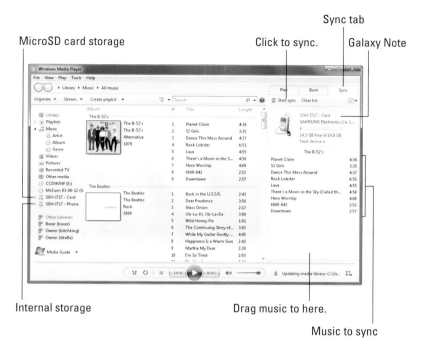

Figure 16-3: Windows Media Player meets the Galaxy Note.

When you have a Macintosh or you detest Windows Media Player, you can use the doubleTwist program to synchronize music between your phone and your computer. For information, refer to the section in Chapter 20 about synchronizing with doubleTwist.

- The phone can store only so much music! Don't be overzealous when copying your tunes. In Windows Media Player (refer to Figure 16-3), a capacity-thermometer thing shows you how much storage space is used and how much is available on your phone. Pay heed to the indicator!

- You cannot use iTunes to synchronize music with Android phones.

- Okay, I lied in the preceding point: You *can* synchronize music using iTunes, but only when you install the iTunes Agent program on your PC. You then need to configure the iTunes Agent program to use your Android phone with iTunes. After you do that, iTunes recognizes the phone and lets you synchronize your music. Yes, it's technical; hence the icon in the margin.

Getting music from the Google Play Store

It's possible to get your music from the same source where you buy your apps, the Google Play Store. Here's how it works:

1. **Open the Play Store app on your phone.**

   It can be found on the Home screen or, like all apps, on the Apps menu. You can also get to the Google Play Music store by touching the Play Store button in the Play Music app. (Refer to Figure 16-1.)

2. **Choose the Music category.**

3. **Use the Search command to locate music you want, or just browse the categories.**

   Keep an eye out for free music offers at the Play Store. It's a great way to pick up free tunes.

   Eventually, you see a page showing details about the song or album, similar to the one shown in Figure 16-4. Choose a song from the list to hear a preview. The button next to the song or album indicates the purchase price, or it says *FREE,* for free music.

4. **Touch the price button to purchase a song or album.**

   Don't worry — you're not buying anything yet.

5. **Choose your credit card or payment source.**

   If a credit card or payment source doesn't appear, choose the option to add a payment method. Sign up with Google Checkout, and submit your credit card or other payment information.

6. **Touch the Accept & Buy button.**

   The album or song is downloaded into your phone.

The Google Play Music notification appears when the album or song has completed its transfer into your phone. You can then use the Play Music app to listen to the new music; find it quickly by choosing the Recent category from the Play Music app's main screen.

✔ All music sales are final. Don't blame me — I'm just writing down Google's current policy for music purchases.

✔ If you plan to download an album or multiple songs, connect to a Wi-Fi network. That way, you don't run the risk of a data surcharge on your cellular plan. See Chapter 19 for information on activating the Galaxy Note's Wi-Fi.

✔ The Google Play Music notification icon is the same one that appears whenever you download a new app for your phone. The notification name, however, is Google Play Music.

✔ You eventually receive a Gmail notice regarding the purchase. The Gmail message lists a summary of your purchase.

✔ Music you purchase from the Google Play Music store is available on any mobile Android device with the Play Music app installed — if you use the same Google account on that device. You can also listen to your tunes by visiting the `music.google.com/` site on any computer connected to the Internet.

✔ For more information on the Google Play Store, see Chapter 18.

More songs by this artist

Return to the music store.   Search.

Share this item.   Album price

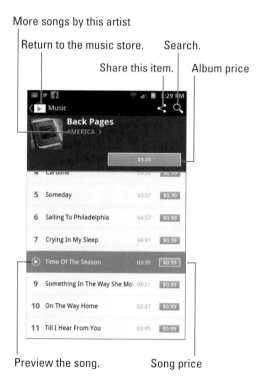

Preview the song.   Song price

Figure 16-4: Buying music at the Google Play Store.

Music Organization

The Play Music app organizes your music by category, artist, album, genre, and so on. Like most humans, however, you probably have favorite songs and tunes that match your mood. You have things that you like to hear in one setting, or songs you prefer to listen to in another. Music is emotional, after all.

To fulfill your personal tastes and moods, you can organize your tunes into playlists. A *playlist* is a collection of tunes you create. You build the list by combining songs from whatever music you have on your phone. You can then listen to the playlist and hear the music you want to hear in the order you want to hear it.

Reviewing your playlists

Any playlists you've already created, or that have been preset on your phone, appear in the Playlists category. To view this category, choose Playlists from the Music Categories menu on the Music app's main screen. You see something similar to Figure 16-5.

Music categories   Add playlist.

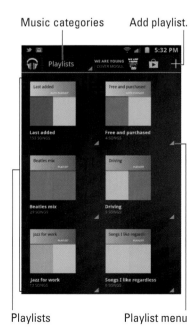

Playlists   Playlist menu

Figure 16-5: Playlists.

To listen to a playlist, long-press the playlist name and choose the Play command from the menu that appears.

You can also touch a playlist name to open the playlist and review the songs that are listed. You can touch any song from the list to start listening to that song.

A playlist is a helpful way to organize music when a song's information may not have been completely imported into your phone. For example, if you're like me, you probably have a lot of songs by "Unknown Artist." The quick way to remedy this situation is to name a playlist after the artist and then add those unknown songs to the playlist. The next section describes how it's done.

Building playlists

The Play Music app features two precreated playlists — Last Added and Free and Purchased, shown earlier, in Figure 16-5. Obviously, having more playlists is a good idea.

Creating a playlist involves two steps. First, you create the playlist. Next, you add songs to the playlist.

Create a new playlist by following these steps:

1. **Choose the Playlists category in the Play Music app.**

2. **Touch the Add Playlist button.**

   Refer to Figure 16-5 for the Add Playlist button's location.

3. **Type a descriptive name for the new playlist.**

   Short names are best.

4. **Touch the OK button.**

   The playlist is created, but it's empty. The next step is to add tunes.

You add songs to any playlist by obeying these directions:

1. **Long-press the song, artist, or album that you want to add to the playlist.**

   When you choose Artist or Album, all songs associated with that artist or album are added to the playlist.

2. **Choose Add to Playlist.**

3. **Choose the playlist.**

4. **Repeat Steps 1 through 3 to continue building the playlist.**

The songs appear in the playlist in the order you add them; you cannot rearrange the order afterward. That's a bummer.

You can continue adding songs to as many playlists as you like. Adding songs to a playlist doesn't noticeably affect the phone's storage capacity.

- ✔ To remove a song from a playlist, long-press the song in the playlist and choose the command Remove from Playlist. Removing a song from a playlist doesn't delete the song from your phone. (See the next section for information on deleting songs from the music library.)

- ✔ To delete a playlist, long-press its name in the list of playlists. Choose the Delete command. Touch the OK button to confirm. Though the playlist is removed, none of the songs in the playlist has been deleted.

Deleting music

To purge unwanted music from your phone, follow these brief, painless steps while using the Play Music app:

1. **Long-press the music that offends you.**

   It can be an album, a song, or even an artist.

2. **Choose Delete.**

   A warning message appears.

3. **Touch the OK button.**

   The music is gone.

 You cannot use your phone to delete music purchased at the Google Play Store. You can, however, remove the songs by visiting the My Music website: `music.google.com`. Click the triangle menu next to an album title, and choose the Delete Album command.

Galaxy Note Radio

Though they're not broadcast radio stations, some sources on the Internet — *Internet radio* sites — play music. Lamentably, the Galaxy Note comes with no Internet radio apps preinstalled. That doesn't mean that you can't add a few yourself. Two that I recommend are

- ✔ TuneIn Radio
- ✔ Pandora Radio

The TuneIn Radio app gives you access to hundreds of Internet radio stations broadcasting around the world. They're organized by category, so you can find just about whatever you want. Many radio stations are also broadcast radio stations, so odds are good that you can find a local station or two.

 Pandora Radio lets you select music based on your mood, and it customizes, according to your feedback, the tunes you listen to. The app works like the Internet site www.pandora.com, in case you're familiar with it. The nifty thing about Pandora is that the more you listen, the better the app becomes at finding music you like.

Both apps are available at the Google Play Store. They're free, though paid versions may also be available.

 ✔ I recommend listening to Internet radio when your phone is connected to the Internet via a Wi-Fi connection. Streaming music can use a lot of your cellular data plan's data allotment.

✔ See Chapter 18 for more information about the Google Play Store.

 ✔ Internet music of the type delivered by the apps mentioned in this section is referred to by the nerds as *streaming music*. That's because the music arrives on your phone as a continuous download from the source. Unlike music you download and save, streaming music is played as it comes in and isn't stored long-term.

What Else Does It Do?

In This Chapter

▶ Setting alarms

▶ Using the calculator

▶ Checking your schedule

▶ Adding an event

▶ Reading eBooks

▶ Playing games

▶ Scribbling on the screen

▶ Recording audio

*W*hat do you call one gadget that serves many purposes? Years back, it would have been a *fantasy,* a *fake,* or a *Swiss army knife.* In the TV show "Star Trek*,"* it was the *tricorder,* which was a combination computer-recording device that made a loud, whistling noise even when Mr. Spock was sneaking around. Today, that device is your *cell phone.*

This chapter covers the smattering of apps included with the Galaxy Note that do interesting and useful things. It answers the question, "What else does it do?"

It's a Clock

The Galaxy Note keeps constant and accurate track of the time, which is displayed at the top of the Home screen and also when you unlock the phone. Because the time is kept accurately, I would take the phone's timekeeping ability as a sure sign that you should toss out every clock in your house. Well, maybe not *every* clock, but you can do without your alarm clock, for certain.

The Clock app is the Galaxy Note's timekeeping headquarters. It features alarm clocks, 'round-the-world clocks, a stopwatch, a timer, and even a plain old desk clock. The only thing it can't do is time-travel, but that option is rumored to be included in the next release.

Figure 17-1 shows the Clock app's Alarm face, with several alarms created and two of them set.

Alarm is not set.

Alarm status

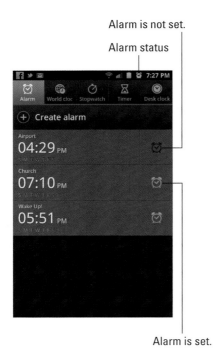

Alarm is set.

Figure 17-1: The Clock app wakes you up.

To set an alarm, follow these steps:

1. **Touch the Alarm tab in the Clock app.**

2. **Choose Create Alarm.**

3. **Describe the alarm.**

   Set the time, determine whether the alarm repeats, choose the tone and volume, and give the alarm a name.

   Because the alarm name appears when the alarm goes off, I set the name to remind me of the reason I'm getting up (or being alarmed). If I need to go to the airport, for example, the alarm name is *Get to the Airport!*

4. **Touch the Save button to create the alarm.**

The alarm appears in a list on the Alarm screen, along with any other available alarms, similar to those shown in Figure 17-1.

Alarms must be set, or else they do not trigger. To set an alarm, touch it in the alarm list. Set alarms have a green Alarm Clock icon by them. (Refer to Figure 17-1.) The icon is your clue that an alarm is set and ready to trigger.

 ✔ Turning off an alarm doesn't delete the alarm.

 ✔ To delete an alarm, long-press it from the list and choose the Delete command.

 ✔ The alarm doesn't work when you turn off the phone. The alarm does, however, go off when the phone is locked.

 ✔ So tell me: Do alarms go *off,* or do they go *on*?

It's a Calculator

One of the oldest, most traditional, and most frighteningly dull cell phone apps is Calculator. Please — don't let the math frighten you.

Start the Calculator app by choosing its icon from the Apps menu. The Calculator appears, as shown in Figure 17-2. Feel free to type various math problems; the phone does the math.

Figure 17-2: The Calculator.

✔ To see advanced calculator functions, turn the phone to its side. In the horizontal display, weirdo math functions appear to the left of the main keypad.

✔ Long-press the calculator's text (or results) to cut or copy the results.

✔ I use the Calculator most often to determine my tip at a restaurant. In Figure 17-2, a calculation is being made for an 18 percent tip on a tab of $56.24, which would have been less had my date not insisted on getting dessert.

It's a Calendar

Nothing beats keeping track of your appointments and schedule, especially when you become rich and famous. The mere act of having kids often requires that you make note of where you need to be and when. To help you stay on time, and to prevent little Molly from spending another tear-filled afternoon stranded at the roller rink, the Galaxy Note offers the handy Calendar app.

Understanding the Calendar

Because the Galaxy Note is tightly tied into Google, you can take advantage of the free feature Google Calendar. This Internet-based calendar and scheduling app neatly folds into the Calendar app on the phone. You can visit Google Calendar by using your computer to go to this web page:

```
http://calendar.google.com
```

If necessary, log in using your Google account. You can use Google Calendar to keep track of dates or meetings or whatever else occupies your time. You can also use your Galaxy Note to do the same thing, thanks to the Calendar app.

Checking your schedule

To see your schedule or upcoming important events, or to know simply which day of the month it is, summon the Calendar app. Samsung stuck a copy of the Calendar app on the Dock at the bottom of every Home screen panel. Touch its icon to behold the magnificence of your schedule.

The Calendar app shows your schedule by month, week, day, or various chunks of time. In Figure 17-3, Week view is shown. You use the tabs on the right side of the screen to choose a different chunk of time to display. Touch the button in the upper-right corner of the screen (illustrated in Figure 17-3) to show or hide the tab.

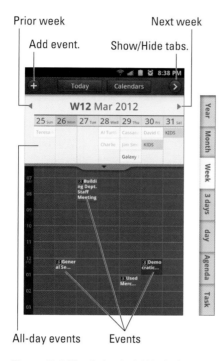

Prior week   Next week

Add event.   Show/Hide tabs.

All-day events   Events

Figure 17-3: The Calendar's Week view.

In Figure 17-3, scheduled appointments appear as colored highlights on various days. Each color is keyed to a different Calendar category. The colors help you locate events by their type or purpose, though using Calendar categories is optional.

Figure 17-4 shows the Calendar app's Month and Day views.

✔ To quickly hop to today's date, touch the Today button found at the top of the screen.

✒ I check Week view at the start of every week to remind me of what's coming up.

✒ Use your finger to flick the Week and Day views up or down to see your entire schedule, from midnight to midnight.

✒ To go to a specific date, press the Menu soft button and choose the Go To command. Use the onscreen gizmo to enter a date, and then touch the Set button.

✒ Various calendar widgets are available: Month, Task, Mini Today, Mini Agenda. See Chapter 22 for information on adding widgets to the Home screen.

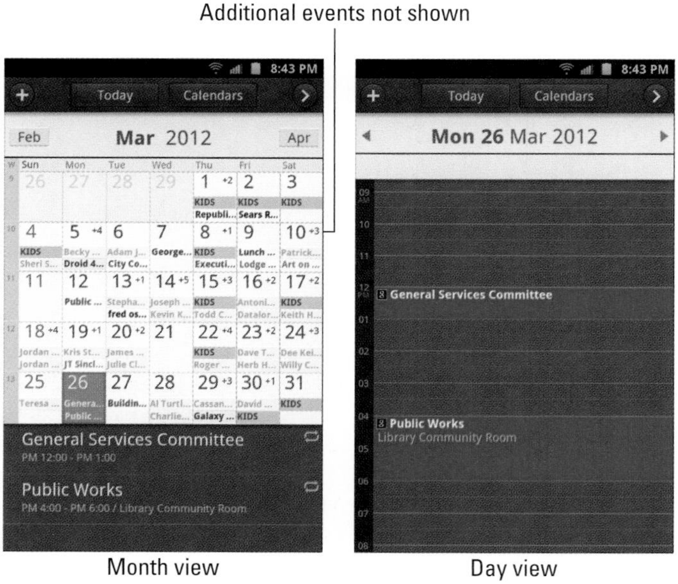

Additional events not shown

Month view   Day view

Figure 17-4: Day and Month views.

Reviewing events

To peruse your upcoming events in list format, tap the Agenda tab on the right side of the screen. You see your schedule as a list of events, as illustrated in Figure 17-5. Rather than list a traditional calendar, the Agenda screen shows only those dates with events and the events themselves.

Search category   Event alarm

Events   Repeating event

Figure 17-5: Agenda view.

To see more detail about an event, touch it. Details about the event appear on the screen, similar to those shown in Figure 17-6. The quality of the details depends on how much information you entered when the event was created. At minimum, the event has a title and a time.

When an event location is specified, you can touch the location to view where the event takes place on the Maps app. From there, it's easy to get directions directly to wherever you need to go. See Chapter 13.

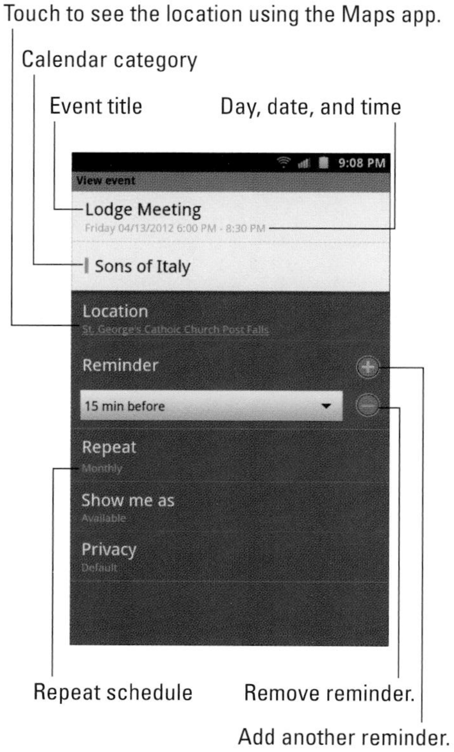

Touch to see the location using the Maps app.

Calendar category

Event title   Day, date, and time

Repeat schedule   Remove reminder.

Add another reminder.

Figure 17-6: Event details.

Creating a new event

The key to making the Calendar app work is to add events: appointments, things to do, meetings, or full-day events such as birthdays and lobotomies. To create a new event, follow these steps in the Calendar app:

1. Touch the Add Event button.

Refer to Figure 17-3 for its location, which is the same no matter which way you're viewing the calendar.

2. Type the event name.

For example, type **Colonoscopy**.

3. **Set the event's starting date and time and then the ending date and time.**

   If the event lasts all day, such as when your in-laws visit you for an hour, place a green check mark in the All Day box.

4. **If the event repeats, such as a regular meeting or appointment, touch the Repeat item to specify how and when the event reoccurs.**

5. **Choose the Calendar event.**

   Calendars are best set up on the Internet using a computer. Basically, they let you organize events by category and color. Also, you can show or hide individual calendar categories when you have a particularly busy schedule.

6. **Set the location.**

   For the location, type a search item similar to one you'd type when searching for an address using the Maps app. If you have the full address, type it in, but often just a street address and zip code work.

7. **Fill in other fields to further describe the event.**

   A good item to set is the event reminder. That way, the phone signals you for an impending date or appointment.

8. **Touch the Save button to create the new event.**

To change an event after it's been created, display its details (refer to Figure 17-6), press the Menu soft button, and choose the Edit command.

To remove an event, display its details and press the Menu soft button. Choose Delete, and then touch the OK button to confirm.

🖝 When you've set a reminder for an event, the phone alerts you. You may see, at minimum, a Calendar Reminder notification, similar to the one shown in the margin. The phone can also be set to sound a ringtone or vibrate for impending appointments.

🖝 To deal with an event notification, pull down the notifications and choose the event. You can touch the Dismiss button to remove event alerts.

🖝 Alerts for events are set by pressing the Menu soft button in the Calendar app and choosing the Settings command. Use the Select Ringtone option to choose an audio alert. Use the Vibrate option to control whether the phone vibrates to alert you of an impending event.

It's an eBook Reader

An *eBook* is an electronic version of a book. The words, formatting, figures, pictures — all that stuff is simply stored digitally so that you can read it on something called an *eBook reader*. The Galaxy Note comes with two eBook reader apps: Play Books, which is Google's own eBook reader, and the popular Amazon Kindle app. Both apps are discussed in this section.

- The advantage of an eBook reader is that you can carry an entire library of books with you without developing back problems.

- Rather than buy a new book at the airport, consider getting an eBook instead, though you can still read a real book during take-off and landing.

- Lots of eBooks are free, such as quite a few of the classics, including some that aren't boring. Current and popular titles cost money, though the cost is often less than the book's real-world equivalent.

- Magazine and newspaper subscriptions are also available for eBook readers.

- Not every title is available as an eBook.

Reading Google Books

The Play Books app allows you to read eBooks purchased at the Google Play Store. The app organizes the books into a library and displays the books for reading on your phone.

The reading experience happens like this:

1. **Open the Play Books app.**

   If you're prompted to turn on synchronization, touch the Turn On Sync button.

   You see your eBook library, which lists any titles you've obtained for your Google Play Books account. Or, when you're returning to the Play Books app after a break, you see the current page of the eBook you were last reading.

2. **Touch a book to open it.**

3. **Start reading.**

   Use Figure 17-7 as your guide for reading a Google Books eBook. Basically, you swipe the pages from left to right.

Touch here to see onscreen information.

Book title and author
(onscreen information)

Touch here to turn
to the next page.

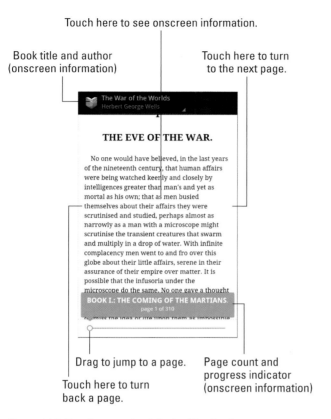

Drag to jump to a page.

Touch here to turn
back a page.

Page count and
progress indicator
(onscreen information)

Figure 17-7: Reading an e-book in the Play Books app.

Also see Chapter 18 for information on purchasing books at the Google Play Store.

Synchronization allows you to keep copies of your Google Books on all your Android devices, as well as at the `http://books.google.com` website.

Using the Amazon Kindle app

The good folks at Amazon recognize that you probably don't want to buy a Kindle eBook reader gizmo because you already have a nifty, portable, do-everything device in your Galaxy Note. Therefore, the Kindle app serves as your eBook reader software and provides access to the vast library of existing Kindle titles at Amazon (`www.amazon.com`).

Upon starting the Amazon Kindle app, you see the Registration screen. Log in using your e-mail address and Amazon password.

If you already have an Amazon Kindle account, after touching the Register button, your phone synchronizes with your existing Kindle library.

Choose a book from the Kindle bookshelf, and start reading. The eBook-reading operation works on the Kindle similarly to the Play Books app (refer to Figure 17-7), though on the Kindle you can highlight text, bookmark pages, look up words in a dictionary, and do other keen stuff that Google will no doubt add to an update of its Play Books app.

✔ Books for the Kindle app are purchased at the Kindle store using your existing Amazon account. In the Kindle app, press the Menu soft button and choose Kindle Store.

✔ Yes, you need an Amazon.com account to purchase eBooks (or even download freebies), so I highly recommend that you visit Amazon to set up an account if you don't already have one.

✔ To ensure that you get your entire Kindle library on your phone, turn on the Wi-Fi connection (see Chapter 19), press the Menu soft button, and choose the Archived Items command.

It's a Game Machine

The secret is out. You can use your Galaxy Note to play games. Not just the old, boring cell phone games but also the sophisticated games that consume your valuable time.

One game is prepackaged on the phone — Canyon Physics. I can't figure it out.

Plenty of understandable and enjoyable games are available at the Google Play Store, including zillions of titles that are popular, free, and captivating. Visit the Google Play Store, and choose the Apps category and then Games. Slide the screen to the left until you see the Top Free category. Have fun.

See Chapter 18 for details on using the Google Play Store to obtain more apps for your phone.

It's a Scribble Pad

When you're desperate to use the S Pen, you need only summon the S Memo app. It's the primary app on the Galaxy Note to take advantage of the S Pen, by letting you doodle, draw, or mark up documents, which you can then save or share to make all the other smartphone owners jealous.

Using the S Memo app

To play or, um, work with the S Pen, start the S Memo app, which is found on the Apps menu. S Memo opens, as shown in Figure 17-8, revealing a slew of precreated documents, plus any others you've created.

New memo (with onscreen keyboard)

New memo

Touch to edit an existing memo.

Figure 17-8: The S Memo app.

To create a new document, touch either of the New Memo buttons at the top of the screen. The only difference between the two is that the text document starts with the onscreen keyboard displayed.

Figure 17-9 illustrates the new memo window. The controls you use to draw an image appear atop the screen, as shown in the figure. You can draw an image from scratch, insert a picture from the Gallery, paste in something from the Clipboard, or take a snapshot of the map.

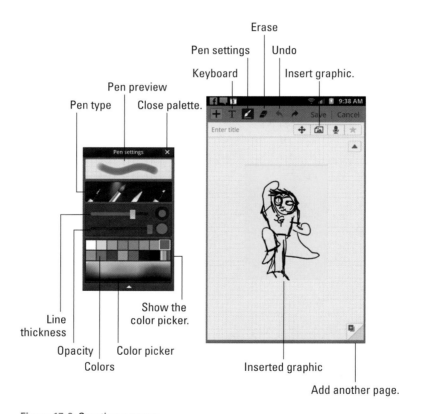

Figure 17-9: Creating a memo.

To get the memos out of the phone, press the Menu soft key and choose the Share Via command. Choose a sharing method from the menu, such as Gmail, Picasa, or Social Hub. Continue using the selected app to share the image; directions for using those apps are found throughout this book.

Touch the Save button to permanently enshrine your work in the Galaxy Note's storage. The memo appears on the main S Memo screen (refer to Figure 17-8), where you can once again summon it for editing, sharing, or whatever.

 ✒ When you desire to quickly scribble something, press the button on the S Pen and tap the touchscreen twice. This action summons the S Memo Lite app, which appears on the screen no matter what else you're doing with your phone.

 ✒ S Memo Lite memos appear on the main S Memo screen, just like any other memos you create.

 ✒ You don't need to use the S Pen to draw your masterpieces. Your finger works but lacks the refinement of the pen — which I suppose explains the difference between painting with a brush and finger painting.

Capturing and scribbling

A common thing to do with the S Pen is to capture a screen image, scribble on that image, and then send the image off, sharing it with friends, enemies, and co-workers. Here's how this operation works:

1. **Summon the screen upon which you want to scribble.**

   It can be anything you see on the Galaxy Note's screen, any app, any window, anything that shows up — even the lock screen (though it doesn't capture well).

2. **Press the S Pen button, and then long-press the touchscreen using the S Pen.**

   You hear a shutter sound, and the screen blinks. You've just captured the screen, which is now saved. Your next step is to mark up that screen-capture image, which looks similar to the one shown in Figure 17-10.

3. **Scribble.**

   Use the controls, illustrated in Figures 17-9 and 17-10, to mess with the image. Scribbling works similarly to how it's done in the S Memo app, though you have no way to write text using the onscreen keyboard on a screen-capture image.

4. **Touch the Share Via button to send the image elsewhere.**

   You can choose Gmail, Facebook, Picasa, or any of the other apps or options displayed on the Share Via menu to forward your masterpiece.

5. **Touch the Save button to save your image.**

Crop

Eraser

Pen / Pen settings   Undo   Scribblings

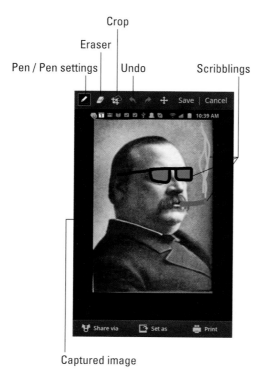

Captured image

Figure 17-10: Scribbling on a screen capture.

Scribbles that you capture in this manner are saved in the Gallery. Look for the album named Capture_Edited for images you've modified. The Capture_Export album contains screen captures you've forwarded using the Share Via menu.

✔ See Chapter 19 for information on printing with your Galaxy Note.

✔ The screen capture you take is copied to the Galaxy Note's clipboard, and it can be pasted into any location that accepts images. See Chapter 4 for more information on cut, copy, and paste on your phone.

It's a Tape Recorder

It makes sense that your Galaxy Note should be able to record your voice. It has a microphone. It has a speaker. It has storage. All it needs is the smarts — the app — to record, and – voila! The app is the Voice Recorder, and it comes preinstalled on your phone, dwelling on the Apps menu.

After opening Voice Recorder, you see the main screen, shown in Figure 17-11. Touch the Record button to begin recording your voice or your surroundings. (In the figure, the app is recording, so the Record button has changed to the Pause button.)

Fancy recording graphics

Record/Pause

Recording library

Figure 17-11: The phone is listening.

When you're done, you see your recording saved in the list. Touch the recording to listen.

✐ Long-press a recording to share, delete, or rename; choose the appropriate command from the pop-up menu.

✐ Recordings are saved in the Sounds folder on the phone's internal storage. They're saved in the 3GPP file format, with the .3ga filename extension.

✐ *Tape recorders* were mechanical devices used to record audio. Your elders may still have a tape recorder handy so that you may look at it with nostalgic awe. Either that, or you can find a tape recorder in any nearby technology museum or antique store.

The Apps Chapter

In This Chapter

▶ Using the Play Store app

▶ Managing apps

▶ Searching for apps

▶ Downloading a free app

▶ Getting a paid app

▶ Reviewing apps you've downloaded

▶ Sharing an app

▶ Updating an app

▶ Organizing the Apps menu

The Windows operating system didn't come to rule the PC world because of Microsoft's ruthless sales. Well, perhaps, but what Windows really had going for it was a wealth of available software, those programs that make a computer worth more than the sum of its parts. When it comes to technology, the gauge of success is software, not computer hardware.

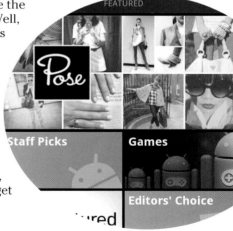

As software makes a computer, apps make a decent smartphone. To meet this end, your Galaxy Note has access to hundreds of thousands of apps, all available for the horde of Android phones out there. You can get new apps to expand the phone's abilities, apps to entertain and distract you, apps to help you get work done. Welcome to the Apps chapter.

The Google Play Store

Your Galaxy Note shipped with about 60 apps preinstalled. It's a pittance. More than 500,000 apps are available at the Google Play Store. Each of them extends the abilities of what your phone can do. Some cost money. Most are free. They're all waiting for you to try, and it starts by visiting the Play Store.

- ✔ The Play Store is also the place to go for downloading videos, music, and books. See Chapters 15, 16, and 17, respectively.

- ✔ You don't even need to know what you want at the Play Store; like many a mindless ambling shopper, you can browse until the touchscreen is smudged and blurry with your fingerprints.

- ✔ You obtain items from the Google Play Store by *downloading* them into your phone. The file transfer works best at top speeds; therefore:

 ✔ I highly recommend that you connect to a Wi-Fi network if you plan to obtain apps, books, or movies. Wi-Fi not only gives you speed but also helps you avoid data surcharges. See Chapter 19 for details on connecting your phone to a Wi-Fi network.

- ✔ The Google Play Store is frequently updated, so its look may change from the way it looks in this chapter. For example, until a few months ago, it was known as *Android Market*, and it may still be referred to as such in your phone's documentation or online.

- ✔ Updated information for this book and the Google Play Store can be found on my website:

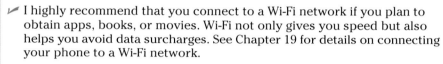

        www.wambooli.com/help/phone

Visiting the Play Store

Your new app experience begins by opening the Play Store app. It's found on the Apps menu, though a shortcut icon may also be on the primary Home screen.

The main screen from the Play Store app is shown in Figure 18-1. The screen lists the overview of all the goodies you can get for your phone. Choose the Apps category to see the Apps main screen, also shown in Figure 18-1. Swipe the screen left or right to browse categories and highlights, such as Top Paid apps, shown in Figure 18-1.

As you browse, you eventually see a list of app tiles, as shown in Figure 18-1. The app tiles give you a quick overview of the app's title, rating, and cost. Touching the tile displays more detailed information, as shown in Figure 18-2.

Go up one level.   App title   Top Paid category

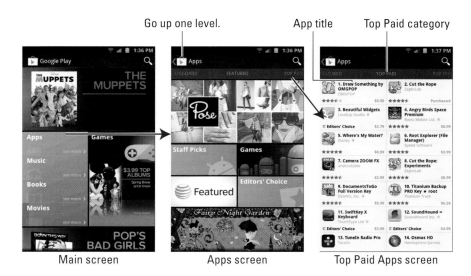

Main screen   Apps screen   Top Paid Apps screen

Figure 18-1: Google Play Store.

Scroll the app's details to read its description, check out its ratings, peruse screen shots, and look at similar or recommend apps. The key things I recommend looking for are its number of downloads and its rating, as illustrated in Figure 18-2.

When you know what you want, such as an app's name or even what it does, searching the Play Store works fastest: Touch the Search button at the top of the Play Store screen. (Refer to Figure 18-1.) Type all or part of the app's name, the book or movie title, or perhaps a description. Touch the Enter key to locate what you're looking for.

- The first time you enter the Google Play Store, you have to accept the terms of service; touch the Accept button.

- Apps that you download are added to the Apps menu, made available like any other app on your phone.

- You can rest assured that all apps that appear in the Play Store can be used on your Galaxy Note. There's no way to download or buy something that's incompatible with your phone.

- Pay attention to an app's ratings. Ratings are added by people who use the apps, like you and me. Having more stars is better. You can see additional information, including individual user reviews, by choosing the app.

- Another indicator of an app's success is how many times it's been downloaded. Some apps have been downloaded tens of millions of times. That's a good sign.

Rating

Install or buy the app.

Video preview

Share button

Return to previous screen.

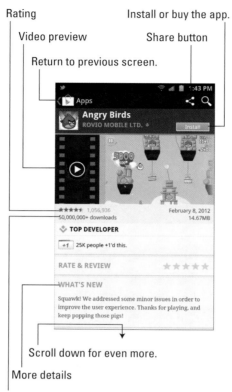

Scroll down for even more.

More details

Number of downloads

Figure 18-2: App details.

    ✔ In addition to getting apps, you can download widgets and wallpapers
    for your phone's Home screen. Just search the Play Store for *widget* or
    live wallpaper.

    ✔ See Chapter 22 for more information on widgets and live wallpapers.

Obtaining a free app

After you locate an app you want, the next step is to download it from the
Play Store into your Galaxy Note. Follow these steps:

**1. If possible, activate the phone's Wi-Fi connection to avoid incurring
    data overages.**

See Chapter 19 for information on connecting your phone to a Wi-Fi
network.

2. **Open the Play Store app.**

3. **Locate the app you want, and open its description.**

   You can browse for apps or use the Search button to find an app by name or by what it does.

4. **Touch the Install button.**

   The button is found at the upper right corner of the app's description screen. (Refer to Figure 18-2.)

   Touching the button doesn't immediately download or install the app.

   After touching the Install button, you're shown the services that the app uses. The list isn't a warning, and it means nothing bad. It simply confirms that the app does what it says it does, and that the Play Store is being honest with you about which resources the app uses.

5. **Touch the Accept & Download button to begin the download.**

   The app is automatically downloaded and installed onto your phone.

6. **Touch the Open button to run the app.**

   Or, if you were doing something else while the app was downloading and installing, choose the Successfully Installed notification, as shown in the margin. The notification features the app's name, with the text *Successfully Installed* beneath it.

At this point, what happens next depends on the app you've downloaded. For example, you may have to agree to a license agreement. If so, touch the I Agree button. Additional setup may involve setting your location, signing in to an account, or creating a profile, for example.

After the initial setup is complete, or if no setup is necessary, you can start using the app.

   ✔ The new app's icon is placed on the Apps menu, along with all other apps on the phone.

   ✔ Peruse the list of services an app uses (refer to Step 4) to look for anything unusual or out of line with the app's purpose. For example, an alarm clock app that uses your Contacts list and the text-messaging service is a red flag, especially if it's your understanding that the app doesn't need to text-message your contacts.

Purchasing an app

Some great free apps are available, but many of the apps you dearly want probably cost money. It's not a lot of money, especially compared to the price of computer software. In fact, it seems odd to sit and stew over whether paying 99 cents for a game is "worth it."

Apps via bar code

Many apps from the Google Play Store can be quickly accessed by scanning their bar code information. You may have seen these *QR Codes* scattered about this book's margins.

How do you scan these codes? Why, with your phone, of course!

The Galaxy Note comes with the AT&T Code Scanner bar code scanning app. It's not my favorite Android bar code scanner, but it works: Start up the app, plow through the information

screens, and, eventually, you see a screen that uses the phone's camera to spy out bar codes. Just point the phone's camera at the bar code until it's focused on the screen. You hear a tone, and then you see a link. For apps, touch the Yes button to open the link on a web page. But instead of a web page, the Play Store opens, and you can quickly download the related app.

By the way, my favorite bar code scanner is the app called, aptly, Barcode Scanner. It's free and easy to use, and it can be found at the Play Store.

I recommend that you download a free app first, to familiarize yourself with the process.

When you're ready to pay for an app, follow these steps:

1. **Activate the phone's Wi-Fi connection.**

2. **Open the Play Store app.**

3. **Browse or search for the app you want, and choose the app to display its description.**

   Review the app's price.

4. **Touch the price button.**

   The price button replaces the Install button for free apps, as shown earlier, in Figure 18-2. The price button represents the app's price. For example, if the app costs 99 cents, the button reads *$0.99.*

   Touching the price button doesn't immediately purchase the app.

5. **Choose your credit card.**

   The card must be on file with Google Checkout. If you don't yet have a card on file, choose the Add Payment Method option. Choose Add Card, and then fill in the fields on the Credit Card screen to add your payment method to Google Checkout.

6. **Touch the Accept & Buy button.**

   Your payment method is authorized, and the app is downloaded and installed.

Never buy an app twice

Any apps you've already purchased from the Google Play Store — say, for another phone or mobile device — are available for download on your current Android phone at no charge.

Simply find the app. You see it flagged as *Purchased* in the Play Store. Touch the Install button and then Accept & Download to install the already purchased app on your Galaxy Note.

After the app is installed, it can be accessed from the Apps menu, just like all other apps available on your phone. Or, if you're still at the app's screen in the Play Store, touch the Open button.

Eventually, you receive an e-mail message from Google Checkout, confirming your purchase. The message explains how to get a refund from your purchase. It works like this: Open the app's info screen (see the section "Controlling your apps," later in this chapter), and touch the Refund button to get your money back.

Be quick on that refund: Some apps allow you only 15 minutes to get your money back. Otherwise, the refund period can be as long as 24 hours. You know when the time limit has expired because the Refund button changes its name to Uninstall.

Also see the section "Removing an app," later in this chapter.

Manage Your Apps

The Play Store app does two important jobs: It's not only where you obtain new apps for your Galaxy Note but also the place you return to for performing app management. This task includes reviewing apps you've downloaded, updating apps, organizing apps, and removing apps that you no longer want or that you severely hate.

Reviewing your apps

It's difficult to look at the Apps menu and determine which apps came with your Galaxy Note and which you've added over time. A better place to look is on the My Apps list found in the Play Store app. Follow these steps:

1. **Start the Play Store app.**

2. Press the Menu soft button and choose My Apps.

The My Apps screen displays two panels. The first, titled Installed (shown in Figure 18-3), lists all apps installed on your phone. Those in need of updating are listed at the top.

Paid app, previously downloaded, not installed

Update all apps configured for automatic updating. App installed on your phone

Touch to see more information or to open or uninstall.

Touch to update. Free app, previously downloaded, not installed

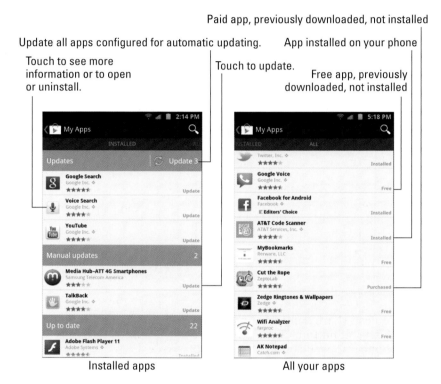

Installed apps   All your apps

Figure 18-3: Your apps.

3. Swipe the screen to the left.

The second panel, titled All, shows all your apps, whether they were downloaded on your Galaxy Note or on another Android device. Apps labeled Installed are found on your phone. Apps labeled Free or Purchased were obtained for other Android devices.

To install one of your previously downloaded apps, choose it from the All panel on the My Apps screen. Touch the Install button, and then touch Accept & Download. Even apps you've already paid for on another Android device can be installed on the Galaxy Note; simply pluck those purchased apps from the list.

Sharing an app

When you love an app so much that you just can't contain your glee, feel free to share it with your friends. You can easily share a link to the app in the Play Store by obeying these steps:

1. **Visit the app on your My Apps list.**

   Refer to the preceding section. Or, the app doesn't have to be on your list of apps; it can be any app in the Play Store. You only need to be viewing the app's description screen.

2. **Touch the Share button.**

   A menu appears, listing various apps and methods for sharing the app's Play Store link with your pals.

3. **Choose a sharing method.**

   For example, choose Messaging to send a link to the app in a text message.

4. **Use the chosen app to send the link.**

   What you need to do next depends on which sharing method you've chosen.

The result of completing these steps is that your friend receives a link. They can touch the link on their phone, or another Android device, and be whisked instantly to the Play Store, where they can view the app and easily install it on their Android gizmo.

You can share multiple apps by viewing the Apps menu and pressing the Menu soft button. Choose the Share App command. You see a list of all your phone's apps. Place a check mark by those you want to share, and then touch the Done button. Continue with Step 3 in the preceding list.

Updating an app

It's the Play Store app's duty to not only deliver new apps to you and help you manage them but also to inform you of app updates. Whenever a new version of any app is available, you see it flagged for updating, as shown in Figure 18-3. Updating the app to the latest version is cinchy.

From the My Apps list (refer to Figure 18-3), touch the Update button to update all apps for which automatic updating is allowed.

Some apps must be updated individually, as shown in Figure 18-3, in the Manual Updates section of the list. To update these apps, touch the green Update button, found to the right of the app's name. (Refer to Figure 18-3.) Touch the Update button on the app's information screen, and then choose Accept & Download.

To make updating easier, open an app's information screen and place a green check mark by the Allow Automatic Updating item.

- ✔ The updating process often involves downloading and installing a new version of the app. That's perfectly fine; your settings and any app information already stored on your phone (data files or high scores, for example) aren't changed by the update process.

- ✔ Updates to apps might also be indicated by the Updates Available notification icon, shown in the margin. Choose the Updates Available notification to be instantly whisked to the My Apps screen, where you can update your apps as described in this section.

Removing an app

You're free to kill off any app you've added to your phone, specifically those apps you've downloaded from the Play Store. To do so, heed these steps:

1. **Start the Play Store app.**

2. **Press the Menu soft button and choose My Apps.**

3. **Slide the screen to the left so that the All category appears atop the list.**

4. **Touch the app that offends you.**

   Choose an installed app. The apps labeled Free or Purchased aren't yet installed on your phone.

5. **Touch the Uninstall button.**

   If you see no Uninstall button, the app is one of the prepackaged apps that are included on your phone, which you cannot remove.

   Paid apps feature the Refund button rather than the Uninstall button — but only for a limited time. After the refund period has lapsed, the Refund button morphs into the Uninstall button.

6. **Touch the OK button to confirm.**

   The app is removed.

The app continues to appear in the All section of the My Apps screen even after it's been removed. After all, you downloaded the app once. That doesn't mean that it's installed.

- ✔ In most cases, if you uninstall a paid app right away, your credit card or account is fully refunded. The definition of "right away" depends on the app and is so stated on the app's description screen. The right-away period can last anywhere from 15 minutes to 24 hours.

> ✔ You can always reinstall paid apps that you've uninstalled. You aren't charged twice for doing so.
>
> ✔ The Galaxy Note has a handful of apps that you cannot remove. They include some of the basic Android apps (such as Phone and Contacts), but also some apps preinstalled by your cellular provider. Only if you hack into your phone using the rooting process can you remove those apps. I don't recommend it.

Controlling your apps

Your Galaxy Note features a secret, technical place where you can review and manage all installed apps. Shhhh! Don't tell anyone or else you'll be kicked out of the Secret Technical Place Club. It's *exclusive*.

To visit the Secret Technical Place, follow these steps:

1. **At the Home screen, press the Menu soft button.**

2. **Choose Settings, and then choose Applications.**

3. **Ensure that no one else is looking.**

4. **Choose Manage Applications.**

5. **Choose the All tab from the top of the screen.**

   A complete list of all apps installed on your phone is displayed — all of them, even secret apps that don't show up on the My Apps list in the Google Play Store.

6. **Touch an application name.**

   The app's info screen appears, showing lots of trivia about the app.

Among the trivia on the application's info screen, you'll find some useful buttons. These are my favorites:

Force Stop: Touch this button to halt a program run amok. For example, I had to stop an older Android app that continually made noise and offered no option to exit.

Uninstall: Touch the Uninstall button to remove the app, which is another way to accomplish the same steps described in the preceding section.

Refund: Freshly purchased apps feature the Refund button rather than the Uninstall button. Touch the Refund button to uninstall the paid app *and* get your money back. Be quick, though: After a given amount of time, anywhere between 15 minutes and 24 hours, the Refund button transforms itself back into the Uninstall button.

Move to SD Card: Touch this button to transfer the app from the phone's internal storage to the MicroSD card. Doing so can help free capacity on the phone's internal storage.

Move to Phone: Touch this button to transfer an app from the MicroSD card to the phone's internal storage. (This button replaces the Move to SD Card button when an app already dwells on the MicroSD card.)

Clear Cache: I've used this button to fix an app that doesn't work or just sits all stubborn on the screen. This trick doesn't work every time, but it's worth a try when an app seems slow or suddenly stops working.

Controversy is brewing in the Android community about whether to store apps on the phone's internal storage or MicroSD card. I prefer internal storage because the app stays with the phone and is always available. Further, shortcuts to apps stored internally don't disappear from the Home screen when you access the media card from your computer.

Apps Menu Organization

Most humans embrace consistency. That's fine because you never, ever, have to mess with the Apps menu, the place to find apps on your Galaxy Note. You can rely on banal predictability: New apps are installed on your phone and inserted into the Apps menu alphabetically. True, that jumbles everything around. So what can you do?

Why! You can eschew consistency and edit the Apps menu. It's cinchy, and it may help resolve some of your frustrations about the icons being jumbled every time a new app is installed.

Changing the Apps menu view

The Apps menu sports three views, as illustrated in Figure 18-4:

Customizable Grid: This view can be modified, as described in the next section.

Alphabetical Grid: This view is probably the one you use now. All apps appears in alphabetical order on a grid. New apps are inserted into the grid alphabetically, which jumbles everything.

Alphabetical List: I believe that no one uses this view. Apps appear in a simple list, requiring endless scrolling that leads to finger fatigue.

Customizable grid   Alphabetical grid   Alphabetical list

Figure 18-4: Different views on the Apps menu.

To change the Apps menu view, press the Menu soft button and choose the View Type command. Select a new view from the list.

Rearranging the Apps menu

The Customizable Grid option for viewing the Apps menu lets you rearrange and order all your phone's apps. Unlike the alphabetical views, the apps stay where you put them. You can even add more panels to the Apps menu and folders, to help keep things organized.

To begin redecorating the Apps menu, press the Menu soft button and choose the Edit command. If you haven't yet chosen Customizable Grid view, touch the Switch button to make the change.

Move an app by dragging its icon with your finger or the S Pen: Long-press the icon, and drag it to a blank part of the same page or to another page, right or left. Figure 18-5 illustrates how the editing screen looks.

Delete icon.

Long-press to drag an icon.

Modify the Dock.

Figure 18-5: Messin' with the Apps menu.

Though you can create folders on the Apps menu to help organize your apps, I don't recommend it. The folders are difficult to manage, and you can easily lose an app in a folder.

Don't delete an app by touching its red Minus button, illustrated in Figure 18-5. If you need to uninstall an app, use the techniques described earlier in this chapter.

When you're done editing the Apps menu, press the Back soft button.

The best way to access and manage your apps is to place shortcuts on the Home screen. See Chapter 22 for details.

Part V
Nuts and Bolts

The 5th Wave   By Rich Tennant

PCS PHONES

"So, what kind of roaming capabilities does this thing have?"

In this part . . .

There are three parts to using your Galaxy Note. The first is communications, which covers using the basic, boring phone as well as the more interesting ways to stay in touch. The second part consists of all the other wonderful things that the device does. The final part is the thing that few people talk about.

No, the final part to using your Galaxy Note isn't forbidden or salacious. It consists of the routine, the configuration, the maintenance, the ancillary information that I call "the nuts and bolts." Though these activities aren't showcased in ads or boasted about over cocktails, they're necessary and useful, and they're covered in this part of the book.

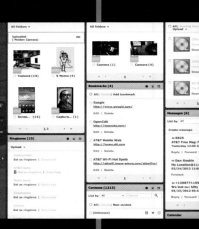

19

Everything Wireless

In This Chapter

▶ Using the digital cellular network

▶ Setting up Wi-Fi

▶ Connecting to a Wi-Fi network

▶ Establishing a mobile hotspot

▶ Sharing the Internet connection

▶ Configuring and using Bluetooth

▶ Printing on your Galaxy Note

*P*hones were born with wires attached. Telephone wires marched from coast to coast. Wires dwelled in the walls of your home. Wires connected the phone to the wall, and connected the handset to the phone's base. Wires were such a big deal that wireless phones of the 1980s were known by the moniker *cordless*. It was the dawn of a new age.

There's no point in having a truly mobile phone if you tether it to something by a wire. Though the Galaxy Note isn't completely wire-free, it's quite close. In fact, all the phone's basic forms of communications are accomplished using wireless methods, including the digital cellular signal, Wi-Fi networking, Bluetooth, and the wireless wizardry covered in this chapter.

It's a Wireless Life

Don't duck. Although if you could see all the wireless communications going on around you, you probably would duck. Or freak out.

An entire spectrum of wireless activity is darting about everywhere, unseen by human eyes. These wireless signals come from all over, even from satellites orbiting the earth. They let you talk, but (most importantly) they let you communicate with the Internet. This section explains how it's all done on the Galaxy Note.

Understanding the digital network

Of the many fees and charges on your monthly cell phone bill, the heftiest one is probably for the cellular data network. It isn't the wireless service you talk on (which is a much smaller charge), but it's important for a smartphone because your Galaxy Note uses the cellular data network to talk with the Internet.

Several types of cellular data network are available to your phone. The current network being used sports an icon that appears on the status bar. Here's a description of the variety of network types and their speed values:

4G LTE: The speed of this fourth generation of digital cellular network is comparable to standard Wi-Fi Internet access. It's fast. It also allows for both data and voice transmission at the same time.

4G / HSPA+: It isn't as fast as the full 4G LTE, but it's still faster than the 3G network. The speed is tolerable for surfing the web, watching YouTube videos, and downloading information from the Internet.

E / EDGE: The slowest data connection is the original.

The Galaxy Note always uses the fastest network available. Whenever a 4G LTE signal abounds, the phone uses it. Otherwise, the 4G data network is chosen, followed by E. Or, when no cellular data network is available, that part of the status bar is blank.

- ✔ When your phone is connected to a Wi-Fi network, it uses that network rather than the digital cellular network. In this case, the digital cellular network's speed icon is replaced on the status bar by the Wi-Fi Connected icon, shown in the margin.

- ✔ The digital cellular signal may still appear when you're using Wi-Fi. That's because some apps use that signal exclusively. Or something.

- ✔ You can still make phone calls when no data network is available. As long as the signal-strength bars on the phone's status bar show that a signal is present, you can receive and make phone calls.

- ✔ Accessing the digital cellular network isn't free. You likely signed up for some form of subscription plan for a certain quantity of data when you first received your Android phone. When you exceed that quantity, the costs can become prohibitive.

✔ The data subscription is based on the *quantity* of data you send and receive. At 4G LTE speeds, the prepaid threshold can be crossed quickly.

Activating the Wi-Fi

Wi-Fi is the same wireless networking standard used by computers for communicating with each other and the Internet. It's popular, and therefore Wi-Fi networks abound. You probably have one in your home or office. Stir in the various Wi-Fi networks at coffee shops, hotels, restaurants, libraries, airports, and elsewhere, and you can easily see how accessing a Wi-Fi network is a useful thing.

Making Wi-Fi work on your Galaxy Note requires two steps. First, you must activate Wi-Fi by turning on the phone's wireless radio. The second step is to connect to a specific wireless network.

Follow these steps to activate Wi-Fi on your Galaxy Note:

1. **At the Home screen, press the Menu soft button.**
2. **Choose Settings and then choose Wireless and Network.**
3. **Choose Wi-Fi Settings.**

   You see the Wi-Fi Settings screen, similar to the one shown in Figure 19-1.

4. **Choose Wi-Fi to place a green check mark by that option.**

   A green check mark indicates that the phone's Wi-Fi radio is activated.

Next, you connect the phone to a Wi-Fi network, which is covered in the next section.

To turn off Wi-Fi, repeat the steps in this section. Doing so turns off the phone's Wi-Fi access, disconnecting you from any networks.

✔ For fast Wi-Fi on-off action, you can use the Power Saving widget. It has various buttons that activate various phone features, most of which help save battery life. See Chapter 22 for more information about adding widgets to the Home screen.

✔ See Chapter 23 for help with extending the phone's battery life.

✔ Using Wi-Fi to connect to the Internet doesn't incur data usage charges.

The phone's Wi-Fi is on.

You'll be alerted to nearby Wi-Fi networks.

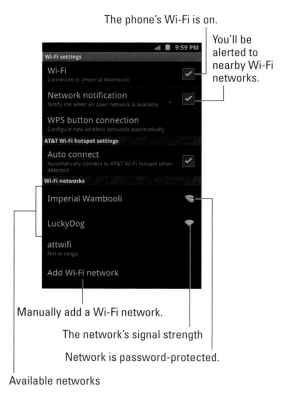

Manually add a Wi-Fi network.

The network's signal strength

Network is password-protected.

Available networks

Figure 19-1: Hunting down a wireless network.

Accessing a Wi-Fi network

After activating the Galaxy Note's Wi-Fi radio, you can connect to an available wireless network. Heed these steps:

1. **Press the Menu soft button while viewing the Home screen.**

2. **Choose Settings and then Wireless and Network.**

3. **Choose Wi-Fi Settings.**

   You see a list of available wireless networks displayed in the bottom area of the Wi-Fi Settings screen. (Refer to Figure 19-1.) When no wireless network is displayed, you're sort of out of luck regarding Wi-Fi access from your current location.

4. **Choose a wireless network from the list.**

In Figure 19-1, I chose the Imperial Wambooli network, which is my office network.

5. **If prompted, type the network password.**

Putting a green check mark in the Show Password box makes it easier to type a long, complex network password.

If the Wi-Fi network supports the WPS setup, you can connect by using the network PIN, pressing the Connection button on the wireless router, or using whatever other WPS method is used by the router.

6. **Touch the Connect button.**

Your phone should be immediately connected to the network. If not, try the password again.

When the phone is connected, you see the Wi-Fi status icon appear atop the touchscreen, as shown in the margin. This icon indicates that the phone's Wi-Fi is on, connected, and communicating with a Wi-Fi network.

Some wireless networks don't broadcast their names, which adds security but also makes accessing them more difficult. In these cases, choose the Add Wi-Fi Network command (refer to Figure 19-1) to manually add the network. You need to input the network name, or *SSID,* and the type of security. You also need the password, if one is used. You can obtain this information from the unfocused young lady with the lip ring who sold you coffee or from whoever is in charge of the wireless network at your location.

- Not every wireless network has a password.

- Some public networks are open to anyone, but you have to use the Web app to get on the web and find a login page that lets you access the network: Simply browse to any page on the Internet, and the login page shows up.

- The phone automatically remembers any Wi-Fi network it's connected to and its network password. The network is automatically connected as soon as the Galaxy Note is within range.

- To disconnect from a Wi-Fi network, simply turn off Wi-Fi on the phone. See the preceding section.

- A Wi-Fi network is faster than the 4G or HSPA+ cellular data network, so it makes sense to connect by Wi-Fi if the only available network is 4G.

- Use Wi-Fi whenever you plan to remain in one location for a while. Unlike a cellular data network, a Wi-Fi network's broadcast signal has a limited range. If you wander too far away, your phone loses the signal and is disconnected.

> ✔ WPS, or Wi-Fi Protected Setup, covers a variety of methods for easily connecting your phone to a Wi-Fi base station.

A Connection to Share

Your Galaxy Note deftly accesses the digital cellular signal. It can get on the Internet from any location where that signal is available. Your other mobile devices, such as a laptop computer? Well, unless these gizmos sport their own cellular modems, it's tough luck. Well, that is unless you bother to *share* the Galaxy Note's Internet connection. This section explains how it's done.

Before proceeding, be aware that the Mobile Hotspot or Internet Tethering options must be enabled on your cellular data plan. Yes, that's an extra cost, one that you probably skipped over when you signed up for the service. If the features aren't enabled, your Galaxy Note cannot perform the tasks described in this section.

Creating a mobile hotspot

The Mobile Hotspot feature allows your Galaxy Note to share its cellular data connection by creating its own Wi-Fi network. Other Wi-Fi devices — computers, laptops, other mobile devices — can then access that Wi-Fi network to enjoy a free ride on the Internet, courtesy of your Galaxy Note.

Well, it may not be free, because the feature comes at a premium price, but you get my point.

To set up a mobile hotspot on your phone, heed these steps:

1. **Turn off the Wi-Fi radio.**

   There's no point in creating a Wi-Fi hotspot where one is already available.

2. **Plug the phone into a power source.**

   The Mobile Hotspot feature draws a lot of power.

3. **At the Home screen, press the Menu soft button.**

4. **Choose Settings and then Wireless and Network.**

5. **Choose Tethering and Portable Hotspot.**

6. **Place a check mark by the Portable Wi-Fi Hotspot option.**

7. **Click the OK button to dismiss the warning.**

8. **If you're prompted, accept the terms and conditions to subscribe to the service that gives your phone mobile-hotspot abilities.**

   You must have the Mobile Hotspot feature enabled on your cellular provider's data plan. If not, you cannot activate the feature.

9. **Name your mobile hotspot and change the password, if you so desire.**

   If you've not yet set up a mobile hotspot, supply some information, such as the name of your hotspot and the password. You can change the name and password that are provided or keep them as is.

   Make a note of the password. You need it in order to log in to the mobile hotspot.

10. **Touch the OK button or the Save button to save your settings and start the hotspot.**

   You're done.

 When the mobile hotspot is active, the Mobile Hotspot notification appears on the phone's status bar, as shown in the margin.

To turn off the mobile hotspot, repeat Steps 3 through 6, but remove the check mark in Step 6.

- ✔ The range of the mobile hotspot is about 30 feet. Things such as walls and molten lava can interfere with the signal, shortening its range.

- ✔ Data usage fees apply when you use the mobile hotspot, and you pay them on top of the fee that your cellular provider may charge for the mobile hotspot service. These fees can add up quickly.

- ✔ Don't forget to turn off the mobile hotspot when you're done using it.

Tethering the Internet connection

A more intimate and direct way to share the Galaxy Note's digital cellular connection is to connect the phone directly to a computer and activate the tethering feature.

Yes, I am fully aware that tethering goes against the wireless theme of this chapter. Still, it remains a solid way to provide Internet access to another gizmo, such as a laptop or desktop computer.

Follow these steps to set up Internet tethering:

1. **Disable Wi-Fi.**

   You cannot tether the Wi-Fi connection, and the phone doesn't let you complete these steps with Wi-Fi on, so disable it. Directions are found earlier in this chapter.

2. **Connect the Galaxy Note to another mobile device by using the USB cable.**

3. **On the phone, at the Home screen, press the Menu soft button.**

4. **Choose Settings and then Wireless and Network.**

5. **Choose Tethering and Portable Hotspot.**

6. **Place a green check mark by the USB Tethering item.**

   Internet tethering is activated. Well, unless your data plan doesn't support it, in which case nothing happens.

The other device should instantly recognize your Galaxy Note as a "modem" with Internet access. Further configuration may be required, which depends on the device using the tethered connection. For example, you may be prompted on the PC to locate and install software for your phone. Do so: Accept the installation of new software when you're prompted by Windows.

 When Internet tethering is active, the Tethering Active notification appears, as shown in the margin. Yes, it's the same notification icon that's used for the Mobile Hotspot feature. Apparently, the production department at AT&T was on vacation that week.

To end Internet tethering, repeat Steps 3 through 6, but remove the green check mark in Step 6. You can then disconnect the USB cable.

 Sharing the digital network connection incurs data usage charges against your cellular data plan. Be mindful of your data usage when you're sharing a connection.

The Bluetooth Way

If the terms *Wi-Fi* and *digital cellular connection* don't leave you completely befuddled, I have another term for you. It's *Bluetooth*, and it has nothing to do with the color blue or dental hygiene.

Bluetooth is a wireless protocol for communication between two or more Bluetooth-equipped devices. Your Galaxy Note just happens to be Bluetooth-equipped, so it too can chat it up with Bluetooth devices, such as those earphone-speakers that make you look like you have a tiny robot parasite on the side of your head.

The dawn of Wi-Fi Direct

Wi-Fi Direct is a competing standard for Bluetooth. Wi-Fi Direct is based on the same Wi-Fi technology that's included in your Galaxy Note, but it doesn't operate the same. Basically, Wi-Fi Direct allows your phone to communicate with other Wi-Fi Direct devices for sharing information, such as transferring photos from the Gallery app to a Wi-Fi Direct-enabled digital picture frame.

Wi-Fi Direct is an emerging technology, though it will probably become more popular. Until it does, Bluetooth remains the best option for connecting local devices, such as headsets and printers, to your Galaxy Note.

Activating Bluetooth

You must turn on the phone's Bluetooth networking before you can use one of those Borg-earpiece implants and join the ranks of walking nerds. Here's how to turn on Bluetooth:

1. **At the Home screen, press the Menu soft button.**

2. **Choose Settings, and then choose Wireless and Network.**

3. **Choose Bluetooth Settings.**

4. **Place a green check mark next to the Bluetooth item.**

   If a little green check mark already appears by the Bluetooth option, Bluetooth is already on.

From the now-he-tells-us department, the quick way to activate Bluetooth is to use the Quick Actions found on the notifications screen: Pull down the notifications, and touch the Bluetooth button. *Voilà.*

To turn off Bluetooth, repeat the steps in this section.

~ When Bluetooth is on, the Bluetooth status icon appears. It uses the Bluetooth logo, shown in the margin.

~ Activating Bluetooth can quickly drain the phone's battery. I recommend using Bluetooth only when necessary and turning it off when you're done.

Using a Bluetooth headset

Bluetooth can be used to pair the phone with a variety of gizmos, including your computer (if it's Bluetooth-equipped) and even Bluetooth printers, as described in the next section. Even so, the most common Bluetooth gizmo to use with a cell phone is a wireless headset.

To make the Bluetooth connection between your phone and a set of those I'm-so-cool earphones, follow these steps:

1. **Ensure that Bluetooth is on.**

   Refer to the preceding section.

2. **Turn on the Bluetooth headset.**

3. **At the Home screen, press the Menu soft button and choose Settings.**

4. **Choose Wireless and Network and then Bluetooth Settings.**

   The Bluetooth Settings screen appears.

5. **Choose Scan for Devices.**

   If you've activated the Motion feature on your Galaxy Note, you can vigorously shake the phone to scan for Bluetooth devices. See Chapter 3 for information on the Shake to Activate feature.

6. **If necessary, press the main button on the Bluetooth gizmo.**

   The *main* button is the one you use to answer the phone. You may have to press and hold the button.

   Eventually, the device should appear on the screen, or you see its code number. In Figure 19-2, the headset is named Nica.

   If you don't see the device, repeat Steps 5 and 6.

7. **Choose the device.**

8. **If necessary, input the device's passcode.**

   It's usually a four-digit number, and quite often it's simply 1234 or 0000.

When the device is connected, you can stick it in your ear and press its main Answer button when the phone rings. Chat away.

If you tire of using the Bluetooth headset, you can touch the Headset button on the touchscreen to use the phone's own speaker and microphone. (Refer to Figure 5-2, in Chapter 5, for the location of the Headset button.)

  ✔ You can turn the Bluetooth earphone on or off after it's been paired. As long as the Galaxy Note's Bluetooth radio is on, the phone instantly recognizes the earphone when you turn it on.

✔ You can unpair a device by locating it on the Bluetooth Settings screen. (Refer to Figure 19-2.) Long-press the name of the device, and choose either the Disconnect or Disconnect and Unpair command.

✔ Don't forget to turn off the earpiece when you're done with it. The earpiece has a battery, and it continues to drain when you forget to turn the thing off.

Allow other Bluetooth devices to see the phone.

Activate Bluetooth.

Bluetooth is active.

Find Bluetooth gizmos.

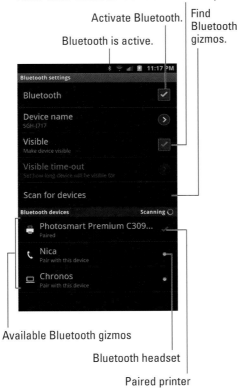

Available Bluetooth gizmos

Bluetooth headset

Paired printer

Figure 19-2: The Bluetooth Settings screen.

Printing to a Bluetooth printer

There are two ways to print something on your Galaxy Note, and both of them probably involve buying something you don't already have. And I'm sure that you just love spending money, so here it is: You need either a Bluetooth printer or a Samsung printer. I don't have a Samsung printer, but I do have a Bluetooth printer, so this section covers only the Bluetooth printing option.

Before you can print, ensure that your Galaxy Note is paired with a Bluetooth printer. (Refer to the earlier section "Using a Bluetooth headset.") Pairing a printer works exactly like pairing a headset: You make the printer discoverable and, possibly, type the printer's passcode on your phone to complete the connection.

You may also need to make the Galaxy Note visible to get it connected to the printer. On the Bluetooth Settings screen (refer to Figure 19-2), place a green check mark by the Visible item. Then direct the printer to search for Bluetooth devices. Choose the Galaxy Note, or device SGH-I717, on the printer's control panel to pair it with the phone.

When the phone and the Bluetooth printer are properly paired, you see the printer listed in the Bluetooth Devices section on the Bluetooth Settings screen, as shown in Figure 19-2. Even if it says *Paired but not connected,* you're ready to go.

Whew.

Assuming that the Bluetooth printer is on and ready to print, obey these steps to print something from your Galaxy Note phone:

1. **View an image in the Gallery, an S Memo, a web page, or a document that you want to print.**

   You can capture any screen on the Galaxy Note by using the S Pen and then paste the image into an S Memo. You can then print the S Memo. See Chapter 17 for details.

2. **Choose the Share Via command.**

   If the Share Via button isn't visible in the app, press the Menu soft button to look for the Share Via command. The command may also be called Share.

   For the Web app, share a web page by pressing the Menu soft button, choosing More, and then choosing Share Page.

3. **Choose Bluetooth from the menu.**

   When no Bluetooth option is on the menu, try using the Send Via command in Step 2. If Bluetooth is missing from the Send Via menu, printing the item using Bluetooth isn't possible.

4. **Choose your Bluetooth printer from the list of items on the Bluetooth Device Picker screen.**

5. **If a prompt appears on the printer, confirm that the phone is printing a document.**

   The document is uploaded (sent from the phone to the printer), and then it prints.

Some Bluetooth printers may require you press a button to proceed with printing. You need to confirm that a document has been sent and that it's okay to print.

✔ The Print command that's found in several apps is linked directly to printing on a Samsung printer. If no Samsung printer is lurking nearby, the phone alerts you that printing isn't possible.

✔ Bluetooth printers sport the Bluetooth logo somewhere.

✔ When you print images from the My Gallery app, I recommend that you load up the printer with photo paper for the best results. You can obtain photo paper at any computer- or office-supply store.

20

Sync, Share, and Store

In This Chapter

▶ Getting the phone and a computer to talk

▶ Mounting the phone as computer storage

▶ Synchronizing media

▶ Wireless file sharing with Kies Air

▶ Copying files between the phone and computer

▶ Understanding phone storage

*Y*ou have a phone. You have a computer. How do you start them talking? Better still, how can you get a picture from your phone into your computer, or vice versa? The answer is that you bind the two with some twine, hire a witch doctor, and howl at the full moon. Though that strategy may not work, it's often how the process seems to go.

It's not that difficult to put your phone and computer on speaking terms. After they're connected, you can share information back and forth, copying files hither and thither and keeping everything synchronized. I've written down the details in this chapter so that you don't have to memorize anything. Just follow the steps. You'll end up saving a lot of money on witch doctors.

Synchronizing...

The USB Connection

The most direct way to mate your phone with your computer is to use the USB cable that comes with the Galaxy Note. Often, the process works smoothly. This section has the details.

Connecting the USB cable

The USB connection is made by using a USB cable, similar to the one that comes in the box with your Galaxy Note. The cable's A end plugs into the computer. The other end, known as the *micro-USB connector,* plugs into the phone's USB hole.

Computer nerds call the USB hole a *port.*

The cable plugs in only one way, so you can't connect the computer and phone improperly, backward, or upside down. That's good.

When your phone is connected via USB cable to a computer, you see the USB Connection notification icon appear, similar to the one shown in the margin. Refer to the later section "Unmounting the phone's USB storage" to see what can be done with this notification.

✔ If possible, plug the USB cable into the computer itself, not into a USB hub. The phone-computer connection works best with a powered USB port.

✔ If you have no USB cable for your phone, you can buy one at any computer- or office-supply store. Get a USB-A-male-to-micro–USB cable.

✔ A flurry of activity takes place when you first connect your Galaxy Note to a Windows PC. Notifications pop up about new software that's installed, or you may see the AutoPlay dialog box, prompting you to install software. Do so.

Making the MTP storage connection

Upon successfully connecting your Galaxy Note to the computer, you most likely see the MTP screen, similar to the one shown in Figure 20-1. MTP typically stands for "Meet the Press," but in the technology world it refers to the Media Transfer Protocol, a set of rules and whatnot for moving media files between gizmos.

There's really nothing you can do with the MTP screen; synchronization takes place automatically, and the screen eventually goes away.

See the later section "Synchronize Your Stuff" to see how to use the basic, USB MTP connection.

Mounting the phone as USB storage

A more traditional approach to the USB connection is to configure the Galaxy Note as a USB storage device. The computer then recognizes the phone as it would a thumb drive, which makes moving files back and forth a lot easier.

USB connection notification

Figure 20-1: The MTP Connection screen.

Here's how to configure your Galaxy Note as a USB storage device mounted into your computer's storage system:

1. **Plug the USB cable into your computer, but don't connect it to your phone.**

   Keep the phone unplugged for now.

2. **At the Home screen, press the Menu soft button.**

3. **Choose Settings and then Wireless and Network.**

4. **Choose USB Utilities.**

5. **Touch the Connect Storage to PC button.**

6. **Attach the USB cable to the phone.**

   You see the happy, green Android icon.

7. **Touch the Connect USB storage button.**

   The Galaxy Note mounts its storage, both internal and the MicroSD card, into your computer's storage system. Upon success, the happy, green Android icon turns into a happy, orange Android icon.

You can now access the phone's storage from your computer:

> **Windows PC:** On a PC, open the Computer or My Computer window to find the Galaxy Note's storage appearing as one or two icons.

Regrettably, the drive letters and names assigned to those icons varies, so I can't tell you specifically which they are. (Blame Microsoft, not Google.)

Macintosh: On the Mac, the phone's internal and external storage appear as two generic disk icons on the right side of the Mac's screen. On my Mac, they're both named NO NAME. One is for internal storage, and the other for the MicroSD card. Which is which? I dunno.

Directions for copying files between your computer and the Galaxy Note's storage are found later in this chapter.

Though its storage is mounted into the computer's file system, you cannot access any information stored on the phone. That means you can't use the address book, view photos in the Gallery, or listen to music, for example. Only after you unmount the storage does that information become available again.

- After you connect the Galaxy Note to a Windows computer, you may see two AutoPlay dialog boxes. That's one for each storage media on the phone — internal and MicroSD. See the later section "Galaxy Note Storage Mysteries" for boring details on the phone's storage.

- When you're done accessing information, you should properly unmount the phone from your computer system. See the next section.

Unmounting the phone's USB storage

When you're done accessing the phone's storage from your computer, you should properly unmount that storage. Obey these steps:

1. **Ensure that you're no longer using the phone's storage or accessing it from your computer.**

   Close any open folder windows, as well as any programs you've opened that are accessing files on the phone.

2. **On a Macintosh, eject the phone's storage: Drag the phone's storage icons to the Trash.**

   This step is important! You must unmount the phone's storage on the Mac before you break the connection on your phone. If you forget, the Mac harangues you with guilt.

3. **On the phone, if you're not viewing the orange Android icon on the USB Mass Storage screen, pull down the notifications and choose the USB item, Turn Off USB Storage.**

4. **Touch the Disconnect Storage From PC button.**

   The phone is unmounted from the computer's storage system.

5. **You can now disconnect the USB cable from the phone, and from the computer.**

   You don't need to remove the cable. The phone's storage is unmounted, so at this point the phone continues to use the USB cable to recharge its battery.

After the phone's storage has been properly unmounted, you're again free to use the phone to its full abilities to access contacts, pictures, and music, for example.

 ✐ There's no need to unmount the phone's USB storage if you're just using the MTP connection, described earlier in this chapter.

 ✐ Never yank out the USB cable. Never! Never! Never! Doing so can damage the phone's storage, which is A Bad Thing. Instead, always properly unmount the Galaxy Note from the computer's storage system when you're done accessing files, as described in this section.

Synchronize Your Stuff

Synchronize can seem like a big, scary word, but it's necessary. You have information on your computer. You have information on the phone. Synchronization (an even bigger, scarier word) is the process of matching up the files on both devices. The method can be pleasant, and it can be ugly. This section explores both.

Synchronizing with doubleTwist

One of the most popular ways to move information between an Android phone such as your Galaxy Note and a computer is to use the third-party utility doubleTwist. This amazing program is free, and it's available at www. doubletwist.com.

doubleTwist isn't an Android app. You use it on your computer, either a PC or a Macintosh. The program lets you easily synchronize pictures, music, videos, and web page subscriptions between your computer and its media libraries and any portable device, such as your phone.

To use doubleTwist, connect the Galaxy Note to your computer using a USB cable. The standard MTP connection is all that's necessary; you don't need to mount the phone as a USB storage device.

Start up the doubleTwist program if it doesn't start by itself. The simple doubleTwist interface is illustrated in Figure 20-2.

Choose items to sync.

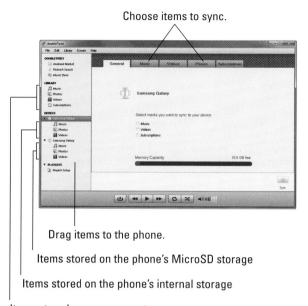

Drag items to the phone.

Items stored on the phone's MicroSD storage

Items stored on the phone's internal storage

Items stored on your computer

Figure 20-2: The doubleTwist utility.

The way I use doubleTwist is to drag and drop media either from my computer to the phone or the other way around. Use the program's interface to browse for media, as shown in Figure 20-2.

✔ doubleTwist doesn't synchronize contact information. Contact information is automatically synchronized between your phone's address book and Google. The information can also be synchronized manually; see the later section "Copying files the manual way."

✔ Information about synchronizing music between your computer and phone is covered in Chapter 16.

Connecting wirelessly with Kies Air

A perfectly wireless way to connect your phone and computer is to use the Kies Air app. As long as both your phone and computer can access the same Wi-Fi network, the connection is made and files can be transferred from the phone to that computer, or from that computer to the phone.

Both your computer and the Galaxy Note must be connected to the same wireless (Wi-Fi) network for the connection to work.

Follow these steps to use Kies Air to share files with your computer:

1. **Ensure that your Galaxy Note is connected to the Wi-Fi network.**

   Refer to Chapter 19 for directions.

2. **Start the Kies Air app.**

   It's found on the Apps menu.

3. **Touch the Start button.**

   Kies Air should immediately recognize your Wi-Fi network. It now sits and waits for an incoming request from your computer.

4. **On your computer, open the web browser app, such as Internet Explorer, Safari, or Firefox.**

5. **On your computer, type the URL listed on the phone's screen into the web browser's address box.**

   On my phone's screen, I see the URL `http://192.168.1.120:8080`.

   After typing the URL into your computer's web browser, you see an Access Request prompt on your phone. The prompt should state the name of the computer that's requesting access.

6. **On your phone, touch the Allow button.**

   The phone and the computer are now connected via the Wi-Fi network.

A web page appears on the computer in the web browser's window, similar to the one shown in Figure 20-3. The web page is being hosted by the phone. It allows access to the phone's resources, as illustrated in the figure.

Browse the various categories on the web page to explore files and media on your phone. To download an item, click the Download link. The item is transferred to your computer just like any file you download from the Internet, though the download comes from your Galaxy Note.

To send a file to the phone, click an Upload link, as illustrated in Figure 20-3. Use the Upload dialog box to find a file. Click to select that file, and then click the OK button to send it from the computer to the phone.

To end the Kies Air connection, touch the Stop button on your phone's screen. You can then close the web browser window on your computer.

   ✔ While the connection is active, you can quickly switch to the Kies Air app on your phone by choosing the Kies Air notification.

   ✔ My guess is that Kies is pronounced "kees." I have no idea what it stands for or whether it's even an acronym.

✔ Don't click the Back button on your computer's web browser screen when using the Kies Air website. Use the controls on the web page itself to navigate.

Items you can sync   View an album.   Copy music to the phone.

Click to return to top level.   Upload a video.   Copy music to the computer.

Categories

Figure 20-3: Kies Air web page on a computer.

Where the phone's files lurk

Files on your phone don't randomly float around, like marbles in a paper bag. Nope, as on your computer, files on the phone are organized into folders. Certain files wind up in specific locations on Android phones. The folders may have slightly different names, but, generally speaking, you can find common files in these locations:

`/download`: This folder contains files you've downloaded using the Web app.

`/DCIM/Camera`: Pictures and videos are stored in this folder.

`/Music`: The Music app organizes your phone's music into this folder. Subfolders are organized by artist.

These folders can exist on either the internal storage or MicroSD card. When you can't find the file or folder you're looking for on one media, look on the other.

Copying files the manual way

When you can't get software on your computer to synchronize automatically, you have to resort to doing the old manual connection. Yes, it can be complex. And bothersome. And tedious. But it's often the only way to get some information out of the phone and on to a computer, or vice versa.

Follow these steps to copy files between your computer and your Android phone:

1. **Connect the phone to the computer as USB storage.**

   Refer to the earlier section, "Mounting the phone as USB storage" for directions. You need to mount the phone's storage to your computer as though the phone were a USB thumb drive.

2a. **On a PC, in the AutoPlay dialog box, choose the option Open Folder to View Files.**

   The option might instead read Open Device to View Files.

   You see a folder window appear, which looks like any common folder in Windows. The difference is that the files and folders in this window are on the phone, not on your computer.

   Use the second AutoPlay dialog box to repeat this process for the phone's other storage (internal or MicroSD).

2b. **On a Macintosh, open the removable drive icon(s) to access the phone's storage.**

   The Mac uses generic, removable drive icons to represent the phone's storage. If two icons appear, one represents the phone's internal storage, and the second is for the phone's MicroSD card or removable storage.

3. **Open a folder window on your computer.**

   It's either the folder from which you're copying files to the phone or the folder that will receive files from the phone — for example, the `Documents` folder.

   If you're copying files from the phone to your computer, use the `Pictures` folder for pictures and videos, and use the `Documents` folder for everything else.

4. **Drag the file icons from one folder window to the other to copy them between the phone and computer.**

   Use Figure 20-4 as your guide.

5. **When you're done, properly unmount the phone's storage from your computer's storage system and disconnect the USB cable.**

   You must eject the phone's storage icon(s) from the Macintosh computer before you can turn off USB storage on the phone.

The phone's internal storage is Drive I on this PC.

The phone's MicroSD is Drive H on this PC.

Specific folders on the phone

Drag files to here to copy to the root.

Files on your computer

Files on the Galaxy Note

Figure 20-4: Copying files to the phone.

Any files you've copied to the phone are now stored on either the phone's internal storage or the MicroSD card. What you do with these files next depends on the reasons you copied the files: To view pictures, use the Gallery; to import vCards, use the Contacts app; to listen to music, use the Music Player; and so on.

✔ It doesn't matter to which storage location you copy files — internal storage or MicroSD card (removable storage). I recommend using the MicroSD card because the phone seems to prioritize its internal storage, and it can fill up quickly.

✔ Quite a few files can be found in the *root* folder, the main folder on the phone's MicroSD card, which you see when the phone is mounted into your computer's storage system and you open its folder.

✔ A good understanding of basic file operations is necessary to get the most benefit from transferring files between your computer and the phone. These basic operations include copying, moving, renaming, and deleting. It also helps to be familiar with the concept of folders. A doctorate in entanglement theory is optional.

Galaxy Note Storage Mysteries

Information on your phone (pictures, videos, music) is stored in two places: on the removable MicroSD card or on the phone's internal storage. That's about all you need to know, though if you're willing to explore the concept further — including the scary proposition of file management on a cell phone — keep reading.

Generally speaking, you use specific apps to access the stuff stored on your phone — for example, the Gallery app to view pictures or the Music app to listen to tunes. Beyond that, you can employ some nerdy apps to see where stuff dwells on your phone.

Using the Downloads app

Any files flown into your phone from the far-flung Internet are found easily by using the Downloads app. It's found on the Apps menu, and it keeps track of any and all files downloaded to the phone, organized by date.

- To view a document, choose it from the list in the Downloads app. The download is opened in whichever app views that type of document: Gallery, Music, or another relevant app. The phone informs you when a document cannot be viewed by any app installed on the phone.

- You can clean up the file list in the Downloads app: Touch the check box next to an item to place a green check mark there. Touch the Delete button to remove the file.

Exploring your phone's files

Your Galaxy Note comes with a file management app, provided for the scary opportunity to explore your phone's files just as you would explore files on your computer. It's the My Files app, and, in fact, it works similarly to the File Explorer in Windows or the Finder on the Macintosh

Using the My Files app works like this:

1. **Start the My Files app.**

   It's found on the Apps menu. The main screen is shown in Figure 20-5.

2. **Browse the files just as you would do on a computer.**

   If you're familiar with computer file management, you'll be right at home amid the folder and file icons: Touch a folder icon to open it and see which subfolders and files dwell inside. Touch a file icon to preview it.

3. **To manage a file or folder, long-press it.**

A menu appears, where you can perform typical file management operations: delete, rename, copy, or move, for example.

Go to Home level.

Root, or Home, level | Go up one level.

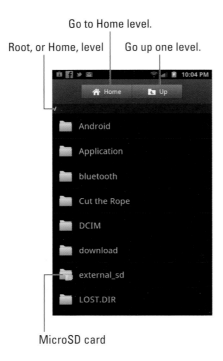

MicroSD card

Figure 20-5: File management with the My Files app.

You can press the Home soft button when you're done being frightened by file management in the My Files app.

✔ The files you see at the top level in the My Files app represent the phone's internal storage. To view files on the MicroSD card, choose the external_sd folder, as shown in Figure 20-5.

✔ You can also examine files and folders on your phone by mounting the phone's storage to a computer system. This method is easier to manage because you have access to a full-size screen and keyboard; plus, a computer mouse to move things around. See the earlier section, "Copying files the manual way."

Take It Elsewhere

*Y*ou can take your phone with you wherever you go. It's small and portable. But whether you can *use* the phone is another question. Wander too far from your cellular provider's signal, and you witness the curiosity of roaming. Then there's the ability to make calls both to and from strange and distant locales. Yep, plenty of issues are involved when you take your Galaxy Note elsewhere.

Where the Phone Roams

The word *roam* takes on an entirely new meaning when it's applied to a cell phone. It means that your phone receives a cell signal whenever you're outside your cell phone carrier's operating area. In that case, your phone is *roaming*.

Roaming sounds handy, but there's a catch: It almost always involves a surcharge for using another cellular service — an *unpleasant* surcharge.

Relax: Your Galaxy Note alerts you whenever you're roaming. The Roaming icon appears at the top of the screen, in the status area. You may even see the word *Roaming* on the lock screen and potentially witness the name of a cellular provider other than AT&T adorning that same screen.

There's little you can do to avoid incurring roaming surcharges when making or receiving phone calls. Well, yes: You can wait until you're back in an area serviced by your primary cellular provider. You can, however, altogether avoid using the other network's data services while roaming. Follow these steps:

1. **At the Home screen, press the Menu soft button.**
2. **Choose Settings.**
3. **Choose Wireless and Network and then Mobile Networks.**
4. **Ensure that the Data Roaming option isn't selected.**

   Remove the green check mark by Data Roaming.

Your phone can still access the Internet over the Wi-Fi connection while it's roaming. Setting up a Wi-Fi connection doesn't make you incur extra charges, unless you have to pay to get on the wireless network. See Chapter 19 for more information about Wi-Fi.

Another network service you might want to disable while roaming has to do with multimedia, or *MMS*, text messages. To avoid surcharges from another cellular network for downloading an MMS message, follow these steps:

1. **Open the Messaging app.**
2. **If the screen shows a specific conversation, press the Back soft button to return to the main messaging screen.**

   (It's the screen that lists all your conversations.)
3. **Touch the Menu soft button.**
4. **Choose the Settings command.**
5. **Remove the green check mark by the Auto-Retrieve option.**

   Or, if the item isn't selected, you're good to go — literally.

When the phone is roaming, you may see the text *Emergency Calls Only* displayed on the lock screen.

Airplane Mode

If you've been flying recently, you're already familiar with the airlines' cell phone rules: Placing a call on your cell phone while on an airborne plane is strictly forbidden. That's because, if you did, the navigation system would completely screw up and the plane would invert and crash into a nearby mountain. The FCC is so certain of disaster that, even if no mountains are around, one will pop up the second you turn on your phone, and the plane will fireball into it.

Seriously, you're not supposed to use a cell phone when flying. Specifically, you're not allowed you make calls in the air. You can, however, use your phone to listen to music or play games or do anything else that doesn't require a cellular connection. The secret is to place the phone in *Airplane mode.*

The most convenient way to place the Galaxy Note in Airplane mode is to press and hold the Power Lock button. From the menu, choose Airplane Mode. You don't even need to unlock the phone to perform this operation.

The most inconvenient way to put the phone into Airplane mode is to follow these steps:

1. **At the Home screen, press the Menu soft button.**
2. **Choose Settings, and then choose Wireless and Network.**
3. **Touch the square by Airplane Mode to set the green check mark.**

   Airplane mode is active.

When the phone is in Airplane mode, a special icon appears in the status area, similar to the one shown in the margin. You might also see the text *No Service* appear on the phone's lock screen.

To exit Airplane mode, repeat the steps in this section. On the Wireless & Network Settings screen, remove the green check mark by touching the square next to Airplane Mode.

✐ Officially, your cell phone must be powered *off* when the plane is taking off or landing. See Chapter 2 for information on turning off the phone.

✐ Bluetooth networking is disabled in Airplane mode. See Chapter 19 for more information on Bluetooth.

✐ You can compose e-mail while the phone is in Airplane mode. No messages are sent until you disable Airplane mode and connect again with a data network. Unless:

✐ Many airlines now feature onboard wireless networking. You can turn on wireless networking for your Android phone and use a wireless network in the air: Simply activate the Wi-Fi feature, per the directions in Chapter 19, after placing the phone in Airplane mode — well, after the flight attendant tells you that it's okay to do so.

✐ A move is afoot to repeal the rules about using cell phones in-flight. If they're repealed, you may be allowed to use your cell phone the entire time you're on the plane, including during landing and takeoff. You may even be allowed to make calls. If the rules change, such limitations will be set by the airlines, not by the government.

Galaxy Note air-travel tips

I don't consider myself a frequent flyer, though I travel several times a year. I do it often enough that I wish the airports had separate lines for security: one for seasoned travelers, one for families, and one, of course, for frickin' idiots. The last category would have to be disguised by placing a Bonus Coupons sign or a Free Snacks banner over the metal detector. That would weed 'em out.

Here are some of my tips for traveling with your cell phone on an airline:

✔ **Charge your phone before you leave.** This tip probably goes without saying, but you'll be happier with a full cell phone charge to start your journey.

✔ **Take a cell phone charger with you.** Many airports feature USB chargers, so you might need only a USB-to-micro–USB cable. Still, why risk it? Bring the entire charger with you.

✔ **At the security checkpoint, place your phone in a bin.** Add to the bin all your other electronic devices, keys, brass knuckles, grenades, and so on. I know from experience that leaving your cell phone in your pocket most definitely sets off airport metal detectors.

✔ **When the flight crew asks you to *turn off* your cell phone for takeoff and landing, obey the command.** That's *turn off,* as in power off the phone or shut it down. It doesn't mean that you place the phone in Airplane mode. Turn it off.

✔ **Use the phone's Calendar app to keep track of flights.** The combination of airline and flight number can serve as the event title. For the event time, I insert takeoff and landing schedules. For the location, I add the origin and destination airport codes. Remember to input the proper time zones. Referencing the phone from your airplane seat or a busy terminal is much handier than fussing with travel papers. See Chapter 17 for more information on the Calendar app.

✔ **Some airlines feature Android apps you can use while traveling.** Rather than hang on to a boarding pass printed by your computer, for example, you just present your phone to the scanner.

✔ **Some apps that you can use to organize your travel details are similar to, but more sophisticated than, using the Calendar app.** Visit the Google Play Store to search for *travel* or *airline* and find a host of apps.

International Calling

You can use your Galaxy Note to dial up folks who live in other countries. You can also take your cell phone overseas and use it in another country. Completing either task isn't as difficult as properly posing for a passport photo, but it can become frustrating and expensive when you don't know your way around.

Dialing an international number

A phone is a bell that anyone in the world can ring. To prove it, all you need is the phone number of anyone in the world. Dial the number using your phone, and, as long as you both speak the same language, you're talking!

To make an international call from your phone, you merely need to know the foreign phone number. The number includes the international country-code prefix, followed by the number.

Before dialing the international country-code prefix, you must first dial a plus sign (+) when using the Dialer app. The + symbol is the *country exit code,* which must be dialed in order to flee the national phone system and access the international phone system. For example, to dial Finland on your phone, you dial +358 and then the number in Finland. The +358 is the exit code (+) plus the international code for Finland (358).

To produce the + code in an international phone number, press and hold the 0 key on the Phone app's keypad. Then input the country prefix and the phone number. Touch the green Dial button to complete the call.

- ✓ You also pay a surcharge for sending text messages abroad. You have to contact your cellular provider to find its text message rates. Generally, providers have two rates — one for sending and another for receiving messages.

- ✓ If texting charges vex you, remember that e-mail is free. There are also alternative ways to chat, such as Google Talk and Skype, both covered in Chapter 12.

- ✓ In most cases, dialing an international number involves a time zone difference. Before you dial, be aware of what time it is in the country or location you're calling.

- ✓ Dialing internationally also involves surcharges, unless your cell phone plan already provides for international dialing.

- ✓ The + character isn't a number separator. When you see an international number listed as 011+20+xxxxxxx, do not insert the + character in the number. Instead, dial +20 and then the rest of the international phone number.

- ✓ International calls fail for a number of reasons. One of the most common is that the recipient's phone company or service blocks incoming international calls or calls from cell phones.

✔ Another reason that international calls fail is the zero reason: Oftentimes, you must leave out any zero in the phone number that follows the country code. So, if the country code is 254 for Kenya and the phone number starts with 012, you dial +254 for Kenya and then 12 and the rest of the number. Omit the leading zero.

✔ Know which type of phone you're calling internationally — cell phone or landline. The reason is that an international call to a cell phone often involves a surcharge that doesn't apply to a landline.

Making international calls with Skype

One of the easiest, and cheapest, ways to make international calls on your Galaxy Note is to use the Skype app. If you haven't already installed it (refer to Chapter 12), install it now to take advantage of its international calling abilities. Search for *Skype* at the Google Play Store, or use the QR Code in the margin to download Skype to your phone.

You can use Skype to contact overseas Skype users at no cost. That's because Skype uses the Internet for basic communications, so as long as you stay under your monthly data usage, Skype-to-Skype calls are free. Refer to Chapter 12 for details.

Beyond Skype-to-Skype calls, you can use Skype Credit to dial internationally to any phone. You can dial from the United States to a foreign country as well as from a foreign country home.

To make an international call, log in to Skype as you normally would. At the main Skype screen, choose the Call Phones command. Punch in the number, including the plus-sign (+) symbol for international access, as described earlier in this chapter and shown in Figure 21-1. Touch the green Call button to make the call.

After the call is connected by Skype, the phone's touchscreen looks similar to the way it looks when you regularly place calls. You can use the keypad, if necessary, mute the call, or put the phone on speaker, for example.

When you're finished with the call, touch the End button.

✔ See Chapter 12 for more information on using Skype with your Galaxy Note.

✔ You're always signed in to Skype unless you sign out. Pressing the Home soft button to switch to another app doesn't sign you out of Skype.

✔ To sign out of Skype, press the Menu soft button at the main Skype screen and choose Sign Out. If the Sign Out command isn't visible at first, touch the More command to find it.

Choose a country. Skype contacts

Skype notification

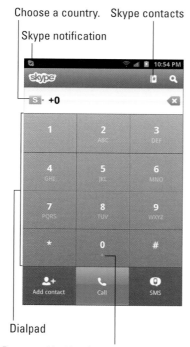

Dialpad

Press and hold to insert a + in the number.

Figure 21-1: Calling internationally with Skype.

Taking your Galaxy Note abroad

The easiest way to use a cell phone abroad is to rent or buy one in the country where you plan to stay. I'm serious: Often, international roaming charges are so high that it's cheaper to buy a simple throwaway cell phone wherever you go, especially if you plan to stay there for a while.

When you opt to use your own phone rather than buy a local phone, things should run smoothly — if a compatible cellular service is in your location. Not every cell phone uses the same network as the Galaxy Note, and, of course, not every foreign country uses the same cellular network. Things must match before the phone can work. Plus, you may have to deal with foreign-carrier roaming charges.

The key to determining whether your phone is usable in a foreign country is to turn it on. The name of that country's compatible cellular service should show up at the top of the phone, where the name of your carrier appears on the main screen. So, where your phone once said *AT&T,* it may say *Wambooli Telcom,* for example, when you're overseas.

- ✔ You receive calls on your cell phone internationally as long as the phone can access the network. Your friends need only dial your cell phone number as they normally do; the phone system automatically forwards your calls to wherever you are in the world.

- ✔ The person calling you pays nothing extra when you're off romping the globe with your Android phone. Nope — *you* pay extra for the call.

- ✔ While you're abroad, you dial internationally. When calling the United States, you use a ten-digit number (phone number plus area code). You may also be required to type the country exit code when you dial.

- ✔ When in doubt, contact your cellular provider for tips and other information specific to whatever country you're visiting.

- ✔ Be sure to inquire about texting and cellular data (Internet) rates while you're abroad.

- ✔ Using your phone over a Wi-Fi network abroad incurs no extra fees (unless data roaming is on, as discussed earlier in this chapter). In fact, you can use the Skype app on your phone over a Wi-Fi network to call the United States or any international number at inexpensive rates.

22

Customize Your Phone

In This Chapter

▸ Changing the Home screen background
▸ Putting your favorite apps on the Home screen
▸ Adding and removing icons and widgets
▸ Setting the phone's locks
▸ Silencing the phone
▸ Modifying phone settings

I figure that only a small portion of people bother customizing anything. And just about all of them work in the technology field. Fulfilling their desires, they make everything customizable, probably because they figure everyone else wants to do so. The problem they run into is that the majority of humanity relies upon consistency. Sure, it may be mediocre and dull, but boring old uniformity is reliable and comforting.

There are plenty of things you can customize on your phone. You can change the look of the Home screen, add extra security, change this, fiddle with that, and modify all sorts of things. Nothing is required, but if you're curious, consider reading this chapter to learn the limits of what's possible. Or never change a thing. That's entirely okay.

It's Your Home Screen

The Galaxy Note sports a roomy Home screen. It has seven Home screen panels that you can adorn with icons, widgets, and wallpapers. As the phone ships, examples of icons, widgets, and wallpaper festoon five of the seven panels. Most people never mess with them, but each of those items is completely customizable. After all, it's *your* Home screen. Why not make it the way you want?

Editing the Home screen

The key to changing the Home screen is the *long-press:* Press and hold your finger on a blank part of the Home screen (not on an icon). The Home screen instantly switches to Editing mode. The Add to Home menu appears at the bottom of the screen, and the Home screen panel shrinks, as shown in Figure 22-1.

Figure 22-1: The Add to Home menu.

You cannot summon the Add to Home menu when the Home screen panel is already full of icons or widgets. Display another panel and try again.

Changing wallpaper

The Home screen has two types of backgrounds, or *wallpapers:* live and traditional. *Live* wallpapers are animated. A not-so-live wallpaper can be any image, such as a picture from the Gallery.

To set a new wallpaper for the Home screen, obey these steps:

1. **Long-press the Home screen.**

   The Add to Home menu appears. (Refer to Figure 22-1.)

2. **Choose the Wallpapers command.**

The Wallpapers menu appears, with these three options:

Gallery: Choose a still image stored in the Gallery app.

Live Wallpapers: Choose an animated or interactive wallpaper from a list.

Wallpaper Gallery: Choose a wallpaper from a range of stunning images (no nudity).

3. **Choose the wallpaper you want from the list.**

When you choose the Gallery option, you see a preview of the wallpaper where you can select and crop part of the image.

For certain live wallpapers, the Settings button may appear. The settings let you customize certain aspects of the interactive wallpaper.

4. **Touch either the Save, Set Wallpaper, or Apply button to confirm your selection.**

The new wallpaper takes over the Home screen.

Live wallpaper is interactive, usually featuring some form of animation. Otherwise, the wallpaper image scrolls slightly as you swipe from one Home screen panel to another.

- If you need to change the wallpaper and all the Home screen panels are full of icons, press the Menu soft button and choose the Wallpaper command.

- You can also change the Galaxy Note's lock screen wallpaper: At the Home screen, press the Menu soft button. Choose Settings, Display, Screen Display. Choose the Wallpaper item in the Lock Screen area. Continue with Step 3 in the preceding list.

- The Zedge app has some interesting wallpaper features. Check it out at the Android Market; see Chapter 18.

- See Chapter 14 for more information about the Gallery, including information on how cropping an image works.

Adding apps to the Home screen

You need not live with the unbearable proposition that you're stuck with only the apps that come preset on the Home screen. Nope — you're free to add your own apps. Just follow these steps:

1. **Visit the Home screen panel on which you want to stick the app icon's shortcut.**

The screen must have room for the icon shortcut.

2. **Touch the Applications icon button to display the Apps menu.**

3. **Long-press the icon of the app you want to add to the Home screen.**

   The phone vibrates slightly, and then you see a preview of the Home screen.

4. **Drag the icon to a blank spot on the Home screen.**

   A copy of the app's icon is placed on the Home screen.

The app hasn't moved: What you see is a copy, or, officially, a *shortcut.* You can still find the app on the Apps menu, but now the app is available — more conveniently — on the Home screen.

See the later section "Rearranging and removing icons and widgets" for information on moving apps around on the Home screen or from one panel to another. That section also covers removing apps from the Home screen.

Slapping down widgets

The Home screen is the place where you can find *widgets,* or tiny, interactive information windows. A widget often provides a gateway into another app or displays information such as status updates, the song that's playing, or the weather forecast. To add a widget to the Home screen, heed these steps:

1. **Switch to a Home screen panel that has room enough for the new widget.**

   Unlike app icons, some widgets can occupy more than a postage-stamp-size piece of real estate on the Home screen.

2. **Long-press the Home screen to summon the Add to Home menu.**

3. **Choose Widgets.**

4. **Scroll the list of widgets to choose the one you want to add.**

   For example, choose the Power Saving widget for quick access to several popular phone features, such as Wi-Fi and Bluetooth and other settings you often turn on or off.

5. **Drag the widget to the Home screen.**

   The widget is plopped on the Home screen.

The variety of available widgets depends on the applications you have installed. Some applications come with widgets, some don't.

~ More widgets are available at the Google Play Store. See Chapter 18.

~ To remove, move, or rearrange widgets, see the later section "Rearranging and removing icons and widgets."

Creating shortcuts

Besides widgets, everything on the Home screen is a shortcut. The app icons? Shortcuts. But the variety of shortcuts doesn't end with apps. You can add shortcuts to the Home screen that help you get at a phone feature or display an informational tidbit without having to dig deep in the phone. That's why they're called *shortcuts*.

For example, I have a shortcut on my Home screen that uses the Maps app's Navigation feature to help me return to my house. I swear that I use the shortcut only when I'm sober.

To add a shortcut, long-press the Home screen and choose the Shortcuts command from the Add to Home menu. (Refer to Figure 22-1.) What happens next depends on which shortcut you choose.

For example, when you choose Bookmark from the Shortcuts menu, you add a web page bookmark to the Home screen. Touch the shortcut to open the Web app and visit that web page.

Choose a direct-dial shortcut to place on the Home screen an icon representing a contact's phone number. Touch that icon and the number is dialed instantly.

You can choose shortcuts to Music and the Maps app (Direction & Navigation), shortcuts to various apps installed on your phone, and shortcuts to common phone settings such as battery use, Wi-Fi, and more.

Rearranging and removing icons and widgets

Icons and widgets aren't fastened to the Home screen. If they are, it's day-old chewing gum that binds them, considering how easily you can rearrange and remove unwanted items from any Home screen panel.

Long-press an icon on the Home screen to move it. Eventually, the icon seems to lift and break free, as shown in Figure 22-2.

Icon being pressed

Drag to left panel. | Drag to right panel.

Drag here to delete.

Figure 22-2: Moving an icon.

You can drag a free icon to another position on the Home screen or to another Home screen panel (left or right), or you can drag the icon to the Remove icon that appears on the Home screen, which deletes the shortcut. (Refer to Figure 22-2.)

Widgets can also be moved or removed in the same manner as icons.

✔ Dragging a Home screen icon or widget to the Remove icon doesn't uninstall the application or widget; the app can still be found on the Apps menu, and the widget can again be added to the Home screen.

✔ Icons aren't removed from the Dock using the method described in this section. You must edit the Apps menu to add or remove Dock icons. See Chapter 18.

✔ When an icon hovers over the Remove icon, ready to be deleted, its color changes to red.

✔ See Chapter 18 for information on uninstalling applications.

Adding and removing Home screen panels

Did I write that the Galaxy Note has seven Home screen panels? My bad — it can have *up to* seven Home screen panels. You're free to remove panels you don't need. And if you need to have seven panels again in the future, you can add them again.

To add or remove Home screen panels, heed these directions:

1. At the Home screen, press the Menu soft button.

2. Choose Edit.

You see an overview of all Home screen panels, similar to the one shown in Figure 22-3.

Drag thumbnails to rearrange.

Primary panel

New panel

Add a new, blank panel.

Figure 22-3: Manipulating Home screen panels.

3. Work the Home screen panels.

You can do these three things:

Remove: To remove a Home screen panel, drag it to the Remove icon. If the panel has icons or widgets, you see a warning. Touch the Yes button to confirm the deletion.

Add: To add a Home screen panel, touch the thumbnail with the Plus Sign icon on it, as illustrated in Figure 22-3. If you don't see a thumbnail with the Plus Sign icon on it, you cannot add additional panels.

Rearrange: Drag a panel around to change the order in which it appears. The thumbnail in the center is the primary Home screen panel.

4. Press the Back soft button when you're done editing.

You must have a Home screen, so you must have at least one Home screen panel.

There's no way to undo a Home screen panel deletion. You have to add a new, blank panel and then repopulate it with icons and widgets.

 The *primary* Home screen panel is the one you return to when you press the Home soft button.

Additional Screen Security

The Galaxy Note features a rudimentary screen lock. The lock isn't that obvious to figure out, but it still doesn't provide true security against anyone who knows the secret. Therefore, to provide more than a modicum of protection, your phone features three alternative locks to choose from: the pattern lock, PIN, or password. Their details are provided in this section.

Finding the screen locks

You'll find that the Galaxy Note's screen locks in a single location: on the Set Screen Lock screen. Heed these steps to visit that screen:

1. At the Home screen, press the Menu soft button.

2. Choose Settings.

3. Choose Location & Security.

4. If an alternative lock isn't yet set, choose Set Screen Lock; otherwise, choose Change Screen Lock.

When an alternative screen lock is already set, you need to work the lock to proceed: Trace the pattern, or type the PIN or password to continue. You're then granted access to the Set Screen Lock screen, which shows four items: None, Pattern, PIN, and Password. Using these items is covered in the next few sections.

📌 The lock you apply affects the way you turn on your phone and wake it up. See Chapter 2 for details.

📌 No locks appear when you answer an incoming phone call. You are, however, prompted to unlock the phone if you want to use its features while you're on a call.

📌 See the nearby sidebar "The lock doesn't show up!" for information on setting the Security Lock timer, which affects when the screen locks appear after you put the phone to sleep.

Removing a lock

To disable the pattern, PIN, or password screen lock on your phone, choose the None option from the Set Screen Lock screen. When None is chosen, the phone uses the standard screen lock, as described in Chapter 2.

Refer to the preceding section for information on finding the None option.

Creating an unlock pattern

The unlock pattern is perhaps the most popular, and certainly the most unconventional, way to lock your phone's screen. The pattern must be traced on the touchscreen to unlock the phone.

To set the unlock pattern, follow these steps:

1. **Summon the Set Screen Lock screen.**

   Refer to the earlier section "Finding the screen locks."

2. **Choose Pattern.**

   If you haven't yet set a pattern, you may see a tutorial describing the process; touch the Next button to skip merrily through the dreary directions.

3. **Trace an unlock pattern.**

   Use Figure 22-4 as your guide. You can trace over the dots in any order, but you can trace over a dot only once. The pattern must cover at least four dots.

4. **Touch the Continue button.**

5. **Redraw the pattern again, just to confirm that you know it.**

6. **Touch the Confirm button, and the pattern lock is set.**

I started here.   The pattern so far

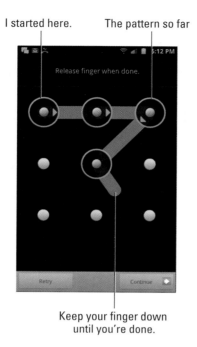

Keep your finger down
until you're done.

Figure 22-4: Setting the unlock pattern.

Ensure that a check mark appears by the option Use Visible Pattern, found on the Location and Security screen. That way, the pattern shows up when you need to unlock the phone. For even more security, you can disable this option, but you *must* remember how and where the pattern goes.

✔ To remove the pattern lock, set None as the lock type, as described in the preceding section.

✔ The pattern lock can start at any dot, not necessarily at the upper-left dot, shown earlier, in Figure 22-4.

✔ The unlock pattern can be as simple or as complex as you like. I'm a big fan of simple.

✔ Wash your hands! Smudge marks on the display can betray your pattern.

The lock doesn't show up!

The pattern, PIN, or password lock screens show up whenever you turn on or unlock the phone. They don't appear, however, when you lock the phone and then quickly unlock it. That's because the time-out value must kick in before the alternative locks appear. When you unlock the phone before the value kicks in, you're met with the standard (or None) unlocking screen for the Galaxy Note.

When you find the lock not showing up in time, or taking too long to set in, you can choose a more appropriate time interval for the way you use the Galaxy Note: From the Home screen, press the Menu soft button and choose Settings. Choose Location & Security, and then choose Timeout. Choose a new time-out value from the list.

Setting a PIN

A *PIN lock* is a code between 4 and 16 numbers long. It contains only numbers, 0 through 9. To set the PIN lock, follow the directions in the earlier section "Finding the screen locks" to reach the Set Screen Lock screen. Choose PIN from the list.

Type your PIN twice to confirm to the doubting computer that you know it. The next time you need to unlock your phone, type the PIN on the keyboard, and then touch the OK button to proceed.

PIN stands for Personal Identification Number.

Applying a password

Perhaps the most secure way to lock the phone's screen is to apply a full-on password. Unlike a PIN (refer to the preceding section), a *password* contains a combination of numbers, symbols, and uppercase and lowercase letters.

Set the password by choosing Password from the Set Screen Lock screen; refer to the earlier section "Finding the screen locks" for information on getting to that screen.

The password you create must be at least four characters long. Longer passwords are more secure but easier to mistype.

You type the password twice to set things up, which confirms to the Galaxy Note that you know the password and will, you hope, remember it in the future. Touch the OK button to lock in the password.

You need to type the password whenever you unlock the phone, as described in Chapter 2. You also type the password whenever you change or remove the screen lock, as discussed in the section "Finding the screen locks," earlier in this chapter.

Some Fine-Tuning

Your Galaxy Note features a plethora of options and settings for you to adjust. You can fix things that annoy you or make things better, to please your tastes. The whole idea is to make your phone more usable for you. Or just ignore making changes, and tolerate all the presets. It's up to you.

Stopping the noise!

Your phone features a bag of tricks designed to silence its speaker. These techniques can come in quite handy, especially when a cell phone's digital noise can be outright annoying.

Vibration mode: You can make the phone vibrate for all incoming calls, which works in addition to any ringtone you've set (and still works when you've silenced the phone). To activate Vibration all-the-time mode, follow these steps:

1. **At the Home screen, press the Menu soft button.**
2. **Choose Settings and then Sound.**
3. **Choose Vibration.**
4. **Choose Always.**

Silent mode: Silent mode disables all sounds from the phone, except for music and YouTube and other types of media, as well as alarms that have been set by the Clock and Calendar apps.

To enter Silent mode, follow Steps 1 and 2 in the previous set of steps, and then place a check mark by the Silent Mode item.

Turn Over to Mute: If you have activated Motion on the Galaxy Note, you can enable the Turn Over to Mute feature. See Chapter 3 for information on the phone's Motion feature.

Changing various settings

This section describes a smattering of settings you can adjust on the phone — all made from, logically, the Settings screen. To get there from the Home screen, press the Menu soft button and choose the Settings command.

You can also view the Settings screen by choosing the Settings app from the Apps menu.

Screen brightness: Choose Display, and then choose Brightness. Use the slider to adjust the touchscreen's intensity. You can choose the Automatic Brightness setting. When this setting is active, brightness is set by using the phone's magical light sensor to determine how much screen intensity is needed.

Screen time-out: Choose Display, and then choose Screen Time-out. Select a time-out value from the list. This duration specifies when the phone locks.

Ringer volume: Choose Sound, and then choose Volume. Use the sliders to specify how loud the phone rings for ringtone (incoming calls), media, system, and notification sounds. Touch OK when you're done.

Adjust the keyboards: Choose Language & Keyboard. Keyboard options are available for each of the phone's keyboards. Choose one to see a screen full of settings and options. Set things that please you, or deactivate those that vex you.

23

Keep It Running

In This Chapter

▶ Checking the phone's battery usage

▶ Making the battery last

▶ Cleaning the phone

▶ Keeping the system up-to-date

▶ Dealing with problems

▶ Finding support

▶ Getting answers to common questions

*Y*ou remember maintenance, don't you? It's the thing you're supposed to do to the lawn mower once or twice a year. It's the reason that businesses exist only to change your car's oil. It's why the coffee maker clogs — because (and you probably didn't know this) you have to clean it out with vinegar at least once a year. That's maintenance.

For your Galaxy Note, maintenance isn't much of a big deal, but as with all maintenance, you avoid it at your own peril. You'll never have to change the oil in your phone, rotate its tires, or pour vinegar into the speaker hole to unclog its pipes. Nope, all you really need to do is read this chapter.

Battery Care and Feeding

Perhaps the most important item you can monitor and maintain on your Galaxy Note is its battery. The battery supplies the necessary electrical juice by which the phone operates. Without battery power, your phone is about as useful as a tin-can-and-a-string for communications. Keep an eye on the battery.

Monitoring the battery

Your phone's current battery status is displayed at the top of the screen, in the status area, next to the time. The icons used to display battery status are similar to those shown in Figure 23-1.

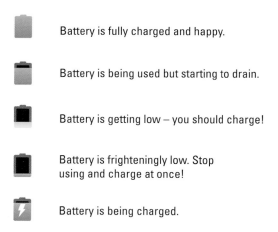

Battery is fully charged and happy.

Battery is being used but starting to drain.

Battery is getting low – you should charge!

Battery is frighteningly low. Stop using and charge at once!

Battery is being charged.

Figure 23-1: Battery status icons.

You might also see the icon for a dead or missing battery, but for some reason I can't get my phone to turn on and display it.

You can check the specific battery level by following these steps:

1. **At the Home screen, press the Menu button.**
2. **Choose Settings.**
3. **Choose About Phone.**
4. **Choose Status.**

The top two items on the Status screen offer information about the battery:

Battery Status: This setting explains what's going on with the battery. It might say *Full* when the battery is full, *Discharging* when the battery is in use, or *Charging* when the battery is being charged. Other text may be displayed as well, depending on how desperate for power the phone is.

Battery Level: This setting reveals a percentage value describing how much of the battery is charged. A value of 100 percent indicates a fully charged battery. A value of 110 percent means that someone can't do math.

Later sections in this chapter describe activities that consume battery power and tell you how to deal with battery issues.

- ✓ Heed those low-battery warnings! The phone sounds a notification whenever the battery power gets low (see the yellow Battery icon shown earlier, in Figure 23-1). The phone sounds another notification when the battery gets *very* low (see the orange Battery icon in Figure 23-1).

- ✓ When the battery is too low, the phone shuts itself off.

- ✓ The best way to deal with a low battery is to connect the phone to a power source: Either plug the phone into a wall socket, or connect the phone to a computer by using a USB cable. The phone charges itself immediately; plus, you can use the phone while it's charging.

- ✓ The phone charges more efficiently when it's plugged into a wall socket rather than a computer.

- ✓ You don't have to fully charge the phone to use it. If you have only 20 minutes to charge and the power level returns to only 70 percent, that's great. Well, it's not great, but it's far better than a 20 percent battery level.

- ✓ Battery percentage values are best-guess estimates. Just because you talked for two hours and the battery shows 50 percent doesn't mean that you're guaranteed two more hours of talking. Odds are good that you have much less than two hours. In fact, as the percentage value gets low, the battery appears to drain faster.

Determining what is sucking up power

A nifty screen on your phone reviews which activities have been consuming power when the phone is operating from its battery. The informative screen is shown in Figure 23-2.

To get to this screen, follow these steps:

1. **At the Home screen, press the Menu soft button.**

2. **Choose Settings, and then choose About Phone.**

3. **Choose Battery Usage.**

   You see a screen similar to the one shown in Figure 23-2.

The number and variety of items listed on the Battery Usage screen depend on what you've been doing with your phone between charges and how many different programs are active.

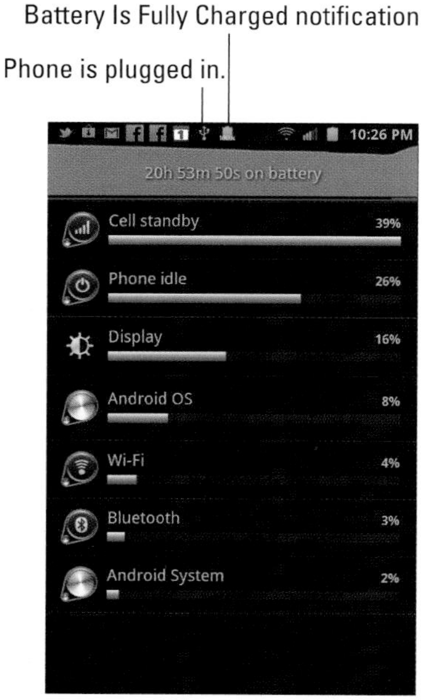

Battery Is Fully Charged notification

Phone is plugged in.

Figure 23-2: Things that drain the battery.

Using power saving tools

The Galaxy Note comes with a handy power-saving feature that you can employ to help squeeze extra juice out of the battery. To use the power saving tools, follow these steps:

1. **At the Home screen, press the Menu soft button.**
2. **Choose Settings.**
3. **Choose Power Saving.**
4. **Place a check mark by the System Power Saving item.**
5. **Touch the OK button to dismiss the notice.**

    Power saving is enabled.

The power saving feature automatically disables certain phone features — specifically, power-draining features — whenever the battery reaches 30 percent capacity. Items that it disables are Wi-Fi, Bluetooth, GPS, and Data Sync. It also throttles the screen brightness.

When power saving is enabled, you see the Power Saving notification icon, as shown in the margin.

To disable power saving, repeat the steps in this section.

If you prefer to customize the power saving settings, choose Custom Power Saving in Step 4. Then choose the Custom Power Saving Settings item to pick and choose which phone features you want to disable. Choose the item Power Saving On At to select which percentage the battery level must drop to before your custom settings kick in.

The Galaxy Note has a Power Saving widget that you can stick on the Home screen. The widget contains buttons to let you control the various features that are automatically set by the power saving feature. See Chapter 22 for information on adding widgets to the Home screen.

Configuring battery-draining settings

Here's a smattering of things you can do to help prolong the battery life in your Galaxy Note:

Turn off vibration options. The phone's vibration is caused by a teensy motor. Though you don't see much battery savings by disabling the vibration options, it's better than no savings. To turn off vibration, follow these steps:

1. **At the Home screen, press the Menu soft button.**
2. **Choose Settings, and then choose Sound.**
3. **Choose Vibration.**
4. **Choose Never.**
5. **Also on the Sound Settings screen: Remove the check mark by Haptic Feedback.**

   The Haptic Feedback option is what causes the phone to vibrate when you touch the soft buttons.

Additionally, consider lowering the volume of notifications by choosing the Volume option. This option also saves a modicum of battery life, though in my travels, I've missed important notifications by setting the volume too low.

Dim the screen. The display is capable of drawing down quite a lot of battery power. Though a dim screen can be more difficult to see, especially outdoors, it definitely saves on battery life.

You set the screen brightness from the Settings screen: Choose Display, and then choose Brightness.

Turn off Bluetooth. When you're not using Bluetooth, turn it off. Or, when you *really* need that cyborg Bluetooth ear-thing, try to keep your phone plugged in. See Chapter 19 for information on turning off Bluetooth.

Turn off Wi-Fi. Wi-Fi networking on the phone keeps you on the Internet at top speeds but drains the battery as it's being used. Because I tend to use Wi-Fi when I'm in one place, I keep my phone plugged in. Otherwise, the battery drains like my bank account at Christmas. Refer to Chapter 19 for information on turning off the phone's Wi-Fi.

Disable automatic syncing. Your phone syncs quite often. In fact, it surprises me when I update something on the Internet and find my phone updated almost instantly. When you need to save battery power and frequent updates aren't urgent (such as when you're spending a day traveling), disable automatic syncing by following these steps:

1. **At the Home screen, press the Menu soft button.**
2. **Choose Settings, and then choose the Accounts and Sync command.**
3. **Remove the check marks by the options Background Data and Auto-Sync.**

When saving battery juice isn't important, remember to repeat these steps to reenable background and automatic synchronization.

Regular Maintenance

There are only two tasks that you can do for regular maintenance on your phone: Keep it clean, and keep important information backed up.

Keeping it clean

You probably already keep your phone clean. I must use my sleeve to wipe the touchscreen at least a dozen times a day. Of course, better than your sleeve is something called a *microfiber cloth*. This item can be found at any computer- or office-supply store.

- ✓ Never use ammonia or alcohol to clean the touchscreen. These substances damage the phone. Use only a cleaning solution specifically designed for touchscreens.

- ✓ If the screen continually gets dirty, consider adding a *screen protector.* This specially designed cover prevents the screen from getting scratched or dirty but also lets you use your finger on the touchscreen. Be sure that the screen protector is intended for use with your specific phone brand.

- ✓ You can also find customized cell phone cases, belt clips, and protectors, though I've found that these add-on items are purely for decorative or fashion purposes and don't even prevent serious damage if you drop the phone.

Backing up your phone

A *backup* is a safety copy of the information on your phone. It includes any contact information, music, photos, videos, and apps you've recorded, downloaded, or installed, plus any settings you've made to customize your phone. Copying this information to another source is one way to keep the information safe, in case anything happens to the phone.

On your Google account, information is backed up automatically. This information includes your Contacts list, Gmail messages, and Calendar app appointments. Because Android phones automatically sync this information with the Internet, a backup is always present.

To confirm that your Google account information is being backed up, heed these steps:

1. **From the Home screen, press the Menu soft button.**

2. **Choose Settings and then Accounts and Sync.**

3. **Choose your Google account.**

4. **Ensure that a green check mark appears by every option.**

   When no check mark is there, touch the gray square to add one.

If you have more than one Google account synchronized with the phone, repeat these steps for every account.

Updating the system

Every so often, a new version of your phone's operating system becomes available. It's an *Android update* because *Android* is the name of the phone's operating system, not because your phone thinks that it's some type of robot.

Whenever an automatic update occurs, you see an alert or a message appear on the phone, indicating that a system upgrade is available. You have three choices:

- ✔ Install Now
- ✔ Install Later
- ✔ More Info

My advice is to choose Install Now and get it over with — unless you have something (a call, a message, or another urgent item) pending on the phone, in which case you can choose Install Later and be bothered by the message again.

You can manually check for updates. Obey these steps:

1. **At the Home screen, press the Menu soft button.**
2. **Choose Software Update.**
3. **Choose Check for Updates.**
4. **Touch the OK button.**

When your system is up-to-date, the screen tells you so; touch the OK button. Otherwise, you find directions for updating the system.

Help and Troubleshooting

Things aren't as bad as they were in the old days. Back then, you could try two sources for help: the atrocious manual that came with your electronic device or a phone call to the guy who wrote the atrocious manual. It was unpleasant. Today, things are better. You have many resources for solving issues with your gizmos, including your Galaxy Note.

Fixing random and annoying problems

Aren't all problems annoying? There isn't really such a thing as a welcome problem, unless the problem is welcome because it diverts attention from another, preexisting problem. And random problems? If problems were predictable, they would serve in office. Or maybe they already are?

Here are some typical problems and my suggestions for a solution:

Your phone has general trouble. For just about any problem or minor quirk, consider restarting the phone: Turn off the phone, and then turn it on again. This procedure will most likely fix a majority of the annoying and quirky problems you encounter.

When restarting doesn't work, consider removing the phone's battery. Wait about 15 seconds, and then reinstall the battery and turn on the phone again.

The data connection needs to be checked. Sometimes, the data connection drops but the phone connection stays active. Check the status bar. If you see bars, you have a phone signal. When you don't see either the 4G LTE, 4G, E, or Wi-Fi icon, the phone has no data signal.

Occasionally, the data signal suddenly drops for a minute or two. Wait and it comes back around. If it doesn't, the cellular data network might be down, or you may simply be in an area with lousy service. Consider changing your location.

For wireless connections, you have to ensure that the Wi-Fi is set up properly and working. Setup usually involves pestering the person who configured the Wi-Fi signal or made it available, such as the cheerful person in the green apron who serves you coffee.

The phone's storage is busy. Most often, the storage — internal or MicroSD card — is busy because you've connected the phone to a computer and the computer is accessing the phone's storage system. To "unbusy" the storage, unmount the phone or stop the USB storage. See Chapter 20.

When the phone's storage remains busy, consider restarting the phone, as described earlier in this section.

An app has run amok. Sometimes, apps that misbehave let you know. You see a warning on the screen, announcing the app's stubborn disposition. Touch the Force Close button to shut down the errant app.

When you see no warning or an app appears to be unduly obstinate, you can shut 'er down the manual way, by following these steps:

1. **At the Home screen, press the Menu soft button.**
2. **Choose Settings, and then choose Applications.**
3. **Choose Manage Applications.**
4. **Touch the Running tab at the top of the Manage Applications screen.**
5. **Choose the application that's causing you distress.**

   For example, a program doesn't start or says that it's busy or has another issue.
6. **Touch the Stop button.**

   The program stops.

After stopping the program, try opening it again to see whether it works. If the program continues to run amok, contact its developer: Open the Play Store app, press the Menu soft button, and choose My Apps. Open the app you're having trouble with, and choose the option Send Email. Send the developer a message describing the problem.

The phone's software must be reset (a drastic measure). When all else fails, you can do the drastic thing and reset all the phone's software, essentially returning it to the state it was in when it first arrived. Obviously, you need not perform this step lightly. In fact, consider finding support (see the next section) before you start:

1. **At the Home screen, press the Menu soft button.**

2. **Choose Settings, and then choose Privacy.**

3. **Choose Factory Data Reset.**

   By itself, the Factory Data Reset option merely resets the phone's software. The information you have on the phone's storage (internal and MicroSD card) remains. That way, the pictures, videos, music, and other types of information saved on the phone's storage aren't erased — unless you complete Step 4.

4. **Optionally, place a green check mark by the option Format USB Storage.**

   Erasing this option isn't required in order to fix phone problems. The only time I've used it is when I've sold a phone or traded it in.

5. **Touch the Reset Phone button.**

6. **Touch the Erase Everything button to confirm.**

   All the information you've set or stored on the phone is purged.

Again, *do not* follow these steps unless you're certain that they will fix the problem or you're under orders to do so from someone in tech-support.

Getting support

Never discount these two sources of support: your cellular provider and the phone's manufacturer. Even so, I recommend phoning your cellular provider first, no matter what the problem.

Contact information for both the cellular provider and phone manufacturer is found in the material you received with the phone. I recommend that you save those random pieces of paper in Chapter 1, which you obviously have read, and then followed my advice, so that you can easily find that information.

From your phone, the contact number for AT&T is 611. From a non-AT&T phone, dial 800-331-0500.

You can also find AT&T support on the web at www.att.com/support.

For hardware support, you can contact Samsung on the web at this address: www.samsung.com/us/mobile/cell-phones

If you have an issue with the Google Play Store, you can visit its support website: http://support.google.com/googleplay

Galaxy Note Q&A

I love Q&A! That's because not only is it an effective way to express certain problems and solutions but some of the questions might also cover areas I've been wanting to ask about.

"The touchscreen doesn't work!"

A touchscreen, such as the one used on your phone, requires a human finger for proper interaction. The phone interprets complicated electromagnetic physics between the human finger and the phone to determine where the touchscreen is being touched.

You cannot use the touchscreen when you're wearing gloves, unless they're specially designed gloves that claim to work on touchscreens. Batman wears this type of glove, so it probably exists in real life.

The touchscreen might also fail when the battery power is low or when the phone has been physically damaged.

For precise interaction with the touchscreen, use the S Pen.

"I lost the S Pen!"

You can get a replacement for the S Pen at the Phone Store where you bought the Galaxy Note, though it isn't cheap. Even so, any stylus designed for use on a touchscreen works with the Galaxy Note. I recently tried the stylus that came with my laptop-tablet convertible, and it worked fine on the phone.

The only drawback to getting a stylus not designed for the Galaxy Note is that it won't fit into the S Pen compartment on the phone.

"The screen is too dark!"

Modern cell phones feature a teensy light sensor on the front. This sensor is used to adjust the touchscreen's brightness based on the ambient light of your location. If the sensor is covered, the screen can get very, very dark.

Ensure that you don't unintentionally block the light sensor. Avoid buying a case or screen protector that obscures the sensor.

If you'd rather manually set screen brightness, from the Home screen press the Menu soft button. Choose Settings, Display, Brightness. Remove the check mark by Automatic Brightness, and then use the slider to manually set the touchscreen's intensity.

"The battery doesn't charge!"

Start from the source: Is the wall socket providing power? Is the cord plugged in? The cable may be damaged, so try another cable.

When charging from a USB port on a computer, ensure that the computer is turned on. Computers don't provide USB power when they're turned off.

"The phone gets so hot that it turns itself off!"

Yikes! An overheating phone can be a nasty problem. Judge how hot the phone is by seeing whether you can hold it in your hand: When the phone is too hot to hold, it's too hot. If you're using the phone to fry an egg, the phone is too hot.

Turn off the phone. Take out the battery, and let it cool.

If the overheating problem continues, have the phone looked at for potential repair. The battery might need to be replaced.

"The phone won't do Landscape mode!"

Not every app takes advantage of the phone's ability to orient itself in Landscape mode. For example, the Home screen doesn't "do landscape" unless it's placed into a car mount.

One app that definitely does Landscape mode is the Web app, described in Chapter 10. So, just because an app doesn't enter Landscape mode doesn't mean that it *can* enter Landscape mode.

Just to be sure, check the Screen Rotation option. The quick way to check is to pull down the notifications. Screen Rotation is a Quick Action button that appears atop the notifications list. Ensure that Screen Rotation is on. If the problem persists, you know for certain that the app doesn't change orientation.

Part VI
The Part of Tens

The 5th Wave — By Rich Tennant

"Well, here's what happened—I forgot to put it on my AK Notepad."

In this part . . .

I love trivia. Not just random fact trivia, but list trivia. And the best list trivia involves lists with ten items — for example, the Ten Tallest Mountains or the Ten Worst Plane Crashes or even Ten Ugly Guys Who Married Gorgeous Women but Absolutely Not Because They Were Insanely Wealthy. If you too love these kinds of lists, this is your part of the book.

In this part, you'll find chapters containing ten items apiece. These chapters aren't simply stuffed with leftovers or odds and ends — you'll find tips, tricks, shortcuts, and useful information to help expand your Galaxy Note experience. And in case you're wondering, sometimes the gorgeous woman marries the homely guy because she loves him.

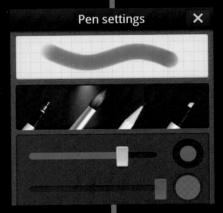

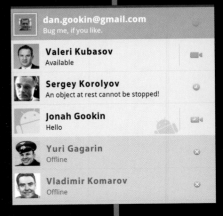

24

Ten Tips, Tricks, and Shortcuts

A tip is a handy suggestion, like "Don't climb the barbed wire fence naked." A trick is an impressive skill that you can show off to others, like "Watch how I can shove two dimes and a nickel in one nostril and pull a quarter out the other." A *shortcut* is a quick way of doing an otherwise time-consuming task, like breaking up via Twitter instead of spending money on a fancy dinner first and then having to sit through all that crying and stuff.

This chapter contains a total of ten tips, tricks, and suggestions for using your Galaxy Note. The idea is to make life easier and more productive for you and your beloved phone so that you can get the most from your investment.

Disable Animations

Who doesn't want a faster phone? Well, people who don't really care about all the onscreen animations. Though this trick doesn't truly speed up your phone, by disabling animations, you help your phone have a peppier feel to it. Heed these directions:

1. **At the Home screen, press the Menu soft button.**

2. **Choose Settings and then Display.**

3. **Choose Animation and then No Animations.**

The animations you've disabled are mostly screen transitions, such as the fade-in effect when you return to the Home screen. It may not be much, but when I disabled animation on my phone, I had a sudden feeling of intense power and well-being. Though that may not happen to you, disabling animations is worth a try.

Use Picasa

Your Google account features Picasa Web, an online photo-hosting site. It's already part of your account, so why not use it?

To ensure that Picasa is configured for your Google account, heed these steps:

1. **At the Home screen, press the Menu soft button.**

2. **Choose Accounts and Sync.**

3. **Choose your Google account.**

4. **Ensure that a check mark appears by the item Sync Picasa Web Albums.**

   If you see no Picasa item, you may have to visit the Internet to set up your Picasa Web Albums account: Visit `picasaweb.google.com`.

You can confirm that your Picasa Web Albums are being synchronized with the Galaxy Note by opening the Gallery app. Look for your online albums on the Gallery's main screen. They're flagged by the Picasa icon, shown in the margin.

Being able to view Picasa Web Albums on your phone is nice. Even nicer is sharing the images you take by uploading them to Picasa. Here's how to do it:

1. **Open the Gallery app.**

2. **View the image that you want to share (upload) on the screen.**

3. **Press the Menu soft button.**

4. **Touch the Share Via button, and choose Picasa from the menu.**

5. **Type a caption for the image.**

   For example, type **Jenny, before the accident**.

6. **Choose the album.**

7. **Touch the Upload button.**

   The picture is sent to the Internet.

All images you upload are available on the Internet. Further, if you have other Android devices, you see your Picasa Web Albums on those devices as well.

- It's possible to upload multiple images at a time. In Step 2, display an album of images, such as the Camera album. After Step 3, touch thumbnails in the album to select multiple photos. Then for Step 4, choose More and then the Share Via command. Choose Picasa from the Share Via menu.

- You should set up and configure your Picasa Web Albums using a computer's web browser. You can have public albums and private albums.

- The image(s) you upload appear twice in the Gallery app. The original image is probably in the Camera album, and the duplicate in whichever Picasa web album you chose. (Refer to Step 6.)

- You can delete the original image for photos you've uploaded to Picasa. See Chapter 14 for details. Even so, remember that you cannot edit Picasa album images on your Galaxy Note.

- *Upload,* which is the opposite of *download,* means to send a file from the phone to the Internet or to another host computer.

Add Spice to Dictation

I feel that too few people use dictation, despite how handy it can be — especially for text messaging. Anyway, if you've used dictation, you might have noticed that it occasionally censors some of the words you utter. Perhaps you're the kind of person who doesn't put up with that kind of s###.

Relax. You can revoke the vocal censorship by following these steps:

1. **At the Home screen, press the Menu soft button.**

2. **Choose Settings, and then choose Voice Input and Output.**

3. **Choose Voice Recognizer Settings.**

4. **Remove the check mark by the Block Offensive Words option.**

And just what are offensive words? I would think that *censorship* is an offensive word. But no — apparently, only a few choice words fall into this category. I won't print them here, because the phone's censor retains the initial letter and generally makes the foul language easy to guess. D###.

Share a Location

After you find that taco stand you're looking for, why not share its location with your friends? It's a Taco Party!

When you use the Maps app to locate a restaurant, coffee house, or hookah den, you make the location known: Touch the location's cartoon bubble to display more information. Choose the command Share This Place. (Scroll down to find it.) Choose a sharing method, such as Social Hub, Gmail, or Messaging. Invite your friends!

Or, if you're searching for a pool of molten lava, invite your enemies!

See Chapter 13 for more information on the Maps app.

Create Direct-Dial and Direct Text Shortcuts

For the folks you contact most frequently, you can create Home screen direct-contact shortcuts. Here's how:

1. **Long-press the Home screen.**

   Choose a Home screen panel that has room for at least one icon.

2. **Choose the Shortcuts command from the Add to Home menu.**

3. **Choose Direct Dial.**

4. **Choose the contact you want to direct-dial.**

   Contacts with multiple phone numbers have more than one listing.

A shortcut to that contact's phone number (with the contact's picture, if the person has one) appears on the Home screen. Touching the shortcut dials the contact's phone number instantly.

Just as you can create a direct-dial shortcut (shown in the preceding section), you can create an icon to directly text-message a contact. The difference is that you choose Direct Message, rather than Direct Dial, in Step 3.

See Chapter 9 for more information about text messaging.

Obtain Apps from Unknown Sources

The Google Play Store isn't the only place from which you can obtain apps for your Galaxy Note — AT&T also has an app store, as does Amazon. But to get apps from these locations, you need to loosen the phone's uptight attitude about where apps come from.

To allow apps to come from locations other than the Google Play Store, follow these steps:

1. **At the Home screen, press the Menu soft button.**

2. **Choose Settings.**

3. **At the Settings screen, choose Applications.**

4. **Place a check mark by the option Unknown Sources.**

5. **Ignore the warning and touch the OK button.**

The phone is now open to obtaining apps from other sources. In fact, if you've tried to run some of the preinstalled apps on your Galaxy Note, you've already been prompted to enable the Unknown Sources option.

✔ Are you taking a security risk? Oh, yes — but only if you're obtaining apps from locations other than well-known outfits such as AT&T, Samsung, or Amazon. In fact, if you're concerned about security and don't plan to get any of those apps, you never need to turn on this setting.

✔ Ironically, you can download Amazon Mobile from the Google Play Store. But to obtain Amazon apps, you need to enable the Unknown Sources setting.

✔ You do not need to enable Unknown Sources when purchasing music from the Amazon MP3 store or when buying books for the Kindle app.

Control the Phone Using Your Voice

The Voice Search app, found on the Apps menu, allows you to bellow verbal orders to your Galaxy Note. Start the app, and you see the main screen, as shown in Figure 24-1. Touch the Help button for suggestions on what you can say.

Figure 24-1: The phone can obey you.

Try out a few of the commands, such as the Call command. The phone may ask you for more detailed information, requiring you to reply "yes" or "no," similar to an annoying voice menu at some Big Impersonal Company.

I admit that this feature is a tad unreliable, especially compared to how well the dictation feature works overall. Still, it's worth a try if you truly want to play Mr. Spock and dictate your commands to a cold, impersonal piece of electronics.

Here are just a few of the phrases you can utter into the phone after starting the Voice Search app and when you see the Speak Now prompt:

- Watch a video
- Listen to *(artist, album, song)*
- Send e-mail to *(contact)*
- Set alarm for *(time)*
- Go to *(address, map location)*

Alas, try as I might, the phone never responds when I say, "Make me a sandwich!"

The Voice Command app shortcut is to press and hold the Search soft button.

I recommend using the Voice Search app over AT&T's Voice Talk app. If prompted to choose between the two, place a check mark in the box Set As Default and then choose Voice Search.

Get Somewhere Quickly

It seems kind of silly. After all, the Galaxy Note's navigation feature helps you get somewhere you've never been. But what about getting home? Especially when the way there was beset with one-way streets, it helps to have a shortcut to get back home.

The navigate-home shortcut also helps when being chased by angry mobs.

To create a location shortcut for your home or office, heed these steps:

1. **Long-press the Home screen.**

   Ensure that you're using a Home screen panel that has room for a new icon.

2. **Choose the Shortcuts command.**

3. **Choose Directions & Navigation**.

   A special screen appears, where you can enter location information.

4. **Type a destination address.**

   Type the address just as though you're searching for something with the Maps app. For your home or office, type the street address and zip code.

5. **Choose a method of transportation.**

6. **Type a name for the shortcut.**

   The name appears below the shortcut's icon on the Home screen, so keep the name short and descriptive.

7. **Choose an icon.**

   All the icons are boring, so it doesn't matter which you select.

8. **Touch the Save button.**

   The shortcut icon is created and pasted to the Home screen.

You can use this technique to create a Home screen shortcut for any location: Your favorite coffee hangout, a pizza joint, the parole office, or any place you frequent. To use the icon, touch it. The phone instantly launches the Maps app and sets you on a course for the destination you typed in Step 4.

Find Your Lost Cell Phone

Despite its mammoth size, someday, you may lose your beloved Galaxy Note. It might be for a few panic-filled seconds, or it might be for forever. The hardware solution is to weld a heavy object to the phone, such as a bowling ball or a tree, yet that kind of defeats the entire mobile/wireless paradigm. The software solution is to use a cell phone locator service.

Cell phone *locator services* employ apps that use a phone's cellular signal as well as its GPS to help locate the missing gizmo. These types of apps are available at the Google Play Store. I've not tried them all, and many of them require a subscription service or registration at a website to complete the process.

Here are some suggestions for cell phone locator apps:

- Wheres My Droid
- Lookout Mobile Security
- Mobile Phone Locator

Visit the Task Manager

If you want to get your hands dirty with some behind-the-scenes stuff on your Galaxy Note, Task Manager is the app to open. It's not for everyone, so feel free to skip this section if you want to use your phone without having to acquire any computer nerd sickness that you have otherwise successfully avoided.

The Task Manager app is found on the Apps menu. If so, you can avoid looking at Figure 24-2, which illustrates the main Task Manager screen.

The Task Manager window shows all the phone's currently running apps, You can see how much RAM (memory) an app is using as well as the CPU power it's consuming.

Other tabs on the Task Manager screen display information about the phone's memory (RAM) and storage. It's a nerd's paradise of trivial information and meaningless facts.

Check storage usage.

Check memory usage.

Running apps

Figure 24-2: Managing tasks.

You can use Task Manager to kill off tasks that are hogging up too much CPU time or memory or that just bug the stuffing from your couch. As illustrated in Figure 24-2, you touch the Exit button to close an app or touch the Exit All button to snuff out all running apps.

✔ Also see Chapter 23 on using the Stop button to kill an app run amok.

✔ The Android operating system does an excellent job of managing apps. If resources are needed for another app, Android automatically closes any open apps as needed. There's no need to futz with Task Manager, unless you just enjoy messing with such a thing.

25

Ten Things to Remember

In This Chapter

▶ Locking the phone

▶ Using landscape orientation

▶ Bring up recent apps

▶ Saving typing time

▶ Minding activities that consume battery power

▶ Checking for phone roaming

▶ Using the + key to dial international calls

▶ Employing soft button S Pen shortcuts

▶ Taking a picture of your contacts

▶ Using the Search command

*I*f only it were easy to narrow to ten items the list of all the things I want you to remember when using your Galaxy Note. So even though you'll find in this chapter ten good things not to forget, don't think for a moment that there are *only* ten. In fact, as I remember more, I'll put them on my website, at www.wambooli.com. Check it for updates about your phone, and perhaps even more things to remember.

Lock the Phone on a Call

Whether you dialed out or someone dialed in, after you start talking, you should lock your phone: Press the Power Lock button. By doing so, you ensure that the touchscreen is disabled and the call isn't unintentionally disconnected.

Of course, the call can still be disconnected by a dropped signal or by the other party getting all huffy and hanging up on you, but by locking the phone, you prevent a stray finger — or your pocket — from disconnecting (or muting) the phone.

Landscape Orientation

The natural orientation of the Galaxy Note is vertical — the *portrait* orientation. Even so, you don't have to use an app in portrait orientation.

Turning the phone to its side makes many apps appear wider, such as the Web app and the Maps app. That's often a better way to see things, to see more available items on certain menus, and if you're using the onscreen keyboard, it gives you larger key caps on which to type.

Not every app supports landscape orientation.

Recent Apps

There's no point in having to switch between an app and the Home screen or between an app and the Apps menu. The better solution is to use the Recent Apps feature, to not only switch between apps but also summon any app you've recently opened.

To quickly access the apps you've recently opened on your phone, press and hold the Home button. You see a screen listing the last several apps you've opened or used. Choose one.

Keyboard Suggestions

Don't forget to take advantage of the suggestions that appear above the keyboard when you're typing text. In fact, you don't even need to touch a suggestion: To replace your text with the highlighted suggestion, simply touch the space key. Zap! The word appears.

The setting that directs the keyboard to make suggestions work is Show Suggestions. To ensure that this setting is active, obey these steps:

1. **At the Home screen, press the Menu soft button.**

2. **Choose Settings.**

3. **Choose Language & Keyboard.**

4. **Choose your phone's keyboard from the list, such as Swype or Android Keyboard.**

   The Samsung keyboard has no Suggestions setting.

5. **Confirm the Suggestion setting:**

   Swype: For Swype, choose Preferences, Word Suggestion, and then ensure that a check mark appears by the Word Suggestion option.

   Android Keyboard: For the Android Keyboard, ensure that a check mark appears by the Show Suggestions option.

Things That Consume Lots of Battery Juice

Several items on your phone suck down battery power faster than an 18-year-old fleeing the tyranny of high school on graduation day:

- ✔ Navigation
- ✔ Long videos
- ✔ Bluetooth
- ✔ Wi-Fi networking

Navigation is certainly handy, but because the phone's touchscreen is on the entire time and dictating text to you, the battery drains rapidly. If possible, try to plug the phone into the car's power socket when you're navigating. If you can't, keep an eye on the battery meter.

When you use an app to view movie or TV show, the screen stays on the entire time. It can drain the battery, perhaps not as quickly as Navigation, but close.

Both Bluetooth and Wi-Fi networking require extra power for their wireless radios. When you need that speed or connectivity, they're great! I try to plug my phone into a power source when I'm accessing Wi-Fi or using Bluetooth. Otherwise, I disconnect from those networks as soon as I'm done, to save power.

- ✔ Technically speaking, using Wi-Fi doesn't drain the battery as drastically as you would think. In fact, the Wi-Fi signal times itself out after about 15 minutes of non-use, so it's perfectly okay to leave Wi-Fi on all day — your phone experiences only a modicum of battery loss because of it. Even so, I'm a stickler for turning off Wi-Fi when I don't use it.

- ✔ See Chapter 23 for more information on managing the phone's battery.

Check for Roaming

Roaming can be expensive. The last non-smartphone (dumbphone?) I owned racked up $180 in roaming charges the month before I switched to a better cellular plan. Even though you too may have a good cell plan, keep an eye on the phone's status bar. Ensure that when you're making a call, you don't see the Roaming status icon on the status bar atop the touchscreen.

Well, yes, it's okay to make a call when your phone is roaming. My advice is to remember to *check* for the icon, not to avoid it. If possible, try to make your phone calls when you're back in your cellular service's coverage area. If you can't, make the phone call but keep in mind that you will be charged roaming fees. They ain't cheap.

Use + When Dialing Internationally

I suppose that most folks are careful when dialing international numbers. On an Android phone, you can use the + key to replace the country's exit code. In the United States, the code is 011. So, whenever you see an international number listed as 011-xxx-xxxxxx, you can instead dial +xxx-xxxxxx, where the x characters represent the number to dial.

See Chapter 21 for more information on international dialing.

S Pen Soft Button Equivalents

I love the S Pen. It's so much more precise than my sausage fingers. Because I enjoy using the Swype keyboard, I can even "type" using the S Pen. It's fun.

What's not fun is my annoying habit of trying to use the S Pen to press the soft buttons. I don't know why, but whatever magic lets the pen write on the screen prevents it from pressing a soft button.

Fortunately, you can employ a few shortcuts using the S Pen button if you miss using the S Pen on the soft buttons. Table 25-1 lists the S Pen action / soft button equivalents.

Table 25-1	S Pen Soft Button Actions
Press This Soft Button	*To Drag the S Pen This Way*
Menu	Upward
Home	Downward
Back	To the left

You must press and hold the S Pen button to work the soft button equivalents.

No S Pen action is equivalent to the Search soft button.

Snap a Pic of That Contact

Here's something I always forget: Whenever you're near one of your contacts, take the person's picture. Sure, some people are bashful, but most folks are flattered. The idea is to build up your Contacts list so that all contacts have photos. Receiving a call is much more interesting when you see the caller's picture displayed, especially a silly or embarrassing picture.

When taking the picture, be sure to show it to the person before you assign it to the contact. Let them decide whether it's good enough. Or, if you just want to be rude, assign a crummy-looking picture. Heck, you don't even have to do that: Just take a random picture of anything and assign it to a contact: A plant. A rock. Your dog. But, seriously, the next time you meet up with a contact, keep in mind that the phone can take that person's picture.

See Chapter 14 for more information on using the phone's camera.

The Search Command

Google is known worldwide for its searching abilities. By gum, the word *google* is now synonymous for searching. So please don't forget that your Galaxy Note, which uses Google's Android operating system, has a powerful Search command.

The Search command is not only powerful but also available all over. The Search soft button can be pressed at any time, in just about any program to search for information, locations, people — you name it. It's handy. It's everywhere. Use it.

Ten Worthy Apps

Nothing stirs up controversy like stating that ten Android apps are more worthy than the 500,000-plus apps available at the Google Play Store. Even so, when I started out with my first smartphone 20 years ago, I wanted to see a list of worthy apps, or even apps recommended by friends. Lamentably, that was long before anyone else had a smartphone of any type, so I was forced to wait. Thanks to the suggestions in this chapter, you don't have to wait to get started with apps on your Galaxy Note.

AK Notepad

It's odd, but for some reason your Galaxy Note doesn't come with a note-taking app. Forget the Mini Diary app — I don't know what it is, but its warning message about incurring charges scared me enough not to bother. Anyway, a good choice for an app to fill the note-taking void is AK Notepad: You can type or dictate short messages and memos, which I find handy.

For example, before a recent visit to the hardware store, I made (dictated) a list of items I needed by using AK Notepad. I also keep some important items as notes — things that I often forget or don't care to remember, such as frequent-flyer numbers, my dress shirt and suit size (like I ever need that info), and other important notes I might need handy but not cluttering my brain.

CardStar

The handy CardStar app answers the question, "Why do I have all these store-reward cards?" They're not credit cards — they're marketing cards, designed for customer loyalty programs. Rather than tote those cards around in your wallet or on your keychain, you can scan a card's bar code using your phone and save the "card" on the phone.

After you store your loyalty cards in the phone, you simply run the CardStar app to summon the appropriate merchant. Show the checkout person your phone, or scan the bar code yourself. CardStar makes it easy.

Dolphin Browser

Though I don't mind using the Web app that comes with the Galaxy Note, it's universally despised by many users. A better and more popular alternative is Dolphin Browser.

Like many popular computer browsers, Dolphin Browser features a tabbed interface, which works much better than the silly multiple-window interface of the standard Web app. It's also faster.

Gesture Search

The Gesture Search app provides a new way to find information on your phone. Rather than use a keyboard or dictate, you simply draw on the touchscreen the first letter of whatever you're searching for.

Start the Gesture Search app to begin a search. Use your finger to draw a big letter on the screen. After you draw a letter, search results appear on the screen. You can continue drawing more letters to refine the search or touch a search result.

Gesture Search can find contacts, music, apps, and bookmarks in the Web app.

Google Finance

The Google Finance app is an excellent market-tracking tool for folks who are obsessed with the stock market or who want to keep an eye on their portfolios. The app offers you an overview of the market and updates to your stocks as well as links to financial news.

To get the most from this app, configure Google Finance on the web, using your computer. You can create lists of stocks to watch, which are then instantly synchronized with your Galaxy Note. You can visit Google Finance on the web at

```
www.google.com/finance
```

As with other Google services, Google Finance is provided to you for free, as part of your Google account.

Google Sky Map

Ever look up into the sky and say, "What the heck is that?" Unless it's a bird, an airplane, a satellite, a UFO, or a superhero, Google Sky Map helps you find what it is. You may learn that a particularly bright star in the sky is, in fact, the planet Jupiter.

The Google Sky Map app is elegant. It basically turns your Galaxy Note into a window you can look through to identify objects in the night sky. Just start the app and hold the phone up to the sky. Pan the phone to identify planets, stars, and constellations.

Google Sky Map promotes using the phone without touching its screen. For this reason, the screen goes blank after a spell, which is merely the phone's power-saving mode. If you plan extensive stargazing with Google Sky Map, consider resetting the screen time-out. Refer to Chapter 22 for details.

Movies

The Movies app is your phone's gateway to Hollywood. It lists currently running films and films that are opening, and it has links to your local theaters with showtimes and other information. It's also tied into the popular Rotten Tomatoes website for reviews and feedback. If you enjoy going to the movies, you'll find the Movies app a valuable addition to your Galaxy Note's app inventory.

QuickPic

Face it: The Gallery app isn't the best or most logical way to view and organize pictures on your phone. It's not the easiest thing to figure out, and I know that I've been frustrated by it endlessly. A better solution is the free app QuickPic. It's fast. It makes sense. I recommend checking it out.

SportsTap

I admit to not being a sports nut, so it's difficult for me to identify with the craving to have the latest scores, news, and schedules. The sports nuts in my life, however, tell me that the very best app for that purpose is a handy thing named SportsTap.

Rather than blather on about something I'm not into, I'll just ask that you take my advice and obtain SportsTap. I believe you'll be thrilled.

Avoiding Android viruses

How can you tell which apps are legitimate and which might be viruses or evil apps that do odd things to your Galaxy Note? Well, you can't. In fact, most people can't, because most evil apps don't advertise themselves as such.

The key to knowing whether an app is evil is to look at what it does, as described in Chapter 12. If a simple grocery-list app uses the phone's text messaging service and the app doesn't need to send text messages, it's suspect.

In the history of the Android operating system, only a handful of malicious apps have been distributed, and most of them were found on phones used in Asia. Google routinely removes malicious apps from the Play Store, and a feature of the Android operating system even lets Google remotely wipe such apps from your phone. So, you're pretty safe.

Generally speaking, avoid "hacker" apps, porn apps, and apps that use social engineering to make you do things on your phone that you wouldn't otherwise do, such as text an overseas number to see racy pictures of politicians or celebrities.

Tiny Flashlight + LED

The Galaxy Note features an LED lamp on its rump, used for flash photography or to brighten up the subject when shooting video. The lamp can also be employed as a rudimentary flashlight, if you have an app such as the popular Tiny Flashlight + LED.

Tiny Flashlight not only lets you manipulate the phone's LED lamp but also offers several features for illumination in addition to diversion and play. It even has a Morse code feature for signaling, well, however few people are left in the world who can read Morse code.

Index

• N •

• O •

• X •

• Y •

• Z •

Notes

Notes

Notes

Notes

Apple & Mac

iPad 2 For Dummies,
3rd Edition
978-1-118-17679-5

iPhone 4S For Dummies,
5th Edition
978-1-118-03671-6

iPod touch For Dummies,
3rd Edition
978-1-118-12960-9

Mac OS X Lion
For Dummies
978-1-118-02205-4

Blogging & Social Media

CityVille For Dummies
978-1-118-08337-6

Facebook For Dummies,
4th Edition
978-1-118-09562-1

Mom Blogging
For Dummies
978-1-118-03843-7

Twitter For Dummies,
2nd Edition
978-0-470-76879-2

WordPress For Dummies,
4th Edition
978-1-118-07342-1

Business

Cash Flow For Dummies
978-1-118-01850-7

Investing For Dummies,
6th Edition
978-0-470-90545-6

Job Searching with Social
Media For Dummies
978-0-470-93072-4

QuickBooks 2012
For Dummies
978-1-118-09120-3

Resumes For Dummies,
6th Edition
978-0-470-87361-8

Starting an Etsy Business
For Dummies
978-0-470-93067-0

Cooking & Entertaining

Cooking Basics
For Dummies, 4th Edition
978-0-470-91388-8

Wine For Dummies,
4th Edition
978-0-470-04579-4

Diet & Nutrition

Kettlebells For Dummies
978-0-470-59929-7

Nutrition For Dummies,
5th Edition
978-0-470-93231-5

Restaurant Calorie Counter
For Dummies,
2nd Edition
978-0-470-64405-8

Digital Photography

Digital SLR Cameras &
Photography For Dummies,
4th Edition
978-1-118-14489-3

Digital SLR Settings
& Shortcuts
For Dummies
978-0-470-91763-3

Photoshop Elements 10
For Dummies
978-1-118-10742-3

Gardening

Gardening Basics
For Dummies
978-0-470-03749-2

Vegetable Gardening
For Dummies,
2nd Edition
978-0-470-49870-5

Green/Sustainable

Raising Chickens
For Dummies
978-0-470-46544-8

Green Cleaning
For Dummies
978-0-470-39106-8

Health

Diabetes For Dummies,
3rd Edition
978-0-470-27086-8

Food Allergies
For Dummies
978-0-470-09584-3

Living Gluten-Free
For Dummies,
2nd Edition
978-0-470-58589-4

Hobbies

Beekeeping
For Dummies,
2nd Edition
978-0-470-43065-1

Chess For Dummies,
3rd Edition
978-1-118-01695-4

Drawing For Dummies,
2nd Edition
978-0-470-61842-4

eBay For Dummies,
7th Edition
978-1-118-09806-6

Knitting For Dummies,
2nd Edition
978-0-470-28747-7

Language & Foreign Language

English Grammar
For Dummies,
2nd Edition
978-0-470-54664-2

French For Dummies,
2nd Edition
978-1-118-00464-7

German For Dummies,
2nd Edition
978-0-470-90101-4

Spanish Essentials
For Dummies
978-0-470-63751-7

Spanish For Dummies,
2nd Edition
978-0-470-87855-2

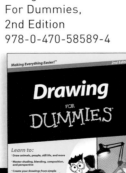

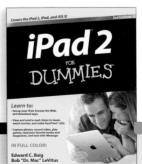

Math & Science

Algebra I For Dummies,
2nd Edition
978-0-470-55964-2

Biology For Dummies,
2nd Edition
978-0-470-59875-7

Chemistry For Dummies,
2nd Edition
978-1-1180-0730-3

Geometry For Dummies,
2nd Edition
978-0-470-08946-0

Pre-Algebra Essentials
For Dummies
978-0-470-61838-7

Microsoft Office

Excel 2010 For Dummies
978-0-470-48953-6

Office 2010 All-in-One
For Dummies
978-0-470-49748-7

Office 2011 for Mac
For Dummies
978-0-470-87869-9

Word 2010
For Dummies
978-0-470-48772-3

Music

Guitar For Dummies,
2nd Edition
978-0-7645-9904-0

Clarinet For Dummies
978-0-470-58477-4

iPod & iTunes
For Dummies,
9th Edition
978-1-118-13060-5

Pets

Cats For Dummies,
2nd Edition
978-0-7645-5275-5

Dogs All-in One
For Dummies
978-0470-52978-2

Saltwater Aquariums
For Dummies
978-0-470-06805-2

Religion & Inspiration

The Bible For Dummies
978-0-7645-5296-0

Catholicism For Dummies,
2nd Edition
978-1-118-07778-8

Spirituality For Dummies,
2nd Edition
978-0-470-19142-2

Self-Help & Relationships

Happiness For Dummies
978-0-470-28171-0

Overcoming Anxiety
For Dummies,
2nd Edition
978-0-470-57441-6

Seniors

Crosswords For Seniors
For Dummies
978-0-470-49157-7

iPad 2 For Seniors
For Dummies, 3rd Edition
978-1-118-17678-8

Laptops & Tablets
For Seniors For Dummies,
2nd Edition
978-1-118-09596-6

Smartphones & Tablets

BlackBerry For Dummies,
5th Edition
978-1-118-10035-6

Droid X2 For Dummies
978-1-118-14864-8

HTC ThunderBolt
For Dummies
978-1-118-07601-9

MOTOROLA XOOM
For Dummies
978-1-118-08835-7

Sports

Basketball For Dummies,
3rd Edition
978-1-118-07374-2

Football For Dummies,
2nd Edition
978-1-118-01261-1

Golf For Dummies,
4th Edition
978-0-470-88279-5

Test Prep

ACT For Dummies,
5th Edition
978-1-118-01259-8

ASVAB For Dummies,
3rd Edition
978-0-470-63760-9

The GRE Test For
Dummies, 7th Edition
978-0-470-00919-2

Police Officer Exam
For Dummies
978-0-470-88724-0

Series 7 Exam
For Dummies
978-0-470-09932-2

Web Development

HTML, CSS, & XHTML
For Dummies, 7th Edition
978-0-470-91659-9

Drupal For Dummies,
2nd Edition
978-1-118-08348-2

Windows 7

Windows 7
For Dummies
978-0-470-49743-2

Windows 7
For Dummies,
Book + DVD Bundle
978-0-470-52398-8

Windows 7 All-in-One
For Dummies
978-0-470-48763-1

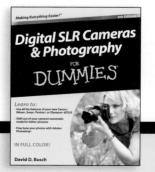

Available wherever books are sold. For more information or to order direct: U.S. customers visit www.dummies.com or call 1-877-762-297
U.K. customers visit www.wileyeurope.com or call (0) 1243 843291. Canadian customers visit www.wiley.ca or call 1-800-567-4797.

Connect with us online at www.facebook.com/fordummies or @fordummies

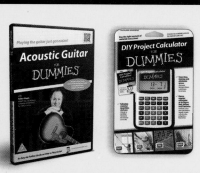

Wherever you are in life, Dummies makes it easier.

From fashion to Facebook®, wine to Windows®, and everything in between, Dummies makes it easier.

Visit us at Dummies.com and connect with us online at www.facebook.com/fordummies or @fordummies